CRIMINAL RESISTANCE?

CRIMINAL RESISTANCE?

Interdisciplinary Research Series in Ethnic, Gender and Class Relations

Series Editor: Biko Agozino, Virginia Polytechnic Institute and State University, Blacksburg, Virginia

This series brings together research from a range of disciplines including criminology, cultural studies and applied social studies, focusing on experiences of ethnic, gender and class relations. In particular, the series examines the treatment of marginalized groups within the social systems for criminal justice, education, health, employment and welfare.

Also published in this series

Apartheid Vertigo
The Rise in Discrimination Against Africans in South Africa
David M. Matsinhe
ISBN 978-1-4094-2619-6

Reconstructing Law and Justice in a Postcolony
Nọnso Okafọ
ISBN 978-0-7546-4784-3

Policing and Crime Control in Post-apartheid South Africa
Anne-Marie Singh
ISBN 978-0-7546-4457-6

W.E.B. Du Bois on Crime and Justice
Shaun L. Gabbidon
ISBN 978-0-7546-4956-4

Democratic Policing in Transitional and Developing Countries
Edited by Nathan Pino and Michael D. Wiatrowski
ISBN 978-0-7546-4719-5

Criminal Resistance?
The Politics of Kidnapping Oil Workers

TEMITOPE B. ORIOLA
University of Massachusetts, Boston, USA

Routledge
Taylor & Francis Group

LONDON AND NEW YORK

First published 2013 by Ashgate Publishing

Published 2016 by Routledge
2 Park Square, Milton Park, Abingdon, Oxon OX14 4RN
711 Third Avenue, New York, NY 10017, USA

Routledge is an imprint of the Taylor & Francis Group, an informa business

British Library Cataloguing in Publication Data
Oriola, Temitope B.
Criminal resistance?: the politics of kidnapping oil workers. – (Interdisciplinary research series in ethnic, gender and class relations)
1. Petroleum industry and trade—Political aspects—Nigeria—Niger River Delta.
2. Insurgency—Nigeria—Niger River Delta. 3. Oil industry workers—Crimes against— Nigeria—Niger River Delta. 4. Political kidnapping—Nigeria—Niger River Delta. 5. Movement for the Emancipation of the Niger Delta (Organization)
 I. Title II. Series
 322.4'2'09669-dc23

The Library of Congress has cataloged the printed edition as follows:
Oriola, Temitope B.
 Criminal resistance?: the politics of kidnapping oil workers/by Temitope B. Oriola.
  pages cm. — (Interdisciplinary research series in ethnic, gender and class relations)
 Includes bibliographical references and index.
 ISBN 978-1-4094-4991-1 (hardback : alk. paper)
 1. Kidnapping—Political aspects—Nigeria. 2. Petroleum industry and trade—Political aspects—Nigeria. 3. Political violence—Nigeria. 4. Nigeria—Politics and government—1960– I. Title.
 HV6604.N6O75 2013
 364.15'409669—dc23

2012043456

ISBN 9781409449911 (hbk)

For Pa Isaac Oriola. Ó dàbò o (goodbye)

Contents

Foreword

by Patrick Bond
Professor of Political Economy
University of KwaZulu-Natal
South Africa

What is the nature of the often successful—albeit momentary—armed resistance to the world's largest transnational oil corporations, in what is probably the most extreme case of eco-social exploitation on Earth? Does violence waged as a struggle tactic in the Niger Delta correspond to historical traditions of Maoist or Guevaraist guerrilla movements, to African nationalist armed struggle, and to Fanon's considerations of anti-colonial violence? Or is there something so unique here, that a profound, fresh scholarship drawing on diverse local and global insights is required?

Temitope Oriola's concept of a 'Resource Frustration' trajectory is based upon his arguments about how 'social banditry' emerged in the Niger Delta. This book is a healthy corrective to the romanticized non-violence fetish of much social movement scholarship as well as that of solidarity movements which arose to support Ken Saro-Wiwa's heroic fight against pollution and underdevelopment of the Ogoni people a quarter century ago. In part because of his tasteful stylistic approach, as well as the extremely rich information and his synthetic capacity, Oriola has produced amongst the finest works yet in the tradition of socio-political framing narratives. This book is, therefore, a vital addition to academic understandings of the Delta conflict, but much more, it offers lessons to anyone interested in Nigeria, Delta solidarity, the oil and security sectors, social movement mobilisation, and environmental justice strategies and tactics.

Writing properly about this controversial subject requires not only a sophisticated politics, but also strong background analysis of conditions that led to widespread discontent. Oriola's contribution to knowledge is understanding kidnapping as a pressure tactic not only in terms of criminology but as a sociological phenomenon in a power struggle between communities and state/capital. It is a highly innovative approach to an otherwise well-researched region of the world.

The crucial challenge is to consider how far the kidnappers of various factions of the Movement for the Emancipation of the Niger Delta (MEND) degenerated into opportunistic activity, in contrast to politically-'liberatory' kidnapping. This is exceptionally complicated given claims and counter-claims. Divisions are rife amongst MEND constituencies and between MEND and various civil society organisations, not to mention state and capital. Opportunistic kidnapping is discredited because of the activities of those seeking merely financial reward, and other resistance tactics—oil bunkering and pipeline sabotage, for example—are similarly fraught given the collateral damage including explosions and ecological devastation. The weapons of the weak are blunt and often face inward.

Why, then, does frustration with the Resource Curse generate such tactics? To get as deep as he does with this study, Oriola first covers international debates on violent/nonviolent social change, followed by a chronological perspective on MEND's development. He then offers a strong narrative focus on the 'framing apparatus' based on rare interviews and focus group discussions, access to exclusive emails, close readings of statements available on the internet, and dissection of official documents. To this balanced assessment of primary data, he adds media coverage and applies sophisticated discourse analysis. The theory he deploys successfully fuses political process framing analysis, the resource mobilization thesis and political opportunity perspectives. It works well, given how many diverse and contradictory factors must be subsumed into the argument.

Oriola's is a complicated conclusion, namely that a combination of 'benevolent leadership' of MEND forces, plus the mix of openness and closedness in terms of Nigerian official avenues for expressing grievances meant kidnapping was a logical and often effective route for the most militant Delta activists. Diagnostic, prognostic and motivational framing strategies were deployed by MEND in order to gain support and a more universal understanding of the affected communities' grievances. He skilfully explores a variety of factors feeding into those grievances: slavery and colonialism (and their legacies of violence), ethnicism and divide-and-conquer politics, the ineffectual character of non-violent resistance, opportunistic political entrepreneurship and corruption, notable instances of political repression, race and class divides, truncated opportunities for accumulation outside oil, ways oil companies and other business agents react and adapt, media coverage, anonymity and organisational fluidity, popular support for the insurgency, geographic terrain (creeks), religious and spiritual traditions, the roles of key individual leaders, gender relations, rhetorical skills, and North-South divisions within Nigeria, amongst others.

From this comprehensive treatment we learn how kidnapping as a tactic developed from decades-old practices of community confrontations with oil companies. We see more clearly why the success of the tactic—especially in times when some MEND kidnap victims evinced a degree of Stockholm Syndrome in which they sympathized with their captors—led to its undermining: criminally-oriented hijackings increased after 2003. And this leads to further questions about what tactics logically follow, and how MEND and successor organisations will adjust their political framings.

The limits of the kidnapping tactic also require strategic and analytical adjustments, because it is logical to move from a classical Not In My Back Yard perspective to broader Resource Curse critiques, including, one day, climate change as a rationale for 'leaving oil in the soil', as is being pursued so well by Environmental Rights Action in Benin City. But to get there first requires moving through the stages of 'Resource Frustration,' a concept that will be of enormous benefit to those both studying and strategizing for the end of the tyranny of oil in Nigeria, and for the limitation of so much other damage done by mineral and petroleum 'riches' elsewhere.

Preface

Insurgent groups specializing in kidnapping oil workers and vandalizing oil infrastructure purportedly as a form of protest against marginalization by the state and transnational oil corporations are rife in the Niger Delta region of Nigeria. This book interrogates the interstitial space between legitimate protest and criminal expropriation in that region.

The data for this project draws upon extensive fieldwork in Nigeria: Interviews and focus group discussions with six sets of actors, including community groups, politicians, journalists, military officials and insurgents. Official statements from the Movement for the Emancipation of the Niger Delta (MEND), the group allegedly spearheading these kidnappings, are also analysed. This data provides insights into how MEND seeks to frame the insurgency as a form of protest. Insurgents seek to portray the situation in the Niger Delta as a form of *war* and oil workers as *enemy combatants*. This metaphor of war is used to frame their violent actions as a form of justifiable repertoire of protest.

The analysis demonstrates that *impression management* pervades kidnapping episodes. The major concern of the Nigerian state is to provide an atmosphere that is sufficiently safe for oil extraction while several insurgent commanders have succeeded in inventing an *alternative political structure* for accessing the conventional structures of society. For others, kidnapping is a dangerous but innovative means of livelihood in a perpetually depressed economy. While the insurgency generates harms for the oil-producing communities, it also creates benefits for some participants. The diffusion of opportunities for self-enrichment among institutional and non-institutional actors suggests that kidnapping in the Delta occasionally serves a *public good*. The combined actions of those who support the existing order alongside the (often violent) challengers have resulted in a synthetic stasis which both paradoxically harms and benefits all parties.

The grievances of the people of the Niger Delta remain legitimate in spite of the infiltration of the movement for environmental justice, basic social fairness and resource control in the Niger Delta by agents who are engaged in the 'struggle' as a means of economic survival. Much has been written about "resource wars" and "resource curse". These theoretical schemata and the social conditions that they ostensibly articulate have taken on a life of their own with varying degrees of agency and rationality accorded the most oppressed actors in real life and death situations. The proposal is that academic and social policy attention shift to what may be conceptually designated as *resource frustration*.

Temitope Oriola
Boston Massachusetts
28 September 2012

Acknowledgments

I owe an irreparable debt to many people. I do not presuppose that a few words would do. Kevin Haggerty has been a source of indescribable motivation. He gave invaluable professional advice at every stage and read all aspects of this work. Thank you for everything. A number of scholars at the University of Alberta Canada contributed to bringing this work to fruition. I am grateful for their willingness to provide timely feedback and constructive criticisms. Many thanks, to Gord Laxer, a scholar with an uncommon intellectual touch. Andy W. Knight has been incredibly supportive and remains a treasured friend. Yasmeen Abu Laban made me think through many standpoints. Clement Dominique provided insightful comments and suggestions. Patrick Bond of the University of KwaZulu-Natal, South Africa also provided helpful comments for which I am grateful.

I appreciate the Department of Sociology, the Faculty of Arts and the University of Alberta for the F.S Chia, Izaak Walton Killam Memorial and the Field Law Leilani Muir Graduate Scholarships, among others that ensured I was fully concentrated on my studies. The International Development Research Centre (IDRC) provided a Doctoral Research Grant that supported my fieldwork in Nigeria.

The support of the people of Agge in Bayelsa state and Okerenkoko in Delta state is gratefully acknowledged. Thank you for sharing your knowledge and experiences. I appreciate the help of General Mobolaji Koleoso, Lt. Col. Timothy Antigha and Col. Rabe Abubakar. Many journalists, informants, and concerned citizens like Ken Saro Wiwa (Jr.), and other research participants made this work possible. Thanks to the editors of the *British Journal of Criminology* and *African Security* for permission to use in this book two of my previously published articles. My friends spread across the world supported me. Thanks to Olufemi Adigun, Tina Okafor, Nduka Ughamadu, Benjamin Ogunmola, Paul Ugor, Nduka Otiono, Idowu and Okezi Ohioze, Abiodun Akindele and family, Olumide Adetunji and family, Nicole Neverson, Wright Eruebi and family, Pastor and Mrs Tokunbo Okunnu, and Sunkanmi Famobio and family. Thank you, Nermin Allam for being a wonderful friend.

My family and friends in Nigeria provided tremendous assistance in the course of this study. They include Reverend Sam Adesua, Wole Adesua, Seun Sotonwa and Tayo Ogunleye. Honourable and Mrs Johnson Alalibo have been immensely supportive as well as Scot Okomi, Morris Alagoa of the Environmental Rights Action and his staff; Benjamin Okaba and Tarilaifa Akpandara. Thanks also to Kayode Odunayo and family, the Fayehuns, Francis Adebayo, Grace Maisamari, the Lawals, the Adeoyes, the Alarapes, the Ighodaros, the Adejumobis, and Alanana Otaki.

Bode Ojo encouraged me to seek graduate studies in Canada. Professor Layiwola Erinosho nurtured this quest and remains a mentor. Charles Adeyanju facilitated the process by providing crucial information and mentorship. I am grateful for and humbled by his continued friendship. Russell Smandych and Kathryn Smandych were the first family I knew in Canada. They remain so to this day. Lori Wilkinson has been a truly reliable friend since my days at the University of Manitoba. My colleagues in the Department of Sociology & Criminal Justice, University of Massachusetts Boston are some of the most supportive people I have ever worked with.

As usual, my family's love twinkling from afar was a constant source of inspiration and their prayers immeasurably supportive. My father passed away four days before this manuscript was due at Ashgate. He was a great father and fine soldier. To my mother; thank you for your kindness and love: This is for you. My siblings; Abosede, Yemisi, Femi and Ayo, motivate me in ways they will never know. To my gorgeous nieces and nephews: Abolade, Eniola, Damilola, Olu and Inioluwa, I hope to make up for the missed birthdays. How may I forget the Omniscient Fountain of Knowledge, Jehovah Mekaddishkem? Words are a poor reflection of appreciation. *E se pupo.* Thank you.

Chapter 1

"Dénouement" as Introduction

I repeat that we all stand before history. I and my colleagues are not the only ones on trial. Shell is here on trial ... The company has indeed ducked this particular trial, but its day will surely come ... for there is no doubt in my mind that the ecological war that the company has waged in the Delta will be called to question sooner than later and the crimes of that war be duly punished ... On trial also is the Nigerian nation, its present rulers and those who assist them. *I predict that the scene here will be played and replayed by generations yet unborn. I predict that the dénouement of the riddle of the Niger Delta will soon come.* The agenda is being set at this trial. Whether the peaceful ways I have favoured will prevail depends on what the oppressor decides: what signals it sends to the waiting public. (emphasis added)

> Kenule Saro-Wiwa, leader, Movement for the Survival of Ogoni People (MOSOP)
> October 31, 1995.

We must avoid falling into the throes of what Adaka Boro foresaw forty years ago. Let them call us terrorists, let them call us bandits but it is important and critical that we remain resolute in the pursuit of the ideals of our fallen heroes like Isaac Adaka Boro, Ken Saro Wiwa and a host of others.

> Asari Dokubo, Leader, Niger Delta People's Volunteer Force (NDPVF)
> November 2009.

On January 11, 2006, four foreign oil workers were kidnapped in an attack on a Shell Petroleum Development Corporation (SPDC, hereafter, Shell) offshore oil facility in Rivers state by a nascent insurgent group, the Movement for the Emancipation of the Niger Delta, (MEND). The attack also led to a daily loss of 120,000 barrels of crude oil (Technical Committee on the Niger Delta 2008). Another attack on Shell facilities in Port Harcourt four days later led to the death of 17 soldiers (Technical Committee on the Niger Delta 2008). By the following month or what became known as "dark February", the Movement for the Emancipation of the Niger Delta (MEND) kidnapped nine expatriate workers of Shell. While insurgents and oil corporations are generally silent about the ransom paid to secure the release of the oil workers, the popular name—"ATM"—given to white oil workers from the geo-political West is an insignia of the times: The release of each of the expatriates costs an average of $250,000.[1] The oil industry in Nigeria collectively spent at least

---

1   See Matthew Harwood (undated). "Perils amid profits in the Niger Delta". URL: http://www.securitymanagement.com/article/perils-amid-profits-niger-delta Accessed 26 January 2011.

$3 billion on security annually at the height of insurgent activities between 2007 and 2009.[2] A donation of $200 million by the Nigerian oil industry to the federal government in February 2011 is only a fraction of the budget of oil corporations for ensuring the safety of their personnel and facilities. These incidents would seem to constitute a new Nigerian business model to a cursory observer monitoring the rise of kidnapping in Nigeria through decontextualized media reports.

However, eleven years before these kidnapping incidents in the Niger Delta, on 31 October 1995, Kenule Saro-Wiwa, the leader of the Movement for the Survival of Ogoni People (MOSOP), a non-violent social movement organization, was engaged in a battle for his life before a military tribunal set up by the regime of General Sani Abacha. Justice Ibrahim Auta, chair of the tribunal concluded the monumental task before him. On trial were 15 environmental and human rights activists—Ogonis from the stupendously oil-rich Niger Delta region of Nigeria. Justice Auta was persuaded that members of MOSOP led by Saro-Wiwa and the National Youth Council of Ogoni People (NYCOP) successfully orchestrated a riot at Giokoo on May 21, 1994. The riot led to the murder of four prominent sons of Ogoni believed to be sympathetic towards the Nigerian state in the festering oil struggle in the Delta—an unpardonable treason in the eyes of the Delta public. The sentence was death by hanging for nine of the activists including Saro-Wiwa. Ever perspicacious and painstakingly *au courant* of history, Saro-Wiwa declared in his final comments at the tribunal that the "dénouement of the riddle of the Niger Delta will soon come. Whether the peaceful ways I have favoured will prevail depends on what the oppressor decides: what signals it sends to the waiting public" (Mbeke-Ekanem 2000:162). Saro-Wiwa argued that the treatment meted out to him and his colleagues would shape the trajectory of the festering Niger Delta crisis.

Nigeria's taciturn maximum ruler, General Sani Abacha, met with the governing body, the Provisional Ruling Council (PRC), to ratify the sentence passed on the Ogoni Nine eight days after the death sentence was delivered. Saro-Wiwa and eight other Ogoni activists were executed on November 10, 1995 before they could appeal the death sentence.

Saro-Wiwa brought the conditions of the people of the Delta to international prominence through the instrumentality of MOSOP and suave use of non-violent tactics in a well-manicured international campaign. A poet, writer, publisher, activist, and entrepreneur, Saro-Wiwa galvanized the disparate elements of the Ogonis—a heterogeneous collection of peoples—into a political force. The hanging of Saro-Wiwa and his kinsmen remains a watershed in the struggle over resource control in the Delta region of Nigeria (Watts 2007; Bob 2005, 2002). Saro-Wiwa also became a symbolic avatar emblematic of the failure of non-violent protest (Bob 2005).

A lot happened that fundamentally challenged the human, material and ideational infrastructure of the Nigerian state in the 14 years separating the

---

2   See Ejiofor Alike. 2011. "Security: Oil firms support FG with $200 in N'Delta", URL: http://www.thisdayonline.com/ Accessed 16 February 2011.

statements that head this chapter from Saro-Wiwa and Asari Dokubo. For all intents and purposes, the Niger Delta effectively became an ungovernable space in the latter part of the 1990s (Watts 2009a, 2008c) as the burgeoning crisis increasingly developed into a mature insurgency (Watts 2009b) from the early 2000s. Pipeline vandalism, illegal oil bunkering, oil facility occupation, and car bombs have become rampant. A frightening proliferation of small arms was also occurring. More importantly, the Movement for the Emancipation of the Niger Delta (MEND), an amorphous, multifaceted amalgam of insurgent groups which demonstrated a devastating clinical precision in executing its intents emerged late in 2005. By early 2006 kidnapping of foreign oil workers assumed a frightening scale. The explicit aim of MEND is to cripple the capacity of the Nigerian rentier petro-state to produce crude oil—its lifeblood.

In an e-mail statement on March 15, 2010, MEND's spokesperson Jomo Gbomo announced a breach of security at the annex of the Delta state government house in Warri, venue of a post-amnesty dialogue organized by the *Vanguard* newspaper. MEND advised the public to avoid the venue and vicinity. MEND detonated two car bombs at the time identified in the e-mail. MEND warned that the "deceit of endless dialogue and conferences will no longer be tolerated" and they hoped they had convinced the Delta state governor Emmanuel Uduaghan that MEND was not a "media creation" as he had asserted. In the end, eight persons were injured and six persons died in the bomb blasts. MEND decided not to detonate the third car bomb ostensibly on humanitarian grounds. Seven months later, as Nigeria marked its 50th independence anniversary from British colonialism, MEND carried out bomb attacks that claimed at least 12 lives. Not known to waste words, even in death, Saro-Wiwa's prognostication was astute: The dénouement had indeed begun.

The Study

Experts working on the causal link between oil (and/or oil dependence) and conflict have found Nigeria's Delta empirically tantalizing (Oyefusi 2008, 2007; Tabb 2007; Collier and Hoeffler 2005; Ross 2003; Collier and Hoeffler 2002; Collier 2000; Collier and Hoeffler 1998; Welch 1995). Since the discovery of crude oil in Oloibiri in the Niger Delta region (situated in Ogbia local government area of the present Bayelsa state) of Nigeria in 1956, many Nigerians have come to wish that this discovery never happened. Oil has fuelled worsening social relations in Nigeria rather than fostering development. The host communities in the Niger Delta (hereafter, the Delta) in particular have seen little beyond violence, state repression, squalor, unemployment and pervasive neglect (Oyefusi 2008; Omeje 2007; Ibeanu and Luckham 2007; Okereke 2006; Okonta 2005; Human Rights Watch 2005; Zalik 2004).

The Delta is rife with a range of rebellious and (quasi)-criminal activities like hot-tapping, illegal oil bunkering, pipeline vandalism, disruption of oil production activities, flow station shut downs, riots, demonstrations, bombings and so on.

This book focuses specifically and primarily on *kidnapping*, recognizing that this phenomenon exists in a wider context. While other forms of violence are visible in the Delta, kidnapping appears to be the newest and one of the most dangerous developments. In addition, groups like MEND that are engaged in kidnapping oil workers claim they do so in protest against the Nigerian state and oil corporations that exploit their communities' natural resource without providing adequate compensation. Hence, MEND and its ilk claim they are kidnapping oil workers in the interest of the people of the Delta. MEND claims to be part of the larger social movement that since the 1960s in the Delta aims to gain resource control for the Delta people.

Kidnapping is a sociologically heterogeneous phenomenon (Caramazza and Leone 1984). Concannon's (2008: 4) delineation of six types of kidnapping provides a foundation for comprehending this complex phenomenon. These are domestic kidnapping (intra-family), political kidnapping (to further a political agenda), predatory kidnapping of an adult, predatory kidnapping of minor, profit kidnapping, revenge kidnapping and staged kidnapping (feigned to cover up another crime). However, kidnappings in Nigeria do not fit into these conceptual schemata. For instance, in Nigeria *domestic kidnapping* mostly functions as *profit kidnapping* and vice versa rather than as an unfortunate methodology for settling family squabbles.

Akpan's (2010) categorization of kidnappings offers a more nuanced explanation of the phenomenon within the Nigerian context. Akpan classifies kidnapping in the Niger Delta into four categories. These are "kidnapping as a general liberation struggle", "kidnapping for economic reasons", "kidnapping as a political tool", and "kidnapping as a new habit of crime" (Akpan 2010: 38–40). This schema inadvertently becomes tautological as the "economic reason" and "new habit of crime" categories are essentially the same. Conversely, the difference between "kidnapping as a general liberation struggle" and "kidnapping as political tool" is difficult to discern.

It is important to note that kidnapping neither exclusively targets oil workers nor geographically bound to the Niger Delta. Kidnapping is common in other parts of Nigeria, especially Anambra in the South East and Lagos in the South West. The targets in these states are business elites, the professional class and other individuals with significant economic capital. This presents a conundrum because while MEND actively engages in kidnapping, it refutes suggestions that it collects ransom for releasing the victims (see Okonta 2006) and vehemently opposes kidnapping for profit (Okaba 2009). Therefore, the type of *kidnapping* this book focuses on must be differentiated from other types of kidnappings in the Delta and other parts of Nigeria.

There are two major types of kidnappings that have little or no relationship to the Niger Delta insurgency. These are *opportunistic kidnappings* and *political vendetta/revenge* kidnappings. While all types of kidnappings have a certain element of opportunism, *opportunistic kidnapping* is in a class of its own. It constitutes a "commerce in human life" rather than an explicitly political act (Jenkins 1985: xx) or "a new habit of crime" (Akpan 2010: 40). The victims often have nothing to do with the conditions of the people of the Niger Delta. Opportunistic kidnappings are sheer business ventures by unemployed young people, who profess no ideological conviction and have no rationale other than economic benefits for their actions.

There are at least three variants of opportunistic kidnappings in Nigeria. First, there are *family-inspired kidnappings, targeted kidnapping of wealthy persons or their family* and *random kidnapping*. In the first case, a fairly wealthy individual may be set up for kidnapping by a member of their family. The family member provides actionable intelligence about the itinerary of the potential victim, their habits, net worth and recent earnings. In the second case, wealthy persons or their family members are targeted exclusively by kidnappers. For instance, in 2009, the father of a former governor of the Central Bank of Nigeria, Professor Charles Soludo, as well as a wealthy businessman Chief Godwin Okeke and Nollywood actor Pete Edochie were kidnapped in separate incidents. They were all released after ransoms were paid by their families, friends and associates. While these cases were well-orchestrated, in the third case, a less-scientific methodology is used. Individuals are kidnapped because of a misfortune of spatial location. Such victims are held until their family members pay for their release.

Political vendetta or revenge kidnappings constitute the second class of kidnappings that must be distinguished from the focus of this book. Political vendetta kidnappings can take the form of intra-elite political rancor. A politician may hire a gang to kidnap an opponent or a member of the opponent's family to create a distraction until an election is decided. In some cases, the homes of political opponents could also be bombed. This could also be a form of punishment for reneging on an agreement. Alternatively, intra or inter-communal feuds may lead to kidnapping members from opposing sides. Whether opportunistic or for political purposes, these kidnappings conform to what Hamilton (1980) calls a deadly political game.

The focus of this book is on kidnappings that are putatively connected to the struggle for emancipating the Niger Delta. This set of kidnappings has fundamental characteristics that distinguish it from the waves of kidnappings mentioned earlier. First, these kidnappings are *constructed* by the insurgents as part of the wider social movement for justice in the Delta. Therefore, apart from monetary demands, insurgents clamor for resource control and provision of basic social goods like roads, schools, hospitals, electricity, etc. from the Nigerian state and oil corporations. Second, oil workers, particularly non-Nigerians or expatriate oil workers are the targets. This precludes kidnapping of Nigerian politicians, business elites and their family members. Third, in the course of these kidnappings, insurgents come into confrontations with the Joint Task Force (JTF), the Nigerian military unit responsible for maintaining security in the Delta, rather than the Nigerian Police. The JTF is concerned with securing oil facilities, ensuring the safety of oil workers by preventing kidnapping and providing an environment that guarantees the continuous extraction of crude oil in the Delta. Other types of kidnappings and the maintenance of security in other parts of

Nigeria are the duties of the police. Fourth, this set of kidnappings involves actors operating in the Delta's creeks with wide connections in the insurgency rather than pockets of individuals acting in isolation across Nigeria. Insurgents kidnapping oil workers are thus members of recognizable groups in the Delta. Finally, this set of kidnappings takes place at the site of oil infrastructure—oil fields, offshore and onshore rigs—and other spaces and symbols of oil extraction in the Niger Delta.

Having divided kidnappings in Nigeria into three broad categories, it is important to point out that there are no reliable figures on the frequency and geographical distribution of all but one of these forms. There is no credible data on incidents of opportunistic and political vendetta/revenge kidnappings in Nigeria. The third category of kidnappings discussed above—kidnappings that are apparently connected to the Delta struggle—are more rigorously recorded by several organizations. One of these is Bergen Risk Solutions. Its June 2010 report indicates that in 2006, 70 oil workers were kidnapped. In 2007, 165 oil workers were kidnapped, while in 2008 and 2009, 165 and 48 oil workers were kidnapped respectively. Between January and June 2010, 31 persons were kidnapped (Bergen Risk Solutions 2010).

MEND is widely believed to be responsible for most of these kidnapping incidents, as stated earlier. However, the level of public support for MEND's kidnapping tactic in the Delta is ambiguous. This book investigates kidnapping in the Delta with a view to ascertaining whether the Delta people view the act as a form of protest or simply the nefarious activity of a few criminals and indeed whether such distinctions make sense in this context. It is also concerned with how MEND frames its activities to garner public support.

This book is concerned with an ostensibly legally irremediable antinomy: On one hand, the Nigerian rentier petro-state has failed to fulfill its obligation to provide basic social goods to its people yet wishes to maintain order. On the other hand, some young men and women in the oil-producing communities have formed militias specializing in kidnapping oil workers purportedly as a form of protest against the ineptitude and negligence of the state and marginalization by transnational oil corporations. The spectacular effervescence of unprecedented violence in the Delta remains the most virile threat to the Nigerian state since the civil war of 1967–1970. For instance, the three core Niger Delta states comprising Bayelsa, Rivers, and Delta have a combined total of at least 120–150 on-going violent conflicts (Watts 2008c; UNDP 2007). The Delta has attracted worldwide attention because of the incessant kidnapping of oil workers by militant youth,[3] pipeline vandalism and destruction of offshore and onshore rigs. These incidents have contributed to rising prices of crude oil in the world market.

---

3   The term "youth" is culturally defined. Indeed, most of the insurgents are in their 20s and 30s but are still referred to as "youth". The term is used in keeping faith with its popular usage in Nigeria. Watts (2007) also notes the problematic nature of what constitutes youth in Nigeria.

How do we understand the *kidnapping* of oil workers in the Niger Delta region? With the stated question as the overarching objective, the following questions are also investigated: How does the political process, particularly the politics of oil and resource distribution and control, in Nigeria, shape kidnappings? What are the opinions of select members of Agge and Okerenkoko communities (as a microcosm of the Delta people) about the kidnapping of oil workers? Following the opinions of community members, is kidnapping of oil workers in the Delta a repertoire of protest or criminal expropriation? What is the profile and *modus operandi* of the Movement for the Emancipation of the Niger Delta (MEND), the group allegedly spearheading kidnapping of oil workers? What are the framing strategies of MEND vis-à-vis kidnappings and other forms of insurgency in the Delta?

Nigeria and its Delta Region

Nigeria is a compelling study in complexity. There are at least 252 "identifiable" ethnic groups (Elechi 2006: 3) speaking over 400 languages with differences in dialects even within the same culture area, a situation unmatched anywhere in Africa (Mensah 2005: 73). Religious practices such as Christianity, Islam and a plethora of African Traditional Religions further heighten the unprecedented diversity.[4] One of the major concerns of Nigerians at home and in the Diaspora is their perception of the country's phenomenal and alarming lawlessness, particularly since the 1980s. With a checkered history of coups and counter coups which brought inexperienced military officers to power and the current "democratic" rule that leaves very much to be desired, the institutional structures of Nigeria are struggling to simply survive (Human Rights Watch 2005b).

Intra and inter communal conflicts are nothing new in Nigeria. In fact, ethnic conflict management is an overbearing aspect of governance in Nigeria. Some of the prominent conflicts in the recent past in various parts of the country include the Tiv-Jukun conflicts in Taraba state (Best, Idyorough and Shehu 2007), the Ife-Modakeke conflict in Osun state (Albert 2007a), and the Zangon-Kataf crisis in Kaduna state (Akinteye, Wuye and Ashafa 2007). The incessant unpredictable ethno-religious crisis in Kano between Christians and Muslims (Albert 2007b) is in a class of its own. Others include the long-standing Warri ownership tripartite debacle among Itsekiris, Ijaws and Urhobo. This particular conflict has had great intensity and urgency since 1997 (Human Rights Watch 2003). The Boko Aram crisis led by extremists opposed to Western education and values (Watts 2009b) is one of the most recent. Boko Haram continues to pose significant problems to the survival of the Nigerian state by engaging in coordinated bombing of churches and government buildings. The consequent death of many Christians heightens the sharp religious divide in Nigeria even though several Muslims have also died in the course of Boko Haram's bombing campaigns. These acts have adversely

---

4   For a history of Nigeria see Falola (1999).

affected the social and economic life of several Northern cities. The UN building in Abuja, Nigeria's capital city was bombed by Boko Haram in August 2011. The group began to target telecommunications infrastructure in 2012.

The execution without trial of Mohammed Yusuf, leader of Boko Haram by police officers accentuates the tenuous observance of the rule of law in Nigeria. In spite of the large-scale violence in these conflicts, they tend to be sporadic, largely isolated and (apart from the on-going Boko Haram crisis) arguably pose little systemic dangers to the corporate existence of Nigeria. The Delta crisis is not reducible to any of the other conflicts in Nigeria as the rationale of the Delta crisis challenges the precarious foundation of the country.

The Niger Delta region exemplifies the diversity of Nigeria. The Delta has roughly 40 ethnic groups who speak over 250 languages and dialects in 13, 329 settlements (Watts 2008b). There are five main linguistic categories in the Delta: Ijoid, Yoruboid, Edoid, Igboid and Delta Cross (Watts 2004b: 7). The Ijaws are the largest ethnic group in the Delta and the fourth nationally after the Hausa-Fulani, Yoruba and Igbo. The Delta region comprises 12 percent of Nigeria's land mass or 112, 110 sq. kms. Nine out of Nigeria's 36 states and 185 out of 774 local government areas belong to the Niger Delta. A total of 60 percent of the Delta population is under the age of 30 making it one of the youngest in the country. There are over 1,500 oil-producing communities in the Delta (Watts 2008b).

About 60 percent of the Gulf of Guinea's oil wealth is in Nigeria—invariably in the Delta region (Lubeck, Watts and Lipschtz 2007). The Delta is an interlocking and stupefying network of pipelines and miscellaneous oil infrastructure. It includes 7000 km of pipelines, 275 flow stations, 10 gas plants, 14 export terminals and four refineries (Watts 2008b). There are over 6,000 oil wells and 606 oil fields (Watts 2008b). The Delta generates about 96 percent of all foreign earnings and 85 percent of state revenues and is fundamental to the existence of the Nigerian state (Oyefusi 2008; 2007; Maxted 2006; Ikelegbe 2001; Ibelema 2000; Obi 1997). At a forum under the auspices of the Nigerian Extractive Industry Initiative, Nigerian National Petroleum Corporation Managing Director Mohammed Barkindo stated that between 1999 and 2009, Nigeria earned an estimated $200.34 billion from oil (Muhammed 2010).[5] Consequently, it is no exaggeration that crude oil from the Delta is essential to Nigeria's existence.

The kidnapping of oil workers in the Delta region has ramifications beyond the African continent. The region has become a turf for highlighting divergent and seemingly irreconcilable national interests of various stakeholders. The interest of the US in the Delta's crude oil is an open secret. At least 15 percent of US overseas oil supply comes from sub-Saharan Africa (Volman 2003), chiefly Nigeria and other countries like Angola, Gabon, Republic of Congo, Chad, Equatorial Guinea, Sudan and Libya (Klare and Volman 2004). Attempts by the United States in "securing" Nigeria's democracy are coterminous with guaranteeing ceaseless oil

---

    5   See Muhammed, Hamisu. 2010. "Nigeria gets $200.34 billion in 10 years from oil", *Daily Trust*, April 1.

flow (Lubeck, Watts and Lipschutz 2007: 1). The US continues to provide military assistance to the federal government of Nigeria for the maintenance of order in the Delta region, which further infuriates the militants.

The Chinese have also become part of the struggle for the Delta's oil. Chinese oil firms obtained four oil-drilling licences at a price tag of $4 billion (US) (Obi 2008) in 2006. This has not gone unnoticed by the militants. MEND detonated a car bomb in Warri Delta state on 29 April 2006 during the visit of Chinese president Hu Jintao to demonstrate its rage against the incursion of the Chinese into the Delta. This was a direct warning to the Chinese to "steer clear of the Niger Delta" and refrain from "investing in stolen crude" (BBC News 2006, cited in Obi 2008: 418). In May of 2007, nine Chinese oil workers were kidnapped, while working for the Nigerian Agip Oil Corporation (Obi 2008). However, the Delta struggle targets all foreign interests and not any specific foreign entity (Obi 2008).

Despite the Delta's importance, the region remains one of the poorest and most marginalized in Nigeria's political structure. Studies speak to the gross marginalization of the peoples of the Delta and their deplorable living conditions although Nigeria makes at least $1.5 billion (US) every week from crude oil sales (Watts 2008a, 2008b; Courson 2007; Joab-Peterside 2007a; Omeje 2004). The alienation of the people from the body politic has also received scholarly attention (Joab-Peterside 2007b; Ikelegbe 2005b).

A Terrorist Gang or Social Movement Organization (SMO)?

Liberal democratic states constitute the epicentre of social movement research in spite of the high level of dissident activities against oppressive regimes in the global south (Alimi 2009; Tarrow 2008). This is intriguing because most episodic or systematic evincing of contentious repertoires of protest takes place in authoritarian regimes, especially in the developing countries of Asia, South America and Africa. The paucity of studies focusing on authoritarian settings is particularly surprising because regime type fundamentally shapes the tenor and dynamics of contentious politics and repertoires of protest (Alimi 2009; Tilly 2003, 2004; McAdam, Tarrow and Tilly 2001; Tilly and Tarrow 2007). The curtailment or wholesale denial of human rights (largely taken for granted in liberal democracies)[6] by authoritarian regimes further buttresses the need to investigate how social movement organizations mobilize under difficult circumstances underscored by threats to life and limb.

Social movement scholars have only recently begun to investigate the trajectories of protest in authoritarian or repressive settings (Earl 2006). There has been a tremendous increase in the number of such studies since the 1990s (Alimi 2009). Interestingly, the scope of most of such studies often stops at the use

---

6   For a minority opinion against the supposed cornucopia of rights, hence, relatively unencumbered protest in democratic societies, see McPhail and McCarthy (2005).

of repressive apparatus by the state to control protest (Earl 2006). The adoption of violent architecture of protest by private, non-state actors has not received commensurate attention. The concomitant effect is an impressive over-production of the admittedly effervescent body of evidence about how some nation-states adopt brutal means to quell protest.

While the likes of Fanon (1968) unabashedly call for the use of violence as a tactic of protest (specifically against colonialism), with very few exceptions, the use of violent repertoires of contention has not garnered sufficient attention in social movement literature (but see Seidman 2001). The reality is that around the world, several SMOs are adopting violent tactics without necessarily eschewing non-violent techniques. Adopting violent tactics need not imply that the movement is declining or sick (Seidman 2001). The South African anti-apartheid movement, for instance, presents a clear case, where violent tactics were used simultaneously with peaceful protest. The use of violent tactics by the ANC has not generated sufficient scholarly analysis (Seidman 2001). It is rarely acknowledged that guerrilla warfare helped shape the more overt peaceful struggle. In fact, the emblem of the movement, the Madiba, Nelson Mandela, owed his earlier rise to limelight to his role as the co-founder and first commander of the African National Congress' (ANC) armed wing, *Umkhonto we Sizwe* (The Spear of the Nation). This militia carried out bombing campaigns that occasionally recorded civilian casualties (Seidman 2001).[7]

The silence of scholars of South African anti-apartheid movement on the use of violent tactics by the ANC demonstrates a trend in social movement theory: the tendency to focus on non-violent popular mass protest (Seidman 2001; see Zunes 1999). In spite of scholars' romanticization of peaceful protest, the line between peaceful and violent protest is not often clear (Seidman 2001). Activists in South Africa adopted violent repertoires after years of failure of peaceful tactics (see Davenport 2005). As the anti-apartheid struggle depicts, current theory does not easily lend itself to analyzing armed struggle in social movements (Earl 2006; Seidman 2001). The ANC and its members, including Mandela, were designated "terrorists" by the US government until 2008. Nevertheless, the ANC currently leads post-apartheid South Africa, as the democratically elected government.

The uprising led by the Zapatista Army of National Liberation (EZLN) Zapatista in Chiapas Mexico represents another theoretical conundrum for social movement scholars who consign groups using violent means into a terrorist category. The uprising was a monumental paradox: an armed militia group mobilized dissidents to fight for democracy (Johnston 2000). About 3000 dissidents captured four cities on January 1, 1994 in protest against the North American Free Trade Agreement (NAFTA), the increasing monopolization of the Mexican economy by

---

7   The ANC and its members, including Mandela, were designated "terrorists" by the US government until 2008. See "US has Mandela on terrorist list" 2008 (April 30). URL: http://usatoday30.usatoday.com/news/world/2008-04-30-watchlist_N.htm Accessed 2 December 2010.

transnational corporations, erosion of Mexican sovereignty, lack of local control over natural resources inter alia (Johnston and Laxer 2003). The Zapatista struggle spurred protests in other cities around the world like Seattle, Prague, and Quebec (Johnston and Laxer 2003). The Zapatistas used what Johnston (2000: 465, 478) describes as "armed pedagogy" or "unconventional combination of pedagogy with armed violence". This strategy entails deliberately limiting the use of violence and sensitizing civil society on the unscrupulous actions of the Mexican state and the need for change (Johnston 2000). By articulating its standpoint through the erudite and eloquent *subcomandante* Marcos among others, the Zapatistas made effective use of speech acts (see Johnston 2006) to garner local, national and international sympathy and support.

Scholars have begun to grapple with this conceptual hiatus. Polletta (2006: 475) argues that "the lines separating movement groups from, say, interest groups, charities, terrorist organizations, unions, nongovernmental organizations, and self-help groups often reflect the idiosyncrasies of how subfields have developed rather than anything intrinsic to the phenomena themselves". She describes non-conventional movements such as neo-Nazis, whose stated aims and objectives challenge the researcher's sensibilities as "awkward movements" (p. 475). While many may recoil at the stated objectives of such movements and the groups that represent them, there are other people who may view them as heroes and champions.

As academics, we often engage with groups that conform with our notions of propriety and morality. This necessarily implies indirectly imposing our reality on the subject. However, as Polletta (2006: 476) points out "there is nothing intrinsically awkward about any movement, group, or tactic. Awkwardness is in the eye of the beholder ... it is a feature of the relationship between researcher and research object". As explained below, in spite of its violent tactics, which have led to the loss of dozens of human lives, MEND construes itself as part of the movement for social and environmental justice in the Niger Delta.

Contextualizing MEND within the social movement for justice in the Delta

Throughout this study, the term *social movement* is used to refer to "strings of more or less connected events, scattered across time and space ... (and) consist(s) of groups and organizations, with various levels of formalization, linked in patterns of interaction which run from the fairly centralized to the totally decentralized, from the cooperative to the explicitly hostile" (Diani 2003: 1). Of course, *no single event or organization in and of itself, however, pivotal, constitutes a social movement*. A social movement encompasses several political actors (with similar or divergent identities and loyalties); a plethora of events linked to a broader theme (for instance, environmental justice) that necessarily challenge or defend an existing order—political, religious, ideational, etc. As Tarrow (1998: 4) points out, social movements are "collective challenges based on a common purpose and social solidarities, in sustained interaction with elites, opponents, and authorities".

Major social movements involve a degree of organization drawing on existing networks, contacts, identities and other social and cultural resources. This underscores the significance of a social movement organization (SMO) without which a movement lacks coherence and direction. Typically, a social movement comprises several SMOs in collective interactions: synergistic, antagonistic or mutually reinforcing. By this description, for example, the Zapatistas do not constitute a social movement but a social movement organization. As an SMO, the Zapatistas aligned itself with the social movement for justice in Mexico's "low intensity democracy",— with its implications for the rule of law (Johnston 2000: 465). The deplorable state of the economy, blatant marginalization of indigenous peoples especially in Chiapas, use of state-sponsored paramilitary squads to exterminate unarmed civilians, land distribution issues and so on (Johnston 2000) were issues that predated the Zapatistas. As a result, a significant number of people could identify with Zapatista's resistance against the corrupt Mexican state and globalization forces as embodied in NAFTA (Johnston and Laxer 2003). The Zapatistas benefitted immensely from mobilizing civil society in Mexico and around the world (Bob 2005). NGOs in particular played crucial roles (Bob 2005). The Zapatistas made partial gains in putting indigenous peoples' issues at the center of public debate as well as the urgency of resource redistribution and mass political participation (Johnston and Laxer 2003; Johnston 2000).

MEND is positioned in the wider social movement for human rights and environmental justice in the Niger Delta in a manner that is similar to Mexico's Zapatistas. The social movement for justice in the Niger Delta dates back to pre-colonial times (Alagoa 1964; Boro 1982; Okaba 2009). The grievances in the Delta include the distribution of oil rents, land rights, environmental pollution by oil corporations, among others (Okaba 2009). The Niger Delta became synonymous with agitations for self-determination and minority rights in the 1950s and 1960s. Prior to the formation of MEND, the social movement in the Delta had created what Ikelegbe (2005a: 251) calls "associational flowering". Civil society in the Delta had become more active and activist in scope on issues affecting the region as a result of several factors. These include first, the transformation of communal and ethnic identity dating back to the period of colonialism into groups based on identity politics; the emphasis on self-help by successive post-colonial governments in Nigeria also led to the establishment of multifarious community development associations (Ikelegbe 2005a). In addition, as the traditional system enacted a coterie of associations such as age grades, women's groups, and even secret cults, such groups expanded their role because of harsh socio-economic and political realities. The intensification of the suffering of the people of the Delta, massive unemployment and grievance have combined to serve as harbinger of groups and associations designed to fight for the rights of Deltans (Ikelegbe 2005a, 2001).

These factors produced three kinds of "vertical categories" (Ikelegbe 2005a: 246). These are first a myriad of local associations of youths, women, long-established traditional age-grade groups, community leaders and others concerned with the micro-economics of members. There are also associations on the community, clan or ethnic group scale. These include the Movement for the Survival of Ogoni People (MOSOP), Ijaw Elders Forum, among others. Finally, there are pan-ethnic, regional and groups with national appeal. This category comprises pro-democracy groups, environmental rights, civil rights, and NGOs (Ikelegbe 2005a). Examples include the Niger Delta Peace project Committee, the Organisation for the Restoration of the Actual Rights of Oil Communities, and many others. Others are home-based NGOs like the Environmental Rights Action, Institute of Human Rights and Humanitarian Law and international NGOs like Amnesty International and Human Rights Watch (Ikelegbe 2005a).

Several studies have focused on the rise of violence in urban centers perpetrated by youth in the Delta ostensibly as a form of protest against oil corporations and the Nigerian state (Oruwari 2006). The frenetic proliferation of gangs, cults and ethnic militias has also garnered scholarly attention (Courson 2007). Some of these groups include: the Izon Youth Council (IYC), Egbesu Boys of Africa (EBA), Feibagha Ogbo, Feibokirifagha Ogbo, Meinbutu Boys, Alagbabagha Ogbo and Torudigha Ogbo. Others are Federated Niger Delta Ijaw Communities (FNDIC), the Niger Delta Militant Force Squad (NDMFS), the Niger Delta Strike Force (NDSF), and the Grand Alliance. Groups like the Niger Delta Coastal Guerillas (NDCG), South-South Liberation Movement (SSLM), the November 1895 Movement, ELIMOTU, the Arogbo Freedom Fighters, Iduwini Volunteer Force (IVF), the Niger Delta People's Salvation Front (NDPSF), the Greenlanders, Deebam, Bush Boys, KKK, Black Braziers and Icelanders are also part of the potpourri. More recently, organizations like the Coalition for Militant Action (COMA), Niger Delta People's Volunteer Force (NDPVF), Joint Revolutionary Council and MEND have become very famous (see Courson 2007: 25).

MEND has become the symbol of an increasingly militant trajectory in the social movement for resource control and environmental justice in the Delta. There are several reasons why MEND should be analyzed as an SMO. First, MEND discursively connects itself to the wider social movement in the Delta. MEND's official statements, which form a part of the data analyzed in this study, make direct reference to the emancipation of the Delta people as its major objective. The four major demands of MEND: convocation of a sovereign national conference, fiscal federalism, socio-economic well-being of the Niger Deltans and environmental justice are the cardinal objectives of the social movement in the Delta aimed at addressing the grievances of the people. These objectives transcend any particular SMO.

Second, MEND is part of the "accumulated history" (Tilly and Tarrow 2007: 57) of the Delta. Historical trends, developments and events are crucial to understanding the repertoires of contention in any social movement. Kidnapping was a "known repertoire of contention" (Tarrow 1998: 71) before the formation of MEND in 2005. Oil-producing communities used the kidnapping of oil workers as a form of protest as early as the 1960s (Okaba 2009) as explained in Chapter 7. Besides, prior to the formation of MEND, protest in the Delta was a combination of peaceful demonstration and increasingly violent and militant tactics like pipeline vandalism and illegal oil bunkering (see Ikelegbe 2005a).

Third, the situation in the Delta established a movement for justice with thousands of willing and versatile young men and women in the Eastern and Western Delta. As argued in Chapter 4, MEND is a mere beneficiary of an army of everyday people ready to take on the Nigerian state and its oil industry. The sheer number of insurgents demonstrates that the wider movement is not a collection of small pockets of people or gangs. For example, MEND's affiliate called "Camp 5" in Gbaramatu Kingdom, Delta state had over 3000 operatives at the height of the insurgency. Although the exact number of insurgents is not known, the Camp 5 operatives are only a fraction of the overall insurgents. One clear yet incomplete indication of the number of insurgents is the over 20,000 people who accepted the government's amnesty program in 2009 and went through rehabilitation in Obubra, Cross River state.

Other evidence that MEND is seen as a platform for engaging the state in the struggle for justice in the Delta can be seen in the overwhelming public support it enjoys. In a 2009 press release on a military action in Agge community, for instance, the JTF lamented how "the militants were neither condemned for attacking JTF troops … nor the community condemned for allowing miscreants to use their area as staging base for attacks … but the JTF was accused of carrying out an attack on Agge community". This statement demonstrates that the Nigerian authorities recognize that the insurgents enjoy a significant level of public sympathy and legitimacy. This is fully discussed in Chapter 4.

Analyzing the enigma called MEND as an SMO *neither implies condoning its violent tactics nor rationalization its actions*. A growing number of scholars recognize that certain groups resort to using violence when opportunities for peaceful protest are blocked (see Seidman 2001; Earl 2006; Alimi 2009). This is generally against the tenor of research by social movement scholars in liberal democratic states, where there exist more patterned and regularized methodologies for protest. Indeed groups that elect to use violence as a form of protest, particularly in authoritarian settings or countries in the interstices of absolute rule and democracy may be on the ascendance and not necessarily declining. As groups like Hamas and Hezbollah demonstrate in their morally bifurcated actions, an organization that is categorized as terrorist—and indeed perpetrates acts of terrorism—may be perceived as heroes and champions by the people in its immediate constituency. Hamas, for instance, is on the terrorist organizations' list of the European Union and many countries, including Canada and the US, yet it is also the democratically elected government in the Gaza Strip. While allegedly sponsoring terrorist acts, Hamas also provides roads, schools and other social services.

MEND is analyzed as an SMO because of the staggering evidence that everyday people in the Delta believe MEND are engaged in the inter-generational Delta struggle for justice in spite of its tactics. In Chapter 3, the current wave of kidnapping in Nigeria is contextualized within its historical and socio-political flows, while taking cognizance of the political opportunities and constraints on insurgents.

Why Investigate Kidnapping of Oil Workers in the Delta? Raison d'être of the Study

This book is situated in the interstitial space between the burgeoning subfield of critical criminology and social movement scholarship. A critical approach to criminology necessarily investigates the role of power, conflict and vested interests in criminality (Ratner 1989). More importantly, critical criminology "brackets" state definitions of *crime* while emphasizing praxis that is not conditional on the total collapse of capitalist society (Ratner 1989: 6).

Insurgents in the Delta organize themselves into groups, consciously mobilize human and material resources and attempt to garner bystander support through various framing strategies. These actors form social movement organizations (SMOs) such as MEND with a clear methodology of protest—albeit violent— rather than the unpredictable demonstrations of anger by mobs in collective behaviour approaches (see Buechler 2004; della Porta & Diani 1999; Smelser 1962, cited in della Porta and Diani 1999). Consequently, a nuanced analysis of MEND and its cohort necessarily entails drawing on a theoretical conjuncture of critical criminology and the political process paradigm of the social movement literature.

This book fills a gulf in our understanding of the Delta crisis. Many studies have focused on oil dependence and civil conflict (Oyefusi 2007; Tabb 2007; Ross 2004; Collier and Hoeffler 2002). Scholars have investigated the probability of or predispositional factors to rebel participation by Delta youths (Oyefusi 2008), and mobilization, leadership and media strategies in the internationalization of the Ogoni struggle (Bob 2002, 2005). The collation and documentation of serious security breaches in the Delta (Bergen Risk Solution 2007, 2006), intensification of civil society participation in the Delta struggle (Ikelegbe 2001) and the rise of violence among youth in the Delta (Human Rights Watch 2005) among others have also generated an impressive assortment of literature. However, to date, very few studies have specifically focused on empirically analyzing the rise of and turn to *kidnapping* in the Delta and how the Delta people view this act by their youths.

Although there are some allusions to the use of violence as *resistance* among youths in the Delta (Ikelegbe 2005b) and the *grievances* of the people, it is quite perplexing that apart from the analysis of the rise and decline of MOSOP and its organizational prowess (see Okonta 2008; Bob 2005, 2002), the on-going Delta struggle has not been concisely embedded in the wider social movement literature. In fact, with only few exceptions (see Ihediwa 2008: 1205; Ikelegbe 2005b), terms like "protest movement" or "resistance" are rarely used in enunciating the rise of militias in the Delta and other parts of Nigeria. Rather than presupposing that kidnapping in the Delta is an aberration, this book investigates kidnapping as a trajectory within the Delta movement dating back to at least the 1950s. Cognizant of historical antecedents and progenitors of the on-going struggle in the Delta, this book avoids the misleading tendency of some studies on militancy in the Delta to essentialize kidnapping rather than investigate the phenomenon as a momentous development in a long-standing tradition of protests within an increasingly intolerable socio-economic climate marked by routine state repression.

As stated earlier, the adoption of violent tactics by social movement organizations often poses a quandary for social movement scholars owing to the romanticization of peaceful tactics of protest (Seidman 2001). Scholars pay scant attention to the intricate relationship between violent and non-violent mechanisms of protest having begun with the presupposition that adopting violent tactics implies that the movement is in decline (Seidman 2001). However, the Delta movement has never been more alive. That said, the strategies adopted by groups like MEND in framing kidnapping have yet to generate deserved attention. To the best of my knowledge, this book is the first to *systematically* explicate the framing strategies of MEND. It investigates the opinions of insurgents who have accepted the amnesty offered by the federal government of Nigeria in 2009 and are now undergoing "rehabilitation". The opinions of 42 of such insurgents help illuminate our understanding of the struggle, how they view their involvement, and the place of MEND in the social movement universe in the Delta.

Kidnapping as a social phenomenon has not received the attention it deserves in the criminological literature (Tzanelli 2006; Turner 1998). Rather problematically, the criminological notion of crime is narrowly conceptualized (Morrison 2006; Agozino 2003), relying on the idea of a subset of society engaging in acts defined as crime, while the rest of society, represented by the state, deploys its might to control crime. In contrast, the study of politically motivated violence should be a central focus of criminologists as it was to the likes of Lombroso, Bentham, Beccaria and other early figures in the discipline's history (Ruggiero 2005).

This book adds to the stock of knowledge about the Delta situation, the resource war literature, political economy and studies on transnational corporations' activities in the developing world. It also makes important contributions to the fields of political science, social movements and studies on resistance from below. It provides an empirical case for the theoretical concepts developed by Tilly (2003, 2004), McAdam, Tarrow and Tilly (2001) and Tilly and Tarrow (2007) and interrogates Hobsbawm's (1969, 1959) concept of "social banditry" in order to ascertain whether those kidnapping oil workers are perceived as modern-day Robin Hoods or common criminals. This book also contributes to understanding the role of the contours and dynamics of the political process in generating protest, framing, dissident rhetoric, and social movement theory in general.

The Delta issue requires urgent attention. There is a great danger of further economic turmoil as corporations are beginning to divest from the Delta because of kidnapping of workers and other security concerns. Chevron, for instance has begun to divest by selling its 380 service stations (oil retail business) to Corlay Global SA (Olanrewaju 2008).[8] Most countries now have strongly worded travel

---

8   See Olanrewaju, Suleiman. 2008. "Chevron to sell off 380 stations in Nigeria", *Saturday Tribune*, September 20. Available at http://www.tribune.com.ng/19092008/news/news3.html Accessed September 20, 2008.

warnings to their citizens wishing to travel to Nigeria because of the Delta situation. The US State Department for instance warns US citizens of "possible dangers of travel to Nigeria, and to note the *continued unstable security situation in the Niger Delta region. American citizens should defer all but essential travel to Delta, Bayelsa, and Rivers states because of the very high risk of kidnapping, robbery, and other armed attacks in these areas.* American citizens who are resident in the Delta are strongly advised to review their personal security in light of the information contained in this Travel Warning when deciding whether to remain"[9] (emphasis added). For a country struggling economically and wishing to attract investors around the world, the Delta situation is not only an unmitigated embarrassment; it is disastrous for Nigeria as a whole.

By contributing to an understanding of the phenomenon of kidnapping in the Delta, it is hoped that this book will contribute to efforts to help rescue Africa's sleeping giant from its major existential threat since the Civil War (1967–70) and prevent yet another theatre of war in Africa. For the masses of the Delta, this is a bottom-up study where popular voices and concerns are articulated. This book is beneficial to the Federal Government of Nigeria, the nine states of the Niger Delta region specifically, and Nigeria as a whole. Non-Governmental Organizations concerned with human rights, indigenous peoples' rights, and resource control, environmentalist groups, scholars interested in activities of transnational corporations, peace and conflict resolution, youth studies, security studies, developing societies/economies and so on will find this book useful. In addition, this book contributes to the growing scholarly literature on failed or failing states (see Joseph 1987).

The focus of this book has international ramifications, as the Delta situation has grievous consequences beyond Nigeria's shores. Not only does the Delta crisis affect global oil supply and price, the harsh reality of kidnapping in the Delta is that the main targets are foreign oil workers from the US, UK and other Western countries. There is no over-emphasizing the fact that if the crisis leads to a complete violent break-up of Nigeria, the concomitant humanitarian crises involving Nigeria's over 170 million people, the largest number of Africans anywhere on earth, will be unprecedented. The sheer number of people—women, children, men, young and old—and the complexity of the geographical terrain with the cost of humanitarian assistance will be very daunting for all concerned.

---

9 United states Department of State. 2007. "Travel Warning: Nigeria". Available at http://travel.state.gov/travel/cis_pa_tw/tw/tw_928.html Accessed September 25, 2008. Warnings such as this are of course interesting considering the high level of gun violence in the US.

Data and Methods

The objectives of this book are addressed through a two-pronged primary data collection method involving interviews and focus group discussions (FGDs). Online sources specifically official e-mails from MEND's spokesperson, Jomo Gbomo, are also used in this book. These sources are augmented with secondary sources such as official reports of Niger Delta Development Commission (NDDC) and newspaper data.

In total, six sets of actors were involved in the primary data collection process. These are community members (made up of men, and women over 18 years), political and environmental justice activists as well as representatives of relevant NGOs and militants undergoing rehabilitation. Others are journalists and military authorities. In all, 42 interviews and 13 FGDs were conducted. Nineteen ex-insurgents were interviewed. Seventy two persons participated in 13 FGDs. The FGDs varied in size from a minimum of two participants to nine. These include 23 ex-insurgents in five FGDs, seven editorial board members of a major newspaper in Nigeria and over 50 community members drawn from Agge community in 2009 and Okerenkoko in 2010.

Agge community in Bayelsa state and Okerenkoko in Delta state serve as the case studies of this research. Agge and Okerenkoko are approached as archetypes of the Delta universe and oil-related violence. Agge community was the site of the August 3, 2008 military action by the federal government of Nigeria's Joint Task Force (JTF). Okerenkoko in Gbaramatu Kingdom has also experienced several JTF actions including incidents in 2003 and 2009.

Although normal ethical protocol requires using pseudonyms in place of real names of research participants, some of the participants in this study were already well-known individuals and agreed to have their names revealed. Some of the participants that were willing to be identified include:

- Ken Saro Wiwa (Jr), presidential adviser and son of the late Ken Saro Wiwa (August 2010)
- General Sarkin Yaki Bello, JTF commander, (August 2010)[10]
- Asari Dokubo, former IYC president and founder of the Niger Delta People's Volunteer Force (NDPVF, July 2010)
- Henry Bindodogha, Leader of the Niger Delta Freedom Fighters (NDFF, July 2010)
- Dr. Ukam Edodi, Director of Planning, Niger Delta Development Commission (NDDC, July 2009)
- Onengiya Erekosima, founder and president, Niger Delta Non-Violent Movement (NDNVM, July 2009)

---

10   Gen. Bello was relieved of his JTF duties in September 2010. He is referred to as JTF commander throughout this book, as he was in charge at the time of conducting this research.

- Alagoa Morris, Project Officer, Environmental Rights Action, (ERA) (July 2009; follow up in August 2010)
- Col. Rabe Abubakar, Coordinator Joint Media Campaign Centre (JMCC), Joint Task Force (JTF, July 2009)
- Lieutenant Colonel Timothy Antigha, Successor to Col. Abubakar as Coordinator Joint Media Campaign Centre (JMCC), Joint Task Force (JTF, July 2010)
- Oboko Bello, President Federated Niger Delta Ijaw Communities (FNDIC)
- Prof. Benjamin Okaba, director, Centre for Niger Delta Studies (CNDS), Niger Delta University, Wilberforce Island, Bayelsa state (July 2009)
- Allen Onyema, president Federation for Ethnic Harmony in Nigeria (FEHN), the NGO appointed by the federal government to provide "Kingian non-violent" training for ex-militants at the Obubra camp, Cross River state (July 2010)
- Paramount chief of Agge community (June 2009)
- Rank and file ex-insurgents directly involved in kidnapping (June – July 2010)

The list above provides only a glimpse of the richness of the data collected and analyzed in this book. Having such a diverse set of participants—activists, military authorities, insurgents engaged in kidnapping, NGO representatives, community leaders—affords the opportunity to cross-check information and provide a sense of the complexity of the Niger Delta movement.

The participants from the community were drawn using snowball sampling. This approach is informed by the nature of the topic of this research and entails relying on participants to recommend others willing to be part of the study. Political activists such as Ken Saro Wiwa (Jr.) and environmental rights activists like Morris Alagoa, who had been very vocal about the Delta issue, however, were selected purposively in light of their explicit engagement with the Delta.

All of the interviews and FGDs were semi-structured. The questions asked in the interviews were open-ended. This gave participants the opportunity to express themselves. It also enabled the researcher to ask follow-up questions. An interview guide was prepared to serve as a compass for the interviews and focus group discussions. Most of the interviews were conducted in Yenagoa, Bayelsa state, Warri, Delta state, Port Harcourt, Rivers state, Obubra, Cross River state, Benin, Edo state and Abuja, the Federal Capital Territory of Nigeria. In all, the fieldwork was conducted in five of the nine Niger Delta states. These are Rivers, Bayelsa, Delta, Edo and Cross River.

E-mails from "Jomo Gbomo"

Although this book uses several secondary sources, one of these sources—e-mails from Jomo Gbomo, MEND's spokesperson, requires a little explication. At my behest, a revered environmental justice activist in the Delta sent an e-mail to

Jomo Gbomo, the spokesperson of MEND, to add my e-mail address to MEND's mailing list. I followed up with an e-mail to Jomo Gbomo directly. On Monday 24 August 2009, Jomo Gbomo responded positively. A total of 30 official e-mails from MEND are analyzed. These e-mails were sent between Monday 24 August 2009 and Tuesday 19 October 2010. There were about 50 persons or organizations receiving these e-mails around the world. The listserv includes media organizations such as al-Jazeera, the *Financial Times* of London, South African Broadcasting Corporation (SABC), Bergen Risk Solutions, Sahara Reporters, Reuters, Bloomberg News, *Newswatch*, the *Daily Trust* and *Next* Newspapers of Nigeria among others.

Scope and Limitations of the Study

This book focuses specifically on kidnapping by MEND and its affiliate insurgent groups in the Delta and not the practice of kidnappings in other parts of Nigeria. Although the phenomenon has run amok in many cities as demonstrated in the kidnapping of several Nollywood actors[11] and business elites mainly outside the Delta, this book does not address such opportunistic kidnappings unconnected to the Delta movement. Such kidnappings are symptoms of a deeper malaise. None the less, they certainly warrant being legitimate subjects of study.

Second, several studies have documented the active involvement of women in resisting the state and transnational corporations in Nigeria (Turner and Oshare 1994) and around the world (Stern 2005; Noonan 1995). Women have often succeeded in protesting issues ranging from unemployment to environmental degradation by sometimes shutting down oil infrastructure through their sheer organisational finesse, determination, and overwhelming numbers (see Ikelegbe 2005a). Although the role of women in the insurgency is analyzed in Chapter 4, this book focuses specifically on the activities of male youths spearheading kidnapping of oil workers. Women's repertoire of protest warrants a book of its own in spite of the insight about women's involvement in the insurgency provided in this book.

Third, the major timeline covered by this study is December 2005 to October 2010. This is not necessarily arbitrary. MEND announced itself to the world in December 2005. Kidnapping at a furious pace was underway by January 2006 until 2008 (see Bergen Risk Solutions 2010). By July 2009, the federal government of Nigeria proclaimed amnesty for interested militants. October 2010 is chosen as

---

11   Nkem Owoh (Osuofia) and Pete Edochie are two of the Nollywood celebrities kidnapped for ransom on 9 November 2009 and 16 August 2009 respectively. Rather bizarrely, a Canadian woman was kidnapped in the Northern city of Kaduna on 16 April 2009. Only Owoh's kidnapping occurred in the Delta. These three incidents fall outside the purview of this study as all three victims were not oil workers and were kidnapped under non-oil related circumstances.

the end date of the study to signal the period the last set of data was collected. Therefore, while mention is made of periods outside this timeframe, especially the pinnacle of MOSOP's ascendance in the 1990s, *the central attention of this book is the incursion of MEND and its ilk into the Delta social movement.*

Fourth, while I expected to be treated as an insider-outsider as a Nigerian conducting fieldwork in the Delta, there were moments when it was obvious that the realities of the Delta people were radically different from what I thought I was familiar with. I will never know the full impact of my identity as a Yoruba—one of the three major ethnic groups widely regarded as benefitting from the misery of the Delta people—on this book. This proactive disclosure is made cognizant that insiderness and outsiderness are never static but a becoming.[12]

Finally, although this book is *primarily concerned with kidnapping of oil workers* in the Niger Delta, there is no escaping other forms of expression of the insurgency such as illegal oil bunkering and pipeline vandalism. However, this is not without its disadvantages. Kidnapping is only a part of a larger and more complex story. This is because kidnapping often occurs concurrently with illegal oil bunkering, oil facility sabotage among other acts. Therefore, focusing on kidnapping is an empirical research choice. None the less, where it is impossible to disentangle other insurgent acts from kidnapping, all the observable collective actions with kidnapping are analyzed.

Organization of the Book

This book is organized into eight chapters. A brief description of Chapters 2 to 8 is provided below:

Chapter 2, Kidnapping as "public good": The Actors, Social Benefits and Harms of Nigeria's Oil Insurgency, is an analysis of kidnapping episodes in the Delta as a spectacular series of theatrical performances within a lethal amphitheatre. The "impression management" roles and performances of two sets of actors in kidnapping incidents in the Delta are problematized. These actors include the Delta communities, interventionists, oil workers, oil corporations, the Nigerian state/ security agencies, insurgents, "quasi-invisible" actors, and insurance companies, among others.

Chapter 3, Criminal Resistance? Interrogating Political Kidnapping, begins with the nature and dynamics of the phenomenon of kidnapping. Two sets of theoretical work are interrogated. First, the conceptualization of *social banditry* by Hobsbawm (1969, 1959) is used to enunciate the phenomenon of kidnapping in the Delta. Second, the Political Process paradigm of the social movement literature is examined. This includes the seminal work of Tilly (2003, 2004),

---

12   For more on my experience while conducting research in the Niger Delta, see "The ambivalent insider/outsider status of academic 'homecomers': Observations on identity and field research in the Nigerian Delta", *Sociology*, 46, 3: 540–48 (with Kevin Haggerty).

McAdam, Tarrow and Tilly (2001) and Tilly and Tarrow (2007) and many others (e.g della Porta and Diani 1999). This is used to examine the rationale behind the adoption of various repertoires of protest. Specifically, the notion of *contentious politics* by Charles Tilly and his collaborators helps to inform an understanding of the dynamics of protest in the Delta and the political opportunity for kidnapping oil workers in the Niger Delta. Factors like inattention to earlier forms of protest, routinization of violence, constitutional reforms, and backfire on state repression, among others are analyzed as major contributors to the rise of kidnapping.

Chapter 4, Car-bombing "with due respect": The Idea Called MEND, is an investigation of the Movement for the Emancipation of the Niger Delta (MEND). An analysis of MEND's origins, its demands, and mode of operation is provided. In addition, using the Niger Delta Freedom Fighters, an affiliate of MEND, the space re-presented by the creeks and its significance in the insurgency is theorized. This is followed by a brief analysis of the role of women in the insurgency.

Chapter 5, Framing the MEND Insurgency, examines the factors inherent in MEND's framing strategies. Specifically, the strong religious overtones, ridicule and irony, among others as a prelude to MEND's framing narrative are articulated. The theoretical achievements in the framing perspective help to explicate MEND's diagnosis of the Delta problem, as well as its prognostic and motivational framing.

Chapter 6, Master Frames in the MEND Insurgency, interrogates the master frames in the MEND insurgency. The imperative of violence frame, the injustice frame and the human/minority rights frames are analyzed. It is submitted that the metanarrative of the MEND insurgency is *the imperative of violence master frame*: insurgents believe the Nigerian state has created a war situation, thus, kidnapping oil workers is an act of war. This chapter also analyzes the environmental justice and the return to (true) democracy master frames in the MEND insurgency. The environmental justice frame enables MEND to accentuate the environmental hazards posed by oil extraction in the Delta, while the return to (true) democracy master frame helps MEND to put itself on a moral pedestal as a force for championing the cause of democratic reforms.

Chapter 7, A Repertoire of Protest or Criminal Expropriation?, is an investigation of how two oil-producing communities, Agge in Bayelsa state and Okerenkoko in Delta state understand the kidnapping of oil workers. It is submitted that any community with at least one recognized *benevolent Insurgent commander* will overtly support the insurgency while any community without a benevolent insurgent commander will overtly oppose kidnapping. Specifically, the messianicity of a charismatic insurgent and pioneer MEND member, Government Ekpemupolo or "Tom Polo" is problematized. The weakness and failure of the Nigerian state, and personal characteristics have made Tom Polo the major figure in the insurgency.

Chapter 8, Summary and Conclusions, reviews the findings of the study, contributions to the discipline and offers suggestions for future research.

Chapter 2

Kidnapping as "Public Good": The Actors, Social Benefits and Harms of Nigeria's Oil Insurgency[1]

Introduction

> Scripts even in the hands of unpracticed players can come to life because life itself is a dramatically enacted thing. All the world is not, of course, a stage, but the crucial ways in which it isn't are not easy to specify. (Goffman 1973: 72)

Erving Goffman's analysis of the minutiae of everyday interactions demonstrates the (melo)drama that undergirds human life (1973, 1967). In presenting themselves in everyday life, people routinely employ "impression management" (Goffman 1973: 208). This involves the expression an individual *gives*, for instance, verbally, and the expression such an individual *gives off* through their actions (Goffman 1973: 2). Unwittingly or consciously, these intertwined phenomena involve deceit and feigning respectively (Goffman 1973). Goffman sees a similarity between the theatrical performances of actors on stage and how individuals act in daily life. He conceives of the social world as a theatre where individuals have roles in on-going collective mutually intelligible performances. Therefore, the presentation of self—how people performatively conduct themselves or play their assigned role—is fundamental to the "normal" functioning of the society. This chapter demonstrates how various actors in the Delta region of Nigeria—pro-establishment and challengers of authority—maintain the *status quo* in spite of overwhelming agitation for social change. The cost on both sides is also highlighted. The aim is to show how a seemingly deplorable social condition is nurtured by those who directly benefit from it as well as those who purport to change it.

The application of Goffman's dramaturgical analysis—or conceptualization of the social world as a theatre of performativity—to interrogating social movements and social movement organizations is not new. A dramaturgical approach helps to understand the "social construction and communication of meaning, including formulating roles and characterizations, managing performance regions, controlling

---

1 A version of this chapter was presented under the same title at the Canadian Sociological Association (CSA) Annual Conference (Congress of Humanities and Social Sciences) at St. Thomas University, Fredericton, New Brunswick, Canada, May 31 – June 4 2011. It was awarded the CSA "Best Student Paper" Prize in the Graduate category.

information, sustaining dramatic tensions and orchestrating emotions" (Benford and Hunt 1992: 37). From this perspective, social movements are "dramas in which protagonists and antagonists compete to affect audiences' interpretations of power relations in a variety of domains" (Benford and Hunt 1992: 38). These dramas are not only "emergent and ongoing phenomena" (Benford and Hunt 1992: 38), they are also mimetic and iterative. This is because actors in social movement dramatic moments attempt to influence other *dramatis personae* and take cues from supporting and opposing sides to enhance their performance and ultimately the outcome of their struggle. The theatrics of definition between insurgents and the Nigerian state is only one instance of this contentious drama in the Delta movement. The Nigerian state vacillates between labeling people who kidnap oil workers as "terrorists" and "militants"[2] while the young people refer to themselves as "freedom-fighters".[3]

In this chapter, kidnapping is analyzed as a spectacular array of performances within an ambience of *contentious politics* manufactured by the intricacies of the political economy of the Nigerian rentier petro-state. Kidnapping in the Delta embodies melodrama. The dramatis personae understand their roles well. The roles are articulately scripted, organically orchestrated and meticulously delivered. The setting of this real-life drama goes beyond the Niger Delta. The whole of Nigeria and the world which suffers increases in prices of crude oil are secondary settings. The Nigerian society, the global oil industry, the human rights community, local and international media as well as countries dependent on fossil fuels are all the audience for this play. However, a set of actors can serve as the audience and participants in a social movement drama (see Benford and Hunt 1992; Goffman 1973). The audience is not totally passive but actively involved as participants.

Without meaning to impugn the intentions of the JTF, other security agencies and concerned civil society groups, what is happening in the Niger Delta is not a singular attempt to quell the social problem posed by kidnapping and other tactics of insurgents, but often a form of *impression management* (see Goffman 1973) that guides the conduct of all the actors. The Nigerian state and other actors involved in the kidnapping drama present a bifocal performance: the front stage, where they privilege a narrative of conscientious efforts to resolve the crisis and the back stage, which suggests that efforts being made only exacerbate and perpetuate incidents of kidnapping. The major concern of the Nigerian state, for instance, is to provide an atmosphere that is sufficiently safe for oil extraction to continue unabated. For others, the play is a dangerous but innovative means of livelihood in a perpetually depressed economy. While the Delta insurgency generates harms for all the actors involved, it also has many benefits for all the participants.

---

2   Interviewee 12.
3   Interviewee 15.

Major Players in the Kidnapping of Oil Workers in the Delta

There are two categories of actors involved in Nigeria's oil insurgency. These are first-order and second-order cast. This categorization is far from whimsical, as shown below. Each of these actors performs different roles. There is also a "dramaturgical cooperation" (Goffman 1973: 82) among the cast in the performance of their roles. The performances are mimetic and iterative as the effectiveness of each set of actors in performing its role often depends on the theatrics of other actors.

First-order cast

This category comprises actors whose performances have the greatest influence on kidnapping episodes. The actors in this category include oil-producing Niger Delta communities, interventionists, oil workers, oil corporations, the Nigerian state/ security agencies, and insurgents. In what follows, these players are introduced and their roles, social benefits and harms they receive from the insurgency and how they manage impressions based on their position in the Delta insurgency are analyzed.

Niger Delta communities

The effects of the insurgency have been "sweet and sour" (Watts 2008b: 2) for members of oil-producing communities as they bear significant negative consequences of the proliferation of insurgent acts in their domain. First, kidnapping and other insurgent acts have become a convenient excuse for government failure in providing security and basic social infrastructure. In one instance, construction giant Julius Berger abandoned the popular East-West road project citing security concerns (See "N/Delta: Julius Berger ordered to refund N6.1 billion", *Nigerian Tribune*, 23 April 2009). State officials are quick to point this out as the reason for the neglect of the region.

The shadow economy around kidnappings creates mutual mistrust and animosities that lead to violence. Oil-producing communities experience violence in at least four major ways. In the first case, several casualties result from the battle over "illegal bunkering territorial space" (Okaba 2009: 12). This relates to the struggle by rival groups over who controls what exploitable space, where oil wells are located. In the second case, the stakes involved in ascending to chieftaincy positions have been raised. This is because of the staggering bribes and other emoluments community leaders supposedly receive for oil drilling to continue. This has resulted in chieftaincy disputes, and intra-community clashes among factionalized groups. In the third case, a series of inter-community clashes over oil-rich land and geographical boundaries has continued to grow in the Delta. This set of conflicts arises partly because the socio-economic relevance and revenue accruable to a community hinge on the number of oil wells it possesses. Finally, kidnapping and illegal bunkering activities have led to JTF operations designed to restore peace. These operations come with significant cost in human lives as innocent civilians die in some of those incidents. *The Sun* newspaper headline of 25 May 2009 captures the "burden of oil" (Courson 2007: 2) vividly: "Niger Delta war: Pa Juweigha, 102, oldest man in Gbaramatu bombed to death".

Consequently, the fear of violence in the Delta communities is high. Although there is no hard evidence suggesting that Yenagoa, for instance, is more dangerous than Lagos, the insurgency and its accompanying hyper-militarization (see Joab-Peterside 2007b) makes violent outbreaks routine. Maintaining law and order in the communities has become a difficult task (see Oruwari 2006; Kemedi 2006; Watts 2004), causing incidents of opportunistic crimes to increase.

However, contrary to popular representation, the Niger Delta communities are not non-agentic docile entities in the processual manufacturing of kidnapping incidents and other repertoires of protest adopted by insurgents. Illegal oil bunkering and kidnapping rarely occur without the active connivance or tacit approval (for instance, by refusing to alert authorities) of community members. The historical resistance of the Ijaws to authority perceived as oppressive is legendary (Ukiwo 2007). In fact, kidnapping as a form of protest was not invented by the so-called "militants" but by oil-producing communities in the predominantly Ijaw-speaking areas of the Delta region (Okaba 2009).[4]

The kidnapping of Chevron staff in a communal protest led by Federated Niger Delta Ijaw Community (FNDIC), a self-avowed "nongovernmental, non-violent, pro-democracy organization" provides evidence suggesting that some Delta communities resort to kidnapping as a "survival strategy". In March 2003, FNDIC mobilized the people of Okerenkoko community against the "application of wrong electoral constituencies and wards". Protesters marched to the neighbouring Kolokuoma community to vent their anger. By 13 March, military reprisal began in Okerenkoko. A detachment of JTF operatives fired at community members on a boat and the people "had to think on how to survive".[5] FNDIC discovered that Chevron:

> provided logistics for them (the military), they fed these people, bought boats for them, you know they used their facilities to attack us. They formed the springboard for the attack on us. So, the decision to survive was either you are in the river fighting or you go to their base and reduce their firepower and that was why the activities, the response activities of the people, the survival activities, was extended. There was no decision to go attacking oil installations but these people provided the springboard of the attack on us.[6]

FNDIC led the people of Okerenkoko community to Escravos, where expatriates working for Chevron were rounded up and held hostage as "human shield" against

---

4   Interviewee 2, 15, 37, 38.

5   Interviewee 38. FINDIC President, Oboko Bello. Personal interview, 25 August 2010, Warri Delta state.

6   Interviewee 38.

the military assault of the JTF in Okerenkoko. This was said to be a "spontaneous mass reaction" as a form of "self-defence".[7] FNDIC believed that the "JTF will not see an oyibo (white) man and shoot because the FG is afraid of the US and Britain".[8] FNDIC kidnapped another set of nine foreign oil workers to protect the people of Gbaramatu Kingdom against renewed JTF attacks in 2006.[9]

Kidnapping also helps neglected oil-producing communities to garner the attention of the Nigerian state. FNDIC's media coordinator, Bolou Custom affirms that kidnapping is "fair game" because "whatever attention the struggle has gotten is because of the kidnapping thing" as it has helped in "amplifying the voice of the people". Besides occasionally kidnapping and using foreign oil workers as human shields, and drawing attention to their living conditions, some oil-producing communities benefit from *responsible* insurgents who use the revenue from kidnapping and illegally bunkered oil to provide social goods for the people. One notable insurgent commander frequently mentioned by ex-insurgents is Mr Government Ekpemupolo, known as "Tom Polo", the founder of the notorious "Camp 5" group, a major affiliate of MEND. A political activist explains that:

> The case of Tom Polo is a good example of a militant who used part of the resources in advancing the cause of his people. He built the palace of the king, did water projects, provided scholarships, generators, and so on. In situations like that ... even with the recent bombardment (by the Nigerian military), because he had the support of the people, he escaped through canoes ...[10]

The public support for Tom Polo in Okerenkoko is interesting because the military raids Tom Polo's activities generated have led to the loss of several lives in his community,[11] a number estimated at over 500,[12] although the JTF denies this claim.[13]

The insurgency has also been a source of employment for some youths in the Delta. For instance, all the participants in this study from Okerenkoko agree that Tom Polo's Camp 5 has been a significant source of productively engaging unemployed youths in the area.[14] Camp 5 is believed to have employed at least 3000 youths at the height of its activities. This is a major social service in a country with a nearly 20 percent unemployment rate.

---

7   Interviewee 38.

8   Interviewee 37. FINDIC media coordinator, Bolou Custom. Personal interview, 24 August 2010. Warri Delta state.

9   Interviewee 37.

10   Interviewee 2.

11   Focus Group 7 and 8. Select men and women in Okerenkoko community. 19 August 2010.

12   Interviewee 34. An ex-militant who worked for Tompolo at Camp 5. He claims that he lost his best friend and some of his colleagues during the attack on their camp by the JTF.

13   Interviewee 12. General Bello, JTF commander.

14   Focus Group Discussion 8; Okerenkoko women.

Similarly, illegal oil bunkering in many oil-producing communities is not an aberration but a widespread and popular social action. The level of participation is astounding: men and women, the elderly and those too young to understand what is happening are all involved in scooping fuel for survival.[15] Many members of oil-producing communities have also mastered the science of processing illegally bunkered crude oil into diesel. This is merely one of the sedimented knowledges handed down from one generation to another in remote oil-producing communities.

Using kidnapping to raise awareness about the plight of the people, provide human shield and gain socially beneficial projects from ransom money constitute the back stage that is seldom revealed to the audience. The front stage, where harms are distributed is the narrative of choice. None the less, as demonstrated in the concomitant harms affecting oil-producing communities, attempts to change the existing marginalization of the people by insurgents have merely led to its reinforcement.

Interventionists

The idea that some social problems, such as poverty and political instability, generate opportunities for material and symbolic profits at the individual and institutional level is neither novel nor surprising (see Gans 1972; Okonta and Douglas 2001; Klein 2007). There are several actors notably politicians, elders, monarchs, and opinion leaders, or "stakeholders", from the Niger Delta and outside the zone, who have foisted themselves on the kidnapping episodes and are reaping from it. This category of actors may be designated *interventionists.* Interventionists enjoy spectacular visibility on radio, television, newspapers, magazines, popular consciousness and public discourse. Their faces have become the insignia of the times. The socio-political relevance of such actors has been bolstered by the intensification of kidnapping as they serve as mediators in such episodes. Kidnapping has also become a titillating windfall for these influential individuals. All manner of peace and reconciliation committees, concerned citizens' groups and NGOs have proliferated in Nigeria. As with many social problems, institutions established to tackle kidnapping have merely joined a performative fray.

There is evidence suggesting that the intermediary role such elites play also provides a feedback loop. An editorial in *The Punch* newspaper on 13 July, 2007 puts it succinctly: "Evidently, from their intermediary roles between militants and their captives in the process of securing the latter's release, some governors, politicians and prominent elders in the region seem to know more about the crime than they are prepared to divulge" (14). One activist shares this assertion:

> I know of a state where the major anchorman between the kidnappers and the state is a commissioner. In all the cabinets in the Niger Delta, you will find at least five per cent made up of former criminals, militant leaders held by the

---

15   Interviewee 19. My decision to take pictures of community members processing crude oil into diesel was met with a friendly but firm resistance by this participant.

politicians to say be with us, we are going to use you at the appropriate time. The government is sustaining them. We have some cases whereby some governors go to their camp, pay them lavishly.[16]

While it is nearly impossible to ascertain the authenticity of the percentage of ex-militants in cabinet positions, what is hardly in doubt is that the rapport between insurgents and some elders and politicians during kidnapping negotiations is rather cozy. The ostensibly seamless incorporation of ex-kidnappers in the body politic suggests a long-standing symbiotic relationship between elected leaders and self-anointed insurgents. Insurgents, it appears, are not necessarily operating within an illegitimate social space; rather, they seem to have all along been at the interstitial space between legality and illegality afforded by what Joseph (1987) calls Nigeria's prebendal political economy.

The demands made by militants for the release of 24 Filipinos kidnapped on January 21 2007 provide an apt case. The militants requested to have automatic political tickets—to allow them run for office through the ruling party—to chair rich local governments such as Bomadi, Burutu, Warri South West and Warri South in Delta state (*Nigerian Tribune* February 13, 2007: 3). They also demanded that "choice political appointments be reserved for some of their leaders" (*Nigerian Tribune*, February 13, 2007: 3). Government officials, JTF top brass and militants were involved in the protracted negotiations. Clearly, militants who request to serve in a political cabinet must have a modicum of comfort with the government of the day and feel sufficiently confident that they can get along without fear of legal harassment.

Kidnapping in the Delta is being performatively staged-managed rather than being curbed. Interventionists and other actors would suffer loss of revenue and, worse still, fizzle into oblivion the moment kidnapping stops. There is no reason to believe such persons would seek to end kidnapping, as that would mean political and economic hara-kiri.

Oil workers
Viewed cursorily, the consequences of kidnapping for oil workers, particularly non-Nigerians, are completely grim. After all, images and imageries of disheveled oil workers paraded in the glare of global television cameras indicate that the kidnapping ordeal is not a pleasant one. The fear oil workers live and work with is tortuous. Many oil workers now live under curfews imposed by their companies for their safety (Houreld 2006). Kidnapping incidents have also affected their families and loved ones. The spouses of some oil workers have left with their children because of fear for their lives. Some are now looking for work outside Nigeria so as to have their families back with them (Houreld 2006). Despite the difficult situation, however, oil drilling by local and foreign workers continues in the Delta.

---

16 Interviewee 2.

In Crelinsten and Szabo's (1979: 3) theoretical formulation, the kidnappers are the "offenders", the Nigerian state and oil corporations are the "active victims" on whom demands are made, while kidnapped persons—in this case, oil workers— are the "passive victim". This configuration hardly captures the Delta situation. Oil workers are not passive victims but *rational actors* in kidnapping episodes. As potential targets or former kidnap victims, oil workers are part of the performativity and economy of kidnapping in the Delta as actors with specific socio-economic interests wittingly entering an essentially war-like situation.

Niger Delta youths had issued warnings about oil extraction in the region. Resolution 4 of the 1998 Kaiama Declaration by Niger Delta youths was demonstrably unambiguous about the imminent situation in the Delta:

> Ijaw youths ... *demand that all oil companies stop all exploration and exploitation activities in the Ijaw area.* We are tired of gas flaring; oil spillages, blowouts and being labelled saboteurs and terrorists. It is a case of preparing the noose for our hanging. We reject this labelling. Hence, *we advise all oil companies staff and contractors to withdraw from Ijaw territories by the 30th December, 1998* pending the resolution of the issue of resource ownership and control in the Ijaw area of the Niger Delta.[17] (emphasis added)

The Kaiama declaration was a glimpse of what was to follow. By late 1998, what Watts (2009a) calls the "tipping point" was obviously drawing ever nearer. Oil workers might not have been expected to flee the Delta on the basis of such threats. The Nigerian armed forces had shown it was capable of offering a protective bulwark for the oil industry against popular dissent in the Delta (see Zalik 2004; Ikelegbe 2001; Osaghae 1995; Welch 1995). After all, oil workers survived the storm generated by the Movement for the Survival of Ogoni People (MOSOP) under the General Abacha administration.

Remaining in the Niger Delta as the level of youth agitation increased in the late 1990s conjures a fundamental train of thought. It suggests that oil workers did not know how serious the situation was and so chose to remain in the Delta. This is hard to comprehend as the Ogoni movement was particularly volatile (Osaghae 1995; Welch 1995) and ended in the state-sanctioned hanging of nine activists, including Ken Saro-Wiwa in 1995 among other extra-judicial killings. The situation was already a humanitarian crisis of epic proportions prior to 1998. From late 1995, the oil workers were essentially drilling "blood oil" (Watts 2008c: 2). This arguably makes oil workers complicit in the extreme repressive tactics of the military regimes of the 1990s. By not rejecting the military's protection and also, condoning the extra-legal activities of private security outfits hired by oil companies to protect their staff at the expense of the rights of the Delta public, oil workers' silence was problematic.

---

17   See Ijaw Youths of the Niger Delta. 1998. "The Kaiama Declaration". URL: http://www.unitedijawstates.com/kaiama.html Accessed 12 May 2010.

Oil workers arguably make a means and end calculation. The working conditions and salaries of staff of foreign corporations are better than those of local workers in home-grown industries (Chirayath and De Zolt 2004; Rothgeb 1995). In many cases, oil workers in the Delta earn at least 20 percent more for commensurate work in the US (Houreld 2006). The level of insecurity has further increased the allowances for housing, transportation and other perks provided the oil workers to ensure that they do not run away from Nigeria (Houreld 2006). These improved salaries are mainly predicated on the likelihood that the expatriates may be kidnapped in the Delta. One oil worker in the Delta admits: "It's mostly the money, and it's a good job … It's not Iraq just yet."[18] This statement is a rare glimpse of the back stage and suggests an economically-driven motive. It also implies that while the Delta is not safe, it is safer than Iraq, where oil drilling manages to go on in spite of the anomic situation.

In Nigeria's Delta, foreign oil workers enjoy a fabulous lifestyle: many are chauffeur-driven in host communities with full security and unqualified access to women—a major source of envy among local men.[19] This lifestyle is one that many such workers cannot afford in their home countries. In one incident, a kidnapped Briton who had retired in the UK was working in the oil industry in Nigeria. His captors were quick to point out that he was out of work in his home country but took the job meant for Niger Delta youths.

Foreign oil workers in Nigeria's Delta live in gated communities with state of the art facilities. The neighboring oil-bearing communities often gaze with envy at life's little wonders—the regular electricity supply, clean water, expensive SUVs, lavish parties, and cash—that oil procures. News of how well the "oyibos" (white people) live gets to community members through some of their family or community members who work for oil companies. The only problem has been that somehow community members were left out of the good life.

Prior to the kidnapping episodes of the 2000s, foreign oil workers benefitted immensely from the normative articulation of race (see Li 2003) in Nigeria. The world was literally at their feet in a post-colonial social, physical and ideational space. While Nigeria did not have direct equivalents of the blatant "racial" issues in North America and Europe, vestiges of slavery, traces of colonialism and the remnants of the social and economic relations these historical moments engendered ensured that white oil workers received an unearned positive social value. Simply put, they were well-positioned in society.

However, race, as Stuart Hall argues, is a "floating signifier". The signifying quality, normative operationalization and discursive construction of race assumed a different trajectory in Nigeria when insurgents realized that the market value—or more precisely, the ransom value—of kidnapped foreign oil workers was extremely

---

18   See Katharine Houreld 2006. "Companies Count the Cost of Kidnapping in Nigeria", URL: http://www.insurancejournal.com/news/international/2006/10/11/73226. htm Accessed 4 February 2011.

19   Interviewee 20.

high. The Nigerian government generally panicked and would use everything in its power, including bribery, to have the foreigners, especially Americans and Britons, released. This period began in 2003 (Okaba 2009).

For the kidnappers, foreign oil workers have a positive market value. However, for the oil workers, a negative market value set in, while still retaining the largely positive social value. The positive social value is a fundamental condition for maintaining the positive market value for kidnappers. Consequently, foreign oil workers, who could fairly move freely in society, became pariahs, albeit lucrative ones. Oil workers became a money-making machinery and/or medium for articulating political demands depending on what group kidnaps them. In this drama, foreign oil workers are perceived as antagonists by the young people involved in kidnapping. As argued in Chapter 3, they are seen as symbols of oppression and an Other par excellence by the people in oil-producing communities.[20] Therefore, for the foreign oil workers, earlier performative roles as the ubiquitous beloved expatriates in local communities adored by young children has given way to greater circumspection amid existential threat.

Transnational oil corporations

The presence of transnational corporations (TNCs) in developing countries has increased with the intensification of global capitalism within the generic rubric of globalization (Conway and Heynen 2006; Dicken 2007). While there is no agreement on the consequences of the spread of transnational corporations in developing countries, the growing abdication of responsibility by nation-states to the corporations and the brazen accumulation of "corporate capital power" by the latter is undeniable (Walcott 2006: 62). Nation-states in the global south have little or no control over TNCs, particularly oil corporations (Turner 1980) within their jurisdictions. State capacity to ensure that transnational corporations comply with the fundamental human rights of citizens and communities in developing countries is appallingly low (Morvaridi 2008). Such states are economic Lilliputians where corporations are concerned.

More fundamental, Girvan (1976) points out that the integration of underdeveloped economies to corporations is *ipso facto* a harbinger of conflict. TNCs increase the susceptibility of developing countries to internal conflict (Ukeje 2004; Turner and Brownhill 2004; Rothgeb 1995). Several reasons are responsible for this. The capital intensive system of production favored by corporations creates fewer jobs than anticipated, technology transfer remains a mirage, since most research and development units of corporations remain in western capitals rather than peripheral countries, and social inequalities are exacerbated as corporations' staff are generally better-off than their local counterparts (Chirayath and De Zolt 2004; Rothgeb 1995). These factors may generate social tensions that can contribute to the outbreak of conflicts.

---

20   Interviewee 19.

TNCs' relationship with the state is "uneasy" and may involve not only competition or conflict, but also collusion (Dicken 2007: 232), especially in weak states. For instance, in apartheid South Africa, TNCs, particularly in the mining sector and other large businesses, actively participated in and immensely profited from the heinous policies of the state (Bond and Sharife 2009). The same corporations have largely embraced the "Black Economic Empowerment" (BEE) policy of the ANC government, which stipulates that 25–30 percent of major businesses should be owned by "previously disadvantaged individuals" following the demise of apartheid (Iheduru 2009: 333).

TNCs often operate "as a law unto themselves" (Morvaridi 2008: 159). Through the tax breaks they generously receive and repatriation of profits to their headquarters in the global north, where at least 90 percent of their headquarters are located (Morvaridi 2008), developing peoples, their economies and environment are left to bear the brunt of the management and production techniques of corporations, particularly in extractive industries (McCulloch 2009, 2005).

There is abundant empirical evidence demonstrating that transnational corporations are not bystanders in the socio-political dynamics of the countries in which they operate. The political and economic catastrophe that befell Latin American countries such as Chile, Argentina, Brazil, Colombia and others in the 1960s and 1970s had the active influence of transnational corporations. The corporations were concerned to ensure that only leaders (military or civilian) who would enact policies favorable to their business interests gained and/or retained political power (see Klein 2007; Persaud 1976). In Chile, for instance, Persaud (1976) explains the active role played by US corporations, Anaconda and Kennecott Copper companies, and International Telephone and Telegraph (ITT) in the build-up to the 11 September 1973 coup against president Salvador Allende. ITT in particular enacted a policy aimed "to bring economic chaos" in Chile (Persaud 1976: 117) because of the socialist tenor of the Allende government even though he was democratically elected and widely popular among Chileans.

More recently, the botched March 2004 coup in Equatorial Guinea was the result of "(c)ompeting interests of oil companies from various states" (Uesseler 2008: 189) vying for an opportunity to better position themselves to access the oil wealth of the poverty-ravaged country. The coup had "financiers from across the globe" (Uesseler 2008: 189). The aim was to unseat Obiang Nguema, who favoured an American oil corporation over its Spanish competitors. Through the instrumentality of TNCs, developing countries, especially in Africa, have become grounds where the divergent and (apparently) irreconcilable socio-political and economic interests of world powers are played out with deleterious consequences for the host nations (see Gibbs 1997).

The Delta region of Nigeria is reputed internationally as a specific instance where TNCs "use their powers to perpetuate or even make worse situations of injustice where states are weak" (Morvaridi 2008: 168) and seen as alien and self-serving (see Jackson 1993) by the people. This as Clinard and Yiger (1980) argue, is partly because TNCs generally thrive mostly in unethical environments (cited in Chirayath and De Zolt 2004).

There are of course conflicting perspectives on the role of TNCs in developing countries. Proponents of the modernization school, for example, argue that TNCs provide the necessary technological and entrepreneurial capacity to stimulate economic growth and alleviate poverty (Wint 2006; Buckley 2006; Buckley and Casson 1991; Rostow 1960). The more critical dependency school (see Frank 1967, Rodney 1973) is however, unequivocal in its denunciation of TNCs' activities. Scholars in this tradition contend that corporations create *underdevelopment* (Onimode 1982, 1988; Nnoli 1982) through heinous exploitation. As TNCs are predominantly foreign owned, scholars of this intellectual persuasion, argue that TNCs' interest is profit maximization and not the development of the host countries. A third school of thought—in the interstices of the modernization and dependency schools of thought—appears in more recent scholarly work and demonstrates that the role of TNCs in developing countries is "mixed" at best (Subhash and Vachani 2006: 8) or ambiguous at worst. TNCs are capable of spurring growth and development yet able to cause wanton destruction in host economies and societies. Using East Asian and Latin American countries, Chan and Clark (1995: 187), for instance, argue that TNCs "can be either enabling or disenabling in the pursuit of national development".

Transnational oil corporations are major actors in the ongoing contentious performances in Nigeria. First, the infrastructure of these corporations comes under severe attacks by insurgents. To prevent such incidents, between 2007 and 2009, for example, the oil industry spent $3 billion annually in Nigeria to secure oil operations.[21] Second, oil corporations have had their production capacity reduced because of the insurgency. This implies a loss of revenue albeit not necessarily a net loss. More significantly, oil corporations are compelled to deal with incessant kidnapping of their workers. This is not merely a problem of economics; it is a source of colossal anxiety for the staff and management of corporations, as they have little inkling about the next target of insurgents. There are indications that oil corporations pay millions of dollars in ransom to effect the release of their kidnapped staff. An elaborate regime of insurance of the lives of oil workers against kidnapping has become more important than ever for oil extraction in the Niger Delta, as explained below. Oil corporations have to establish teams to engage in the complex negotiation process of securing the release of their workers when kidnappings occur. All of these constitute an almost incalculable risk and burden on oil corporations operating in the Niger Delta.

While these are only a few of the many reasons to commiserate with oil corporations as undeniable *victims* of kidnapping episodes in the Delta, the corporations are again not passive victims. Their victimhood is also quite questionable. The oil industry is highly problematic around the world. The process of securing oil blocks, contracts and miscellaneous allocations comes with

---

21   See Ejiofor Alike. 2011. "Security: Oil firms support FG with $200 in N'Delt", URL: http://www.thisdayonline.com/ Accessed 16 February 2011.

impressive graft and patronage. Amoral deals were not uncommon in the hay days of the military, for instance. Oil corporations were a crucial part of the "shadow economy". There is no reason to assume that greater transparency now prevails.

As major actors in the Delta imbroglio, oil corporations are construed by host communities as the "bad guys" who cause the first harm. Oil corporations start off—wittingly or unwittingly—on the side of an entity that has little goodwill among the people, as joint-venture partners of the Nigerian state. The situation is exacerbated by the decrees, rules and regulations, such as the Land Use Act of 1978, that generally impinge on the land rights of the Delta people but provide a façade of legality for the oil industry. Besides, oil extraction even under the most environmentally-conscious administration is not particularly friendly to the ecosystem. However, oil corporations attempt to manage public perceptions through various social programs such as offering scholarships and building schools. Shell, for instance, is punctilious about articulating its social responsibility.[22] The back stage (Goffman 1973), however, comprises serious environmental hazards, including hundreds of oil spills and cooperation with the state to guarantee ceaseless oil flow mainly at the cost of the rights of the people.

The Nigerian state and its security agencies
For the Nigerian state and security agencies, the mission in the Niger Delta comes with a huge cost. One newspaper headline captures the grim situation: "11 Soldiers, 16 Agip Workers Missing" *This Day* 19 June 2007, p. 1. The missing soldiers were never found. The JTF command was still exhuming bodies believed to be soldiers' for DNA verification as of 2010.[23] For instance, during an interview with General Bello, the following conversation ensued:

> *General Bello*: Tom Polo was the foremost militant leader in Niger Delta, the strongest ever. He killed 18 of our personnel ... luckily I have some pictures here which I want to share with you just for you to see. Come and see, these are just last week, and these are just the remains of some of the exhumed bodies (shows me pictures on his digital camera of military medical personnel in a laboratory working on some corpses). They are trying to do DNA on them ... This is just last week when I was in Warri (Delta state).

> *Interviewer*: Soldiers?

> *General Bello*: Yes, our soldiers who were killed by the militants. That is what caused the problem in Camp 5 (Tom Polo's camp). These are the remains; this mayhem just last Friday ...

---

22   See Shell Nigeria. (Undated). "Shell in the community", URL: http://www.shell.com.ng/home/content/nga/environment_society/shell_in_the_society/ Accessed 19 May 2011.
23   Interviewee 12; General Bello, Commander JTF. Personal interview, Yenagoa, Bayelsa state, August 2010.

Interviewer: This leads me to the former question, what has been the human and material cost of the JTF operation in the Niger Delta; how enormous?

General Bello: Very, very enormous, you know, very, very enormous. I mean, I wonder in all honesty which country will sit back and allow its security force to be killed with impunity.

The Nigerian army believes that one insurgent commander, Tom Polo, killed at least 18 soldiers.[24] Casualty figures are officially guarded state secrets but General Bello assures that "you'll be amazed at the number of military personnel and security personnel that have been killed; you'll be amazed at the number of innocent people that have been killed".

General Bello's assertion above is the front stage and the preferred narrative of the security agencies. This speaks to the enormous human and material cost of combating kidnapping. At the back stage, however, the phenomenon is an unprecedented profitable enterprise.

There are two kinds of actors within the Nigerian government and its security agencies. These are institutional and individual actors. At the institutional level, the Nigerian state benefits from the insecurity created by kidnapping of oil workers as it can point to the crisis as the reason for its failure to provide basic social services in the Delta. This is important because many of the services were absent before the start of the insurgency. The crisis thus presents a convenient and credible excuse. For instance, the withdrawal of Julius Berger from constructing the East-West road is constantly cited by actors working for the government as evidence that the government means well but has been hampered by the insecurity created by insurgents.[25]

Second, the Delta crisis is a major training ground for the Nigerian army. As a force uninitiated in guerrilla and amphibious warfare, the Delta insurgency provides opportunities for the Nigerian army, in particular to become accustomed to these increasingly ubiquitous phenomena. The JTF commander General Sarkin Yaki Bello points out that "it is a guerrilla warfare that we are fighting. Militancy is not put on somebody's head, they don't wear uniform, they don't wear anything".[26] The military also benefit from being furnished with state-of-the-art military equipment in the quest to combat the insurgency in the Delta by the Nigerian state and foreign powers, especially the US and the UK.[27]

Third, the Delta crisis is arguably a financial windfall for security agencies like the JTF, police, State Security Service and many others. This is because the

---

24   Interviewee 12.

25   Interviewees 10 and 12.

26   Interviewee 12. General Sarkin Yaki Bello, JTF Commander. Personal interview, Yenagoa, Bayelsa state, August 2010.

27   Interviewee 10. Lt. Col. Timothy Antigha, Coordinator Joint Media Campaign Centre (JMCC) of the JTF, personal interview, July 2010.

crisis necessitates making provisions for a "security vote" in the defense budget or as addendum to the budget. A security vote includes huge sums of money for "logistics" for which no full disclosure is required in Nigeria. The clandestine nature of the security vote may ensure that it lacks accountability.[28]

The state security agencies also benefit from the donations provided by oil corporations. In February 2011, for instance, the oil industry collectively donated $200 million to the federal government to maintain security in the Delta. This is different from what each oil corporation provides in support to the JTF and military services such as the Army and the Navy. Oil corporations routinely support the state security agencies with non-monetary items such as trucks, boats, communication and other security equipment, bulletproof vests, among others.[29]

At the individual level, the Delta situation is lucrative for several actors operating from privileged positions in government. Top government officials function as interventionists in kidnapping episodes.[30] As the former armorer of the NDPVF, the group that began kidnapping puts it:

> even some of the government functionaries saw it as a business. They will not be at the background, but underneath they are there. Because when the ransom is to be paid, they will be the people that will take the ransom. Within that interval, they also have their own share.

In addition, the state of insecurity in the Delta has had the unintended consequence of intensifying illegal oil bunkering or theft. To be clear, illegal bunkering existed before kidnapping and other contentious acts got out of control but the sheer magnitude has increased. Under the state of insecurity, top military brass, business and political elite use their access to power, military hardware and ironically responsibility for maintaining security to also siphon fuel. Rank and file soldiers are routinely required to look away as vessels carrying illegal crude oil leave Nigeria's shores for the international black market.

The JTF posting has become a lucrative one in the military. It is essentially a meal ticket in spite of the obvious risks involved in maintaining peace in the Delta. Rank and file soldiers speak of the exciting allowances, possibilities of participating in illegal oil bunkering and opportunities for executing contracts on behalf of senior officers while on JTF duties.[31] One soldier revealed that soldiers in Bayelsa state in particular receive more robust allowances and "if they post you there you don hammer be that ... They don't go to any peacekeeping operation. They make their money there." "You don hammer" means that that individual has become rich. Although his statement about becoming rich in the Delta may well be

---

28   Interviewee 1.

29   See Ejiofor Alike. 2011. "Security: Oil firms support FG with $200 in N'Delt", URL: http://www.thisdayonline.com/ Accessed 16 February 2011.

30   Interviewees 1 and 2.

31   Interviewee 6. JTF soldier. Personal interview, Yenagoa, July 2009.

exaggerated, the soldier confirms that he has made several efforts to get deployed to the JTF but lacks the "connections". Suffice to state that the JTF mission in the Delta contributes to favoritism and god-fatherism in the Nigerian military, particularly the Army.[32]

Insurgents

"Freedom-fighters", "militants", "combatants" or insurgents are fundamental players in the kidnapping of oil workers in the Delta. The histrionicity of insurgents displaying kidnap victims as valuable commodities or enemy combatants and affirmation of their machismo, prowess in the creeks and organizational finesse has captured global imagination. For many insurgents kidnapping, illegal oil bunkering, pipeline vandalism among other acts in the Delta are mere parts of an ongoing deadly "game".[33] The glitz and razzmatazz of erstwhile commanders (explained below) in the insurgency come with a huge price tag. For instance, 10 operatives of MEND died in the August 2006 clash with the JTF (Technical Committee on the Niger Delta 2008). A *Daily Champion* front page headline provides a picturesque depiction of the cost: "JTF kills 18 militants" (14 April 2009, p. 1).

Kidnapping has helped raise awareness about issues in the Delta but has also become formidable money-maker for some insurgents. Former Inspector General of Police Mike Okiro estimates the total ransom cash collected by insurgents at $100 million or N1.5 billion between 2006 and 2008 (*This Day*, April 1 2009). The demands made after kidnapping episodes range from the entertaining to the utilitarian. For instance, in 2007, the militants who kidnapped a Briton and an American demanded "10 cartons of Red Label, 10 cartons of Black Label and N500,000 to even start any physical interaction with them" as well as a total ransom money of N1.8billion (*Nigerian Tribune* 25 January 2007: 3).

A conversation with the armorer of NDPVF demonstrates the dramaturgical awareness of the actors:

> *Interviewer*: Thank you very much, let's look at a series of international issues. Let's talk about kidnapping of oil workers, particularly, foreigners. What can you tell us about that?
>
> *Response*: We never believed in kidnapping, but, as I told you earlier on, it is one of the strategies; at the early stage we used it.
>
> *Interviewer*: Ok. The Niger Delta People's Volunteer Force, you adopted kidnapping at first?
>
> *Response*: Yes

---

32   Participant observation of five JTF soldiers on duty at the David Ejoor Barracks, July 2009.

33   Interviewee 20.

Interviewer: And this was 2002

Response: Yes. And we know all the kidnapping we did was never to extort money from anybody, but it was part of the strategies we adopted to use. But, *when we saw that other groups started coming on stage, we resolved to leave the stage for them.* They took the kidnapping as a business venture. Somebody kidnapped even a two year or two month old baby, you can't say that is constructive and we condemn it in its entirety. We condemn it in its entirety. And, during that time, it is not something that has been done by one particular person, it is collective, because we don't just get up from our houses and say let us do this, because we have the backings of the Ijaw people. Because they know that we are fighting for their freedom. We are fighting for all the benefits of our children that are yet unborn. (emphasis added)

This demonstrates that the NDPVF quit the kidnapping "stage" when other insurgent groups began to kidnap people indiscriminately. It recognized that kidnapping children would earn it a bad reputation and decided to stop kidnapping people altogether to maintain their credibility.

The insurgency in general and kidnapping in particular have raised the level of social relevance of otherwise everyday people. Insurgents have become indispensable to the smooth-running of society and demand respect because they participated in the struggle. For example, on Monday, 6 August, 2007, Inspector General of Police (IGP), Mike Okiro, addressed a press conference in which he announced that 17 hostage-takers had been arrested. Asari Dokubo was a special guest at the press conference. Dokubo used the occasion to reiterate the militants' demands, and the imperative of kidnapping in the struggle though he did not condone kidnapping toddlers. He added that he was there to inform the IGP of his impending trip to Saudi Arabia for medical treatment as required by his bail conditions. The public watched the wonder of the ostensibly good rapport between the chief law officer and a major insurgent commander.

Conversely, insurgents have successfully manufactured an alternative political structure, which assists them in upward mobility in the conventional structure of the Nigerian society. A former insurgent puts it clearly: "I believe this struggle was what gave us a voice and without this struggle most persons that are known abroad, within and outside this country wouldn't have been known".[34] Insurgents have found more than a voice. Many of those who have left the "stage" have retired in comfort. For instance, former MEND commanders, "Africa" and "Boyloff" lived in the Bayelsa state government house in Yenagoa in 2010 under the protection of the state governor. Henry Bindodogha founder of the NDFF is senior special assistant to the Edo state governor on surveillance and waterways security. This makes him a member of the political class in Edo state with all the appurtenances of power. In Delta state, the support of a former MEND commander,

---

34 Interviewee 15.

Mr Government Ekpemupolo or Tom Polo is fundamental to successfully vying for public office. His younger brother, George Ekpemupolo chairs Warri South-West Local Government. Evidence that Tom Polo has nominees in the Delta state cabinet is overwhelming.[35] Individuals who were under state scrutiny less than five years ago are now in a position to make and implement the policies of the same government they fought and whose soldiers they sometimes killed. The alternative political structure created through the instrumentality of the insurgency allows ex-wanted criminals to be in a position to legitimize their past acts deemed criminal by the state they now help to run. This constitutes the back stage which insurgents are quick to de-emphasize.

However, at the front stage, insurgents maintain that they took up arms to fight for the rights of the people and not for personal aggrandizement. The reality is that young men who would have remained unknown and unsung have become folk heroes because of the insurgency. Some ex-insurgents are able to use the conventional structures of society they hitherto loathed because of its failure at equitable distribution of resources to share the largesse of office to the people of their communities. In this sense, participating in the insurgency becomes functional for the insurgents and their communities whose members were routinely excluded from the executive of the state. For instance, Henry Bindodogha claims to be the first person of Ijaw extraction in Edo state to attain the rank of senior special assistant to the governor in more than a generation.[36] Consequently, several insurgents have actually succeeded in joining the ranks of political elites to maintain the existing order while supposedly attempting to effect radical change.

Second-order cast

The second-order cast comprises actors whose roles are dependent on the first-order cast. This category includes the Nigerian society, "quasi-invisible" actors, insurance companies, researchers, the media, and private military corporations.

Nigerian society
The negative consequences of the Niger Delta unrest on the Nigerian society are enormous. Apart from routine travel warnings issued by many countries against Nigeria, the economy, which relies heavily on crude oil production, was almost completely brought down at the height of the insurgency. Besides, the insecurity generated by kidnappings in the Delta has been feasted upon in other parts of Nigeria. Instances of opportunistic kidnappings were spreading, especially in South East Nigeria. This has created real terror in the minds of people and strongly regulates their lives.

However, an entirely new language in the popular culture lexicon can be traced to the etymological context provided by kidnapping. Chief of the new words is

---

35   Interviewees 20 and 2.
36   Interviewee 19.

the notion of being "kidnappable". An individual's "kidnapability" hinges on the person's social class, economic, cultural and symbolic capital, among others. To be kidnappable means to have certain financial resources, occupy a valuable position in the public or private sector and/or share consanguineous relationships with the rich and powerful. Being *kidnappable* appears sinister but is discursively construed as pleasantly tantalizing in Nigeria. A kidnapped person is no ordinary mortal; being kidnappable is a measure of a person's social worth and connections in Nigeria's prebendal system.

At an editorial board meeting of a major national newspaper, the "security question" in the Niger Delta was the subject of discussion. The meeting coincided with the period when four Nigerian journalists were kidnapped. The journalists regained their freedom a few days later and claimed they had been robbed of 3 Million Naira by the kidnappers. The kidnappers stated in the newspapers that they collected only N1.6 Million Naira from the journalists. The public was surprised that journalists had and could carry such huge sums of money in cash. The following conversation occurred between two of the seven editorial board members in attendance:

Member 1: Kidnapping is a public good.

Member 2: I am not a journalist. I never understood things. I have never seen 1.6 Million Naira in my life. The kidnappers were incensed that the journalists lied against them and came out to denounce the journalists' claim. Can you imagine? I want to be kidnapped, so I can say I had 3 Million Naira in my boot (trunk).

Member 1: You are eminently qualified to be kidnapped.

Conversations like the one above permeate public discourse. People joke about their "kidnappability", "ransom value" and so on. Parents jokingly warn their teenage children to return home on time to avert being kidnapped.

The statement by "Member 1" that "kidnapping is a public good" requires further elucidation. From the Niger Delta to South West Nigeria and Abuja, the idea that kidnapping is a lesser evil compared to armed robbery is shockingly common. The argument holds that kidnappings are more discriminatory and targeted than robberies, which often occur at random. Only suitable victims are kidnapped while armed robbers are not always as methodical as kidnappers. Thus, robberies are believed to have decreased because of the increase in kidnapping incidents and therefore, the latter is functional to those who do not have the requisite capital— political, economic, symbolic and cultural—to be kidnappable.

"Quasi-Invisible" actors
The term *Quasi-invisible* is used to signify the tendency of this set of actors to operate in subterranean ways even though their roles are obvious to any keen observer. There are three quasi-invisible actors fundamental to the kidnapping

episodes in the Niger Delta. These are the international community,[37] international arms merchants and illegal oil cartels.

Generally, the international community is a reductionist term for the US, the UK and a handful of Western and/or developed countries able to command respect around the world. The presence of the international community in the Delta crisis is noticeable even in its absence. The imprimatur of the international community is present in the Delta crisis as major players in the oil market, home countries of transnational oil corporations operating in the Delta or the countries of citizenship of kidnapped foreign oil workers in Nigeria. One way or the other the international community is strategically positioned in the Delta crisis as insurgents deliberately target its attention:

> The most important thing is that the message, the signal, has been sent to the international community. That is one of the greatest things we have achieved but there is virtually no quarters in the whole world that the Niger Delta issue is not known ... we have achieved that.[38]

Insurgents are consciously engaged in a performative hailing of the international community. American and British hostages are particularly prized trophies theatrically displayed in the creeks for the world's view.[39] The premium placed on oil workers from the US and the UK coincides not only with the citizenship of most of the oil workers but also the relationship of the Nigerian state with these powers and their relative strength in the comity of nation-states. The reduction in the production capacity of oil corporations affects world oil prices and often has an instantaneous effect on the international community, particularly against the backdrop of political instability in the Middle East. None the less, the international community, particularly the UK is implicated through its historical ties with the Nigerian state, their double-speak on human rights and environmental justice as well as their unrelenting thirst for Nigeria's sweet crude. The influence of the US and the UK on the Nigerian state also makes these countries culpable in the Delta crisis. Consequently, the international community is not a passive or apathetic agent in episodes of kidnapping in the Niger Delta.

If the international community is nebulous in scope, international arms merchants play an even more indeterminate yet fundamental role in the kidnapping episodes in the Delta.[40] International arms merchants specialize in reaping dividends from conflict zones around the world. They provide the necessary arsenal for prosecuting kidnapping episodes and the insurgency in general in the Delta. International arms merchants supply most of the AK47, rocket launchers,

---

37   It is recognized that the term "international community" is rather vague and misleading.

38   Interviewee 15. Chief of Staff to Asari Dokubo.

39   Interviewee 19.

40   Of course, not all arms merchants operate illegally.

anti-aircraft missiles and other weapons used in the Delta. They receive payment in cash in their preferred currency, the US Dollars, or generous oil barges.

The illegal oil cartels have local and international tentacles. They purchase oil at cheap rates from insurgents. They often pay in cash or sometime in arms and ammunitions. There is thus a close alignment between international arms merchants and illegal oil cartels. In some cases, the same persons perform the two roles concurrently. Such individuals collect oil in exchange for arms in their transactions with the insurgents.[41] Kidnapping in the Niger Delta is a lucrative business venture for the arms merchants and oil cartels. The former in particular simply move on to other conflict zones when business dries up in any location. It is interesting to note that the identity of the arms merchants and oil cartels are rarely, if ever revealed. This speaks to the symbiotic relationship between these two sets of merchants and their clients.

Insurance companies/brokers
As stated earlier, oil corporations have adopted an elaborate regime of insurance against the kidnapping of their workers. Not surprisingly, insurance companies and their brokers are major beneficiaries of attempts to deal with the risk of being kidnapped in the Delta. Insurance companies' actions are some of the most secretive in the kidnapping episodes in the Delta. One insurance brokering firm Bellwood Prestbury explains on its website that: "Kidnap insurance is a highly confidential area of cover. If it is publicly known that you carry kidnap and ransom insurance, particularly in lawless or known terrorist areas, you run the danger of heightening the possibility of becoming a target".[42] Therefore, the probabilistic calculations here are not public information. For good measure, Bellwood Prestbury advertises the numerous incidents of kidnapping in Nigeria in a piece "Kidnapping in Nigeria – on the increase?" and advises persons interested in protecting themselves while in Nigeria to call their "experienced team".[43]

Lloyds, an insurance company offering kidnap and ransom insurance (K&R) for businesses and workers at risk in Nigeria, assures that: "You or your client does not need to be a head of state, or a rock star to be a target!"[44] Lloyds offers individuals, corporations, missionary groups, financial institutions and educational institutions two categories of K&R policy. These are personal or family policy and corporate policy. Lloyds considers several risk contingencies in arriving at

---

41   Interviewees 20 and 26.

42   See Bellwood Presbury. "Kidnap insurance—Are you at risk?" URL: http://www.bellwoodprestbury.com/specialist-insurance/kidnap-ransom-insurance/ Accessed 4 February 2011.

43   See "Kidnapping in Nigeria – on the increase?" URL: http://www.bellwoodprestbury.com/news-events/news/article/kidnapping-in-nigeria-on-the-increase-61/ Accessed 4 February 2011.

44   See "A Kidnap and Ransom Insurance Plan", URL: http://www.eglobalhealth.com/kidnap-ransom-extortion-insurance.html Accessed 7 February 2011.

the premium for each client. These include the company's worldwide assessment of risk. Hence, at least 59 countries are designated "high risk". The high risk countries include Nigeria, Afghanistan, Indonesia, Israel, Russia, Yemen, among others. Other factors considered include the duration of stay in the risk zone, details of the applicant's itinerary, and why they are travelling. The calculations are highly individualized based on a number of actuarial factors including age, income, occupation, rank or position, citizenship, value of personal assets or value of business assets, among others. The maximum benefit Lloyd pays in the case of a kidnapping incident cannot be greater than the sum of individual or business assets. The premium calculation also depends on how clients respond to questions such as: "Has there ever been any prior kidnapping, extortion, or detention incident? Has there ever been any threat or attempt at a kidnapping, extortion, or detention? Are there any current threats or incidents regarding kidnapping, extortion, or detention? Are any of the proposed insureds likely kidnapping prospects because of business, outside interests, or other activities?"[45]

Each individual client is objectivized and rendered actuarially visible and knowable. Hence, what industry they operate in (oil and gas rather than the educational sector, for instance), how much they earn annually, places they visit, their citizenship (for example, an American will be a more likely target in the Delta than a Nigerian), how much they are worth, etc. are indicators of the level of risk each subject faces. These questions are posed purportedly in the best interest of the subject. Multiple aspects of an individual's life history, including taste, occupational accomplishment, lived social space, social class, future plans and even self-assessment of risk are collected in a remarkably composed one-page document. The nodal and ostensibly insignificant pieces of information are put together in a manner reminiscent of Haggerty and Ericson's (2000) "surveillant assemblage". The product is a powerful apparatus for rendering the subject concrete, transparent and totalizable. By appending their signature on an innocuous form, an individual affirms that no information has been left out as the assessment and acceptance of the risk of the subject depends on this honest and voluntary submission. By so doing, the individual invites a coterie of experts to use their voluntarily supplied auto-biography to know, theorize and make risk forecasts about their life-world. In a constellation of activities, the subject is responsibilized, surveiled, stabilized through their life trajectories and flows, depersonalized and processually invented as a risk statistic.

For insurance companies, of course, the concerns are neither theoretical nor privacy-related. A K&R premium at Lloyds begins at $600 and can be over $1000. The operation in the Delta region is only one of the growing numbers of social spaces where insurance capital reaps bountifully from a social problem. The premiums paid on the corporate K&R policies adopted by oil corporations in

---

45   "A Kidnap and Ransom Insurance Plan", URL: http://www.eglobalhealth.com/kidnap-ransom-extortion-insurance.html Accessed 7 February 2011.

Nigeria is an increasingly significant source of operation cost (Houreld 2006) and generates huge profits for the insurance companies.

Researchers, academics and global security information companies

Many researchers, research institutions and global security companies have become actors in the kidnapping drama in the Delta. While they are largely second-rate cast or relatively passive actors—to the extent that their performances are determined by what other actors such as the insurgents, the Nigerian state and the Delta communities display—they play a crucial role in terms of the representation of the insurgency in the Delta. For some researchers or academics, the performances in the Delta have provided a source of fascinating research focus and agenda. We will never know the number of honors' theses, master's theses and PhD dissertations based on the Delta insurgency.

However, the benefits to this category of actors go beyond graduate theses or documentation. Some, particularly private global security information companies that engage in intelligence gathering, processing, documentation and dissemination make considerable profit from the ongoing Delta insurgency. For example, in response to my request for security information garnered about the Delta, the head of one of such companies based in Europe assured me during a transatlantic telephone conversation that the series of publications from the analysis of the data generated from the Delta crisis (such as the number of kidnapping incidents, location, etc. and forecast) was his company's "bread and butter". He asked for an official request for the data by e-mail. In response to my e-mail, he included two of his company's publications but noted that "alas, we cannot give you the full updates and reports as they are commercial items. If you have a budget, we will of course be pleased to sign you up for a subscription". He provided a link to his company's website. The website shows that a monthly subscription for the company's "Niger Delta Security Report" costs $822 (US). The company also produces a "Quarterly Maritime Review" that is available at the same price. While this company provides other consultancy services, the Delta insurgency appears to be its major cash cow. Consequently, there are many such actors who are rarely on the stage but are benefitting from the ongoing performances in the Delta as a "normal" and legitimate part of their everyday business.

The media

Social movements and the media are "interacting systems" (Gamson and Wolfsfeld 1993: 114). The media fundamentally shapes movement outcomes in terms of the level of media coverage or seriousness attached to movement actors, disseminating an SMO's framing and presenting the movement in a way that elicits public sympathy (Gamson and Wolfsfeld 1993). This means that the relationship between social movements and the media is asymmetrical as the publicity of collective actions and ultimately the success of movements are dependent on effective and favorable media coverage (Gamson and Wolfsfeld 1993). Despite the dependence of movements on media representation, social movements produce compelling spectacles that the media cannot ignore.

The Delta insurgency is an unqualified media spectacle. The kidnapping of oil workers in the Delta is a major "media event" (see Fiske 1996). Local and international media organizations have positioned themselves as important actors in the Delta. Media organizations are also courted by insurgents as the latter seek maximum coverage and sympathetic representation of their activities. The immediacy, personalization, and extraordinariness (see Knight 2004) of the Delta insurgency confer a significant news value on it and make the Niger Delta insurgency a news gold mine.

As noted in Chapter 1, MEND has a listserv of about 50 media organizations and individuals around the world. Media organizations like al-Jazeera, the *Financial Times* of London, the South African Broadcasting Corporation, and the *New York Times* among others are part of this elite list. These organizations receive up-to-date information about the activities of MEND. As MEND announces its bombing campaigns in advance, the media organizations use the notices to produce cutting edge news. MEND insurgents occasionally grant coveted interviews to media organizations. Al-Jazeera's exclusive interview with former MEND leader, Henry Okah, is only one of such rare media events.[46] Such interviews generate huge viewership and boost the journalistic credentials of correspondents. Some journalists like Michael Peel of the London *Financial Times* have also bolstered their credentials by writing books about their experiences covering the Delta region.

Private military corporations

Private military corporations and miscellaneous security companies are major players in the kidnapping episodes in the Delta. The state of insecurity of oil infrastructure and oil workers particularly after the hanging of the Ogoni Nine in 1995 has ensured a steady stream of business for security companies in the Delta. Companies offering security services such as serving as escort while equipment and staff of oil corporations are transported, guarding oil installations, watching over the homes of management staff and offices became increasingly significant actors in the Delta by the early 2000s. Such companies benefit from the insurgency by making profits from the security problems. They act in collaboration with oil corporations to guarantee the free flow of oil. The impression created by the private military companies is that they are essential to smooth oil extraction. However, alongside the JTF, such companies exacerbate the security problems by often brutally suppressing protest by members of oil-producing communities and over-militarizing the Delta (Bot 2008).

One of such companies that specialize in providing security services in the oil and gas industry is the UK's Libertine Global Solutions. The company's vision statement states that it focuses "predominantly on operations within Africa,

---

46   See "Al-Jazeera's exclusive interview with Nigeria's rebel leader", URL: http://www.youtube.com/watch?v=47yGCz_QZRg Accessed 14 February 2011.

specifically Nigeria and the Niger Delta region, there are currently ongoing discussions with the Nigerian government on future operations".[47] Therefore, for companies such as Libertine Global Solutions, the Delta insurgency has been a tremendous business opportunity.

This chapter analyzes the roles of the actors in the Delta insurgency. The actors include first-order cast like oil-producing Niger Delta communities, interventionists, insurgents, oil workers, oil corporations, and the Nigerian state/ security agencies. Others are second-order cast, such as the Nigerian society, "quasi-invisible" actors, insurance companies, researchers, the media and private military corporations. How each of these actors derives benefits from and/or is negatively affected by kidnaping in the Delta is demonstrated. While not questioning the intentions of the JTF or any of the numerous civil society groups, the actions of all those involved as highlighted above is contributing to the maintenance of the status quo dominated by insurgent acts like kidnapping and illegal oil bunkering. A major argument in this chapter is that impression management is the organizing principle adopted by the actors in the kidnapping episodes in the Delta. The main concern of the Nigerian state is to provide an atmosphere that is sufficiently safe for oil extraction to continue unabated. Several young men who took up arms and became insurgent commanders have succeeded in inventing an alternative political structure for accessing the conventional structures of society. For others, the drama is a dangerous but innovative means of livelihood in a perpetually depressed economy. While the Delta insurgency generates harms for some actors, particularly the oil-producing communities, it also creates benefits for some participants. As stated earlier, a journalist described kidnapping as "public good"[48] because of the diffusion of opportunities for self-enrichment among institutional and non-institutional actors.

Consequently, in spite of the rhetoric of restoring law and order by the Nigerian state and agitations for radical transformation of society by non-state actors, the analysis suggests that ending the insurgency is not in the interest of most of the actors involved. Many of them have become entrenched in the ongoing insurgency and will suffer considerable economic and/or symbolic loss should it end. The performances of these actors—state, para-state and non-state—in the Delta amphitheater arguably guarantees that the insurgency may not end any time soon. This analysis is a useful way of rethinking the intractability and persistence of the Delta crisis beyond the essentialized dichotomy between the centripetal and centrifugal forces in parts of the literature. The thesis is that the actions of the challengers of authority and those who support the existing order produce a common outcome—a synthetic stasis, which negatively affects yet benefits many of the actors concerned.

---

47   See Libertine Global Solutions Ltd. "Company Statements", URL: http://www. libertinesecurity.com/company-statement.php Accessed 7 February 2011.

48   Member 1; focus group discussion with seven editorial board members of a major national newspaper.

Chapter 3

Criminal Resistance? Interrogating Political Kidnapping[1]

Introduction

Today is a great day, not only in your lives, but also in the history of the Niger Delta. Perhaps, it will be the greatest day for a very long time. This is not because we are going to bring the heavens down, but because we are going to demonstrate to the world what and how we feel about oppression. Remember your 70-year-old grandmother who still farms before she eats; remember also your poverty-stricken people; remember, too, your petroleum which is being pumped out daily from your veins; and then fight for your freedom.

Isaac Jasper Adaka Boro (23 February, 1966).

This chapter focuses on two major sets of theoretical work that have a bearing on resistance by people on the margins of society. These are Hobsbawm's *social banditry* and the concept of *contentious politics* in the political process paradigm of the social movement literature. Three major objectives are accomplished in this chapter. First, the literature on political kidnapping is critically examined to highlight its nature and dynamics. Second, the conceptualization of *social banditry* by Hobsbawm (1969, 1959) is used to enunciate and problematize the phenomenon of kidnapping. This is followed by an appraisal of Hobsbawm's theoretical schema with a view to illuminating its relevance to kidnapping in the Delta. Third, the seminal work of Tilly (2003, 2004), McAdam, Tarrow and Tilly (2001) and Tilly and Tarrow (2007) and others (della Porta and Diani 1999) within the rubric of social movement studies are used to explicate why insurgents adopt certain kinds of repertoires of protest within a cocktail of possible tactics. The notion of *contentious politics* by Charles Tilly and his collaborators also help to provide an understanding of the dynamics of protest in the Delta.

---

1   An abridged version of this chapter was presented under the title "Criminal Resistance? The Politics of Kidnapping of Oil Workers in Nigeria" at XVII International Sociological Association (ISA) World Congress of Sociology, Gothenburg, Sweden, July 11–17, 2010.

The Complexity of the Phenomenon of Kidnapping

The term *kidnapping* is a very complex social phenomenon (Crelinsten and Szabo 1979). Kidnapping involves seizing people with force and holding them against their will illegally (Turner 1998: 146). It is an act that typically involves three parties (Crelinsten and Szabo 1979: 3), the offender, the passive victim and the active victim. The passive victim is the kidnapped person(s), while the active victim is the party to whom the kidnappers make economic or political demands (Crelinsten and Szabo 1979: 3). Concepts like abduction (Sanchez 2006) and hostage-taking (Crelinsten and Szabo 1979) are often used interchangeably with kidnapping. Political kidnapping is the abduction of individual(s) for the purpose of forcing a state (or non-state agent) to comply with some specific demands. In this sense, the abducted individuals are not the primary targets of the kidnappers, but only a means to a political end (Crelinsten and Szabo 1979).

   Kidnapping is an act of violence. Kidnappers do their victims violence by holding them against their will. Such violence may assume a political dimension. As Ruggiero (2006) understands it, political violence is "an attempt to give hostile outbursts an organizational structure and a rational, calculable trend, so that uncoordinated hostility is slowly turned into military action (highly specialized and integrated), towards a predictable end" (105). He argues that political violence can occur if there are existing cleavages and strains or avenues pertinent to expressing dissent. Ruggiero (2006: 1) differentiates between *institutional violence* and *anti-institutional violence* (Italics in original). Institutional violence is the use of "authorized force" to create or maintain law and order, hence constituting "violence from above", while anti-institutional violence is the use of "unauthorized force" which constitutes "violence from below" (p. 1). When protesters turn to violent means in order to advance their grievances, this demonstrates a challenge to established authority and may be deemed "threatening and criminal" (Soothill, Peelo and Taylor 2002: 144; Ruggiero 2006). In a cross-national study of Italy and Germany, della Porta (1995: 3) describes political violence as "a particular repertoire of collective action that involved physical force, considered at that time as illegitimate in the dominant culture". In this sense, political violence is a systematic tool of group behavior. This may be expressed in the form of riots, civil insurgencies or disturbances, mass killings, (Skurski and Coronil 2006: 1) terrorism, wanton destruction of property, bombings, kidnapping or "disappearances" and repression of dissent. Political violence often has state complicity (Skurski and Coronil 2006) making it a very nebulous concept (Skurski and Coronil 2006: 1). This is because the state may resort to the use of disproportionate or illegitimate force in its attempt to maintain order and thus engender further dissent (Flyghed 2002). Conversely, where and when non-state actors or groups turn to militancy in their quest for political change, the action or inaction of the state is a major contributory factor (della Porta and Diani 1999; Clutterbuck 1978). Kidnapping to further a political objective is one of the many forms political violence may take (Hamilton 1980).

Historically, there was no known political motivation behind kidnapping (Hamilton 1980), but since the 1970s, the media has been awash with kidnappings involving diverse political motivations (Turner 1998). Economic and political motivations for kidnapping are often intertwined (Turner 1998; Jenkins 1985; Capotorto 1985; Caramazza and Leone 1984; Clutterbuck 1978). Kidnapping of Western soldiers, journalists and aid workers in countries like Iraq and Afghanistan is becoming routine. Citizens of the US are particularly targeted because of widespread anti-American sentiments in the Middle East. Nevertheless, some view kidnapping as more a "commerce in human life" than a political action (Jenkins 1985: xx). Others recognize that there are guerrilla groups that utilize kidnapping as a form of political action to make demands on the state (Turner 1998; Capotorto 1985), as kidnapping is a weapon of the weak (Baumann 1985, 1973). Thus, "victims of political kidnapping are chosen for what they represent, rather than who they are" (Concannon 2008: 164). Latin American countries arguably provide the gold standard of kidnapping in the world (Sanchez 2006; Purnell 1985; Baumann 1984, 1973; Clutterbuck 1978). Countries like Venezuela, Mexico, Argentina and most notoriously, Colombia (Sanchez 2006; Braun 2003) are exemplars of societies where dumbfounding social inequality exist, states are either weak or have not fully succeeded in monopolizing the use of force and thus have to compete with kidnapping rings and miscellaneous crime lords, who have turned kidnapping to a profitable enterprise. The kidnapping rate in Colombia tripled between 1995 and 2000, with 16, 500 people kidnapped between 1999 and 2004 (Posado-Carbo 2004). The rise of "express kidnapping" in countries like Colombia and Mexico among others has guaranteed relative equal opportunity in the spread of kidnap victims as members of the middle class are no longer spared (Sanchez 2006: 184). In this scenario, potential victims are randomly picked up on the streets and taken to the nearest ATM to withdraw their entire daily limit (Sanchez 2006).

Not surprisingly, structural issues like low income, lack of educational opportunities among other related factors (Oyefusi 2008; Turner 1998) and excessive use of violence by the state in controlling dissent are major contributors to kidnapping and attendant violence in Latin America (Sanchez 2006). Where distribution of wealth from scarce commodities, particularly mineral resources is involved in rentier petro-states like Nigeria (Watts 2007), agitations for resource control by resource-rich communities may degenerate into violence such as kidnapping for political purposes.

Hobsbawm's (1969, 1959) influential work on "social banditry" demonstrates that historically, there have always been men of the ilk of the Robin Hood fable on the margins of society who take to banditry as a form of resistance against the state or the wealthy. Hobsbawm describes social banditry as a "universal and virtually unchanging phenomenon, something that is little more than endemic peasant protest against oppression and poverty: a cry for vengeance on the rich and the oppressors ... a righting of individual wrongs" (1959: 5). Social bandits are poor people regarded as criminals by the state, but "*considered by their people as heroes, as champions, avengers, fighters for justice, perhaps even leaders of liberation*, and in any case as men to be admired, helped and supported" (1969: 13, emphasis added). The significance of social bandits rests on their being seen as the "people's champions" (1959: 21) by members of their society. Without this relation of trust, social bandits become common criminals.

Bandits tend to be drawn from the army of unemployed young men who are single and live in inaccessible areas such as mountains, trackless plains, creeks and waterways (Hobsbawm 1969: 1–35). Banditry is also common in societies going through a process of evolutionary transformation from tribal and kinship organizations to modern capitalist and industrial forms. It tends to occur when the government is weak and divided, and when entire communities wish to resist the destruction of their way of life. Thus, banditry is a form of self-help to right perceived wrongs and avenge cases of perceived injustice between the rich and the poor and the strong and the weak (Hobsbawm 1969: 1–35). Also, banditry flourishes in periods of impoverishment and economic crisis. Social banditry, therefore, is precipitated by perceived injustice (1959: 16). The bandit, Hobsbawm (1969) argues, is a figure of social rebellion and provides resistance against the rich, foreign conquerors or oppressors.

Hobsbawm further argues that social banditry has next to no organization or ideology and is totally adaptable to modern social movements. (1959: 5). For Hobsbawm, "bandits consist largely of peasants and landless labourers ruled, oppressed and exploited by someone else—lords, towns, governments, lawyers or even banks." (1969: 15). He emphasizes that social bandits are *reformers not revolutionaries*. They may become revolutionaries when they become the symbol or spearhead of resistance by a whole community. They may also become revolutionary because they are part of society that is largely passive in the face of oppression but whose members generally dream of being free (1969: 22). More tellingly, Hobsbawm predicted in 1969 that "it is not impossible that it (banditry) may arise in sub-Saharan Africa on a more significant scale than we have had on record in the past" (1969: 19).

Hobsbawm (1969, 1959) writing decades ago might well have had in mind Nigeria, South of the Sahara. His theoretical constructs provide useful tools for analyzing kidnapping of oil workers and the general turn to militancy in the Delta. Nigeria is undergoing devastating economic times in which lived existence largely functions on the basis of kinship networks, familial connections and ethnic identification (Okereke 1993; Maier 2000), rather than impersonal bureaucratic structures (Joseph 1987). It is also a country transitioning from a rural-based economy (see Olayiwola and Adeleye 2005) to a modern state. As a result, there are basic problems of unemployment, under-developed infrastructure (Ikelegbe 2001; Ibelema 2000; Obi 1997), and dependency (Onimode 1988, 1982) particularly in rural areas, such as the Delta communities which have a high level of poverty and low quality of life (Omeje 2007; Ibeanu and Luckham 2007; Okereke 2006; Okonta 2005; Zalik 2004).

Consequently, the necessary conditions Hobsbawm (1969, 1959) hypothesizes for the rise of social banditry are palpably present in Nigeria. However, what is unclear is whether oil-producing community members perceive militants kidnapping oil workers as social bandits in the Hobsbawmian sense—as freedom fighters, the people's warriors and avengers of injustices meted to the poor of the Delta. Therefore, one of the fundamental objectives of this book is to interrogate members of two Niger Delta communities namely, Agge, and Okerenkoko, with a view to ascertaining their perceptions of the activities of insurgents, particularly concerning kidnapping, whether or not they think the recourse to kidnapping is a form of resistance, mere criminality or a more complicated hybrid phenomenon.

Hobsbawm's analysis of social bandits, however, has been criticized for his use of literary and folkloric sources and secondary data obtained from government documents (Slatta 2004: 27). His portrayal of the social bandit is based on myths, legends and poems which have questionable relationship to reality (Bettez-Gravel 1985). The use of government documents to analyze such issues is also fraught with problems, as the government can (and often does) label opposition movements bandits (Slatta 2004).

Attempts to find historical groups and personalities approximating Hobsbawm's social bandit have yielded little supporting evidence (O'Malley 1979; Blok 1972). For instance, Mkandawire (2008) finds no connection between African rebels and Hobsbawm's social bandits. Hobsbawm's bandits are predominantly peasants based in rural areas engaged in struggles against the wealthy, while rebels in Africa tend to develop in urban centers (Mkandawire 2008). Similarly, in a synthesis of studies in Latin America utilizing the concept of social banditry, Slatta (1987) concludes that additional models explicitly engaged with political and guerrilla bandits are required to supplement Hobsbawm's theory. One fundamental finding of Slatta (1990) is that while banditry can be an expression of discontent and a form of political action, it is not the prerogative of the rural poor. Slatta (1990) finds that rural elites are also involved in the intricate web of social banditry. Therefore, at least in Latin America, banditry cuts across class lines as bandits have ties to regional and local power holders (Slatta 1990). In addition, Hart (1987) investigates social banditry in Islam using secondary data from Morocco, Algeria and Pakistan. He finds that many of the case studies do not fit into Hobsbawm's theoretical schema and hence questions its universal applicability.

This study departs from Hobsbawm's approach by empirically investigating *how members of MEND are viewed in their local communities*. As noted, the notion of positive evaluation by community members is fundamental to the status of rebels as *bandits* rather than common *criminals* (see Hobsbawm 1969, 1959). This foundational distinction is central to Hobsbawm's theoretical formulation of social banditry. For this reason, in terms of how MEND is perceived, the opinions of community members is privileged rather than the views of NGOs, political and environmental justice activists, politicians, military authorities and other elites. This is not only a theoretical specification, but also an empirical prescription. This is because MEND claims that its struggle is to liberate the poor people in the rural oil-producing communities of the Delta and often condemns the elites of the Niger Delta for helping to oppress their people. Therefore, it is crucial to know whether MEND merely claims to be representing the poor people of the Delta while carrying out an essentially expropriative crime. Thus, there is no a priori assumption that MEND enjoys popular support among members of the community. This book avoids the limitations inherent in relying solely on secondary data as some of Hobsbawm's critics point out (see Hart 1987) by gathering primary and secondary data.

Approaches to Social Movements

Challenges to authority (violent or non-violent) and political violence in general are largely absent as topics of analysis in conventional criminology. Criminologists focus mainly on acts defined as criminal by the state (Ruggiero 2006). One must necessarily turn to the social movement literature to gain an informed theoretical understanding of why certain groups of individuals—and not everyone going through similar frustrating social experiences—engage in coordinated efforts to protest against constituted authority or resort to establishing groups that are actively involved in violence in order to make claims on the state.

There are at least four main theoretical standpoints in research on social movements concerned with why, how and when challengers of authority develop. The four dominant perspectives are:

(A).   The collective behavior perspective (see Buechler 2004; Smelser 1962, cited in della Porta and Diani 1999). This approach considers social movements as by-products of rapid waves of social transformation (della Porta and Diani 1999). Using a biological analogy, social movements are perceived to be generated by an imbalance in the equilibrium of society (Smelser 1962). Therefore, collective action is taken to be crisis behavior (Buechler 2004; della Porta and Diani 1999).

(B).   The Resource mobilization approach (see Edwards and McCarthy 2004; McAdam 1982; McCarthy and Zald 1977) focuses on the rationality of collective behavior. From this perspective, social movements are not mere reactionary phenomena but deeply rational and "normal" part of the political system (McAdam 1982). Hence, collective action is not a symbol of dysfunction of the polity but a choice people consciously make (Tilly, Tilly and Tilly 1975). This approach rejects the reduction of social movements into the irrationality of crowd behavior, and refutes the notion that social movements are non-institutional behavior (Buechler 2004; McAdam 1982). It also emphasizes the purposefulness of organized action, the significance of mobilization of available resources and the costs and benefits of engaging in social movement activities (della Porta and Diani 1999; McCarthy and Zald 1977).

(C). The political process paradigm (Meyer 2004; Tilly 1995. This is discussed in the next section).

(D). The new social movement approach focuses on post-industrial societies (see Pichardo 1997; Aronowitz 1992; della Porta and Diani 1999). As traditional Marxian class divisions have broken down with increasing embourgeoisement of the proletarian class, the focus of new social movements is the "reclamation of autonomous spaces, rather than material advantages" (della Porta and Diani 1999: 12). This approach examines the link between nascent social movements and wider socio-economic structures, the impact of culture and its identitarian dimensions (Pichardo 1997; see also Aronowitz 1992). New social movements are critical of the social order, pretensions to democracy and representativeness without professing any ideology (della Porta and Diani 1999: 12; Pichardo 1997).

All of these approaches are concerned with the "mechanisms which translate various types of structural tension into collective action" (see della Porta and Diani 1999: 2). While these approaches have their strengths, the political process paradigm in particular provides a grounded theoretical perspective that appears well-suited for interrogating the rise of kidnapping of oil workers in Nigeria.

Political Opportunity for Kidnapping Oil Workers in Nigeria

The political process approach views collective behavior as rational action. It examines the relationship between social movements and their situatedness in specific socio-political milieu (Meyer 2004). The political process comprises the interactions between institutional political actors, the state and its agents like the police and protest groups (della Porta and Diani 1999: 9). This approach stresses the salience of the political opportunity structure or the concatenation of actors—antagonists, protagonists and bystanders on the political stage and the context of their interactions (see Kriesi 2004).

The term *political opportunity* is used here in its broadest sense. Tarrow's (1998: 76–7) definition is theoretically and empirically useful: "consistent—but not necessarily formal, or permanent—dimensions of the political environment that provide incentives for collective action". Political opportunity often refers to the relative openness of the institutionalized political system, the (in)stability of elite alignments inherent in the polity, and the presence or absence of elites (McAdam 1996a: 26; Goodwin and Jasper 1999). An even more problematic aspect of political opportunity is state capacity and the apparatus of repression (McAdam 1996a: 26; Goodwin and Jasper 1999).

Increasing legitimate political space for non-violent protest may serve as an effective mechanism for consigning a movement to irrelevance as the movement loses a key ingredient—"outrage" (Tarrow 1998: 84). On the other hand, it is easier to mobilize against a regime that assaults and jails peaceful protesters (Tarrow 1998). This suggests that political opportunity—in this case, repression—can be a positive or negative development vis-à-vis challengers of authority and those who seek to maintain the status quo.

For instance, Amnesty International refused to take up the Ogoni people's cause "because no Ogoni had been killed or jailed" when Saro-Wiwa attempted to garner international NGO support for MOSOP's activities in 1991 (Bob 2005: 72). In fact, Amnesty International required documentary evidence of "conventional killings"—pictures and videos of actual dead bodies of peaceful protesters—instead of the broader oral accusations of cultural genocide and "unconventional killing" that Saro-Wiwa claimed (Bob 2005: 73, 75). By 1993, Saro-Wiwa had won the support of many international NGOs partly because of the brutal suppression of the rights of the Ogonis by the Nigerian military (Bob 2005). More recently, the Israeli naval commando attack on the "Freedom Flotilla" organized by the Free Gaza Movement in May 2010 demonstrates how political opportunity may come in the form of a tragedy. The attack claimed the lives of nine people, who were predominantly Turkish citizens. A *New York Times* report on May 31 2010 captures where blame was assigned in the global imaginary: "Deadly Israeli Raid Draws Condemnation".[2]

Political opportunity emerged largely because of repression and loss of human lives in both MOSOP and the Free Gaza Movement. In the case of MOSOP, the attack by state forces produced incontrovertible evidence that ensured a steady stream of the pictures and videos international NGOs had demanded. Many of these organizations also sent their staff to collect more information and wrote scathing reports against the Nigerian state and the oil corporations, particularly Shell (see Bob 2005, 2002). Therefore, the repression that MOSOP suffered in 1993 positively transformed it from a struggling obscure group to an internationally-recognized champion of environmental justice and human rights.

For the Free Gaza Movement, a similar kind of negative political opportunity resulted in positive developments that advanced the cause of the group against its opponents: An otherwise friendly country, Turkey, recalled its ambassador to Israel and cancelled scheduled military exercises with Israeli forces. In addition, several anti-Israeli demonstrations occurred around the world, the UN Security Council held an emergency session to discuss the attack, and a number of Israeli political elites considered the flotilla attack a public relations disaster for Israel. In this sense, the response of the Israeli commandos to the flotilla provocation created a political opportunity for the Palestinian cause.

This is not the first work to point out that political opportunity may not necessarily be restricted to a positive development such as the availability of influential allies. Tarrow (1998: 80), for instance argues that "there are aspects of

---

2   See *The New York Times*. 2010 (May 31). "Deadly Israeli raid draws condemnation", URL: http://www.nytimes.com/2010/06/01/world/middleeast/01flotilla.html Accessed 21 June 2011.

repressive states that encourage some forms of contention" in spite of the risks to dissidents. This means that although repression is generally intended to discourage contention; it may end up producing the opposite effect (see Tarrow 2007). In the same vein, an open political space may inadvertently guarantee that movements lack vitality (see Tarrow 1998).

Eisinger (1973) investigates the race and poverty riots in the US in the 1960s. This is a path-breaking work. He demonstrates why some cities in the US had widespread riots while others did not (Meyer 2004). The relative openness of urban governments was, for him, the key variable determining the incidence of riots. Municipal governments that had avenues for addressing grievances were able to prevent riots, while those with simultaneously *open* and *closed* structures or avenues for addressing grievances had a greater chance of being theatres of riots. Cities with completely closed structures for addressing grievances had a low likelihood of riots because they were able to repress and thus dissuade dissidents (Meyer 2004). Subsequent works by Tilly (1978) also demonstrate this curvilinear relationship between protest and political opportunity (Meyer 2004).

Similarly, the Nigerian political terrain demonstrates both closed and open characteristics. The Nigerian state has been neither completely authoritarian nor fully democratic at least since May 29, 1999, when democratic rule was restored after years of military dictatorships. Consistent with postcolonial spaces, the Nigerian state often operates as a "private indirect government" (Mbembe 2001: 66), where, in a classic Weberian sense, the state does not exist. However, as a rentier state, concerned with ensuring ceaseless flow of oil, the Nigerian state uses every means at its disposal, including denying the land rights of the peoples of the oil-producing region, corruption and repression of dissidents.

Therefore, it is worth accentuating that in terms of categorizing it as an authoritarian or a democratic state—with its implications for political opportunity—Nigeria is none of the above. It is a hybrid of mimetic fabricated notions of democracy and the moral fibre of authoritarianism. What constitutes social order becomes elusive and highly contestable (see Comaroff and Comaroff 2006). Nigeria's liminality and intersticiality among these two ideal types pose a considerable quandary for the theoretically puritanical. This assertion is fundamental as the political opportunities for kidnapping in the Delta region is analyzed. How repression and constraints have created political opportunities for kidnapping, rather than blocking such avenues is demonstrated. This means that factors that would conventionally be regarded as constraints, such as brutal suppression, have yielded openings for kidnapping. This chapter also considers how the simultaneously open and closed political system contributes to kidnapping episodes.

In what follows next in this chapter, drawing on the political process model, how major shifts, fragmentations, fractures, and even strictures in the socio-political and economic mechanics of Nigeria have inadvertently and at some levels directly contributed to the rise of kidnapping in the Delta is explicated. The relative openness of Nigeria's institutionalized political system, the (in) stability of elite alignments inherent in the polity (see Goodwin and Jasper

1999), the presence or absence of elites and the state's capacity and apparatus of repression (McAdam 1996a; Goodwin and Jasper 1999) are underscored. How the trajectory of collective action—in this case kidnapping—is moulded by variations in opportunities is also highlighted (Koopmans 1999). Variation in opportunity is investigated as a function of interactions of social movements with political and institutional actors (see Koopmans 1999). Kidnapping is not a mere expression of the strategic initiatives of MEND and associate groups like NDPVF but a product of Nigeria's political process (see Koopmans 1999; Noonan 1995). *The overarching theme is that the socio-political configuration and the economic permutations in the Nigerian society have helped to produce kidnappers.*

Implicit in the analysis is the cacophony of contentious politics in Nigeria centered on crude oil and the control and distribution of profits from its exploitation. *Au courant* of the "collective interaction" (McAdam, Tarrow and Tilly 2001: 5) among contending claim makers in Nigeria and its *"episodic" "public"* and *"manifestly political"* nature, the objects or targets of the claims and counter-claims, and the role of third parties (Tilly and Tarrow 2007: 4) in the oil struggle in Nigeria is explicated. Kidnapping in the Delta is a form of *"collective political struggle"* (McAdam, Tarrow and Tilly 2001: 5). It is thus only one *"contentious repertoire"* among several *contentious performances* (Tilly and Tarrow 2007: 11) available to insurgents in Nigeria.

In addition, *why* an excessively strong repertoire embodied in kidnapping takes place in the Delta is explained. This entails investigating the relative strength of the Nigerian state vis-à-vis political and structural changes (see Tilly and Tarrow 2007: 21). The role of the Nigerian government as a major actor at the epicenter of this toxic real life drama is examined cognizant that contentious repertoires vary by regime type (Tilly and Tarrow 2007: 57). The analysis considers the impact of decades of military dictatorships, the seldom-successful democratic experiments and "accumulated history" (Tilly and Tarrow 2007: 57, 158) of spectacular waves of violence in Nigeria to gain an informed understanding of why kidnapping emerged. Close attention is paid to the features of the Nigerian state characterized as "political opportunity structure" (Tilly and Tarrow 2007: 57). The following socio-political, economic and historical factors were essential components in establishing opportunities for kidnapping oil workers as well as other violent insurgent acts in the Delta.[3]

Inattention to earlier forms of peaceful protest

The emphasis on how traditional actors (e.g. state agents) and non-state actors (e.g. activists) interact and the relationship between institutionalized systems of interest representation and emerging forms of collective action is a major attraction

---

3   While some of these factors are widely recognized in the literature and popular discourse, they remain pertinent to any analysis of the current trajectory of insurgency in the Delta.

of the political process approach (della Porta and Diani 1999). In the Delta, the interactions between state agents and challengers of authority have evolved over the years. The evidence suggesting that earlier forms of protests in the Delta were peaceful is compelling. Delta communities wrote petitions, sent delegations to the federal and regional/state governments against the activities of oil corporations, as well as directly to the oil corporations (Osaghae 1995). These forms of protests were generally peaceful. In some cases, access routes to oil installations were blocked as a means of protest (Ikelegbe 2001). Despite being overwhelmingly ineffective, such protests did yield some token amenities from oil corporations (Ikelegbe 2001). Representatives of the Delta were disadvantaged in relation to the oil corporations and the communities" "leadership and agitation were treated with disdain, denied access and ignored, compromised by inducements while negotiations either failed or agreements if any were broken" (Ikelegbe 2001: 441). In addition, litigations by communities against the oil corporations began as communal agitations were ignored (Frynas 2000). The failure of the Nigerian state to accede to peaceful protest is constantly cited by present-day insurgents as a major reason why they took up arms against the state and began kidnapping oil workers.[4]

Routinization of violence

Another part of the context for the rise of kidnapping is that violence in the Delta as well as the whole of Nigeria has long been a staple of daily life. The Portuguese shipped the first consignment of slaves from the Niger Delta around 1480 (Falola 1999). The slave trade was most heinous and its devastating effect gruesome in the Niger Delta where the last slave ship departed from Brass in 1854 (Falola 1999). The British signed a treaty with the Niger Delta in 1884 and formed the "Protectorate of the Oil Rivers" in 1891 (Falola 1999) essentially for oil, at this period palm oil. However, this was only after Delta states like Opobo, Brass, Bonny, Elem Kalabari, Okrika, and Itsekiri were vanquished (Falola 1999). Many of the kingdoms, especially Opobo led by the Jaja of Opobo and Itsekiri under the leadership of Chief Nana put up stiff resistance. In the end, through a combination of the sheer magnitude of violence, military might, trickery and encouragement of internal strife in each kingdom, the British incorporated the Delta into its colonial project that would later become Nigeria (Falola 1999).

This era of British imperialism marked the high point of the socio-genesis of violent resistance against outsiders in the Delta. Many other events in Nigeria's political process have also contributed to making violence routine, mundane and unspectacular in the Delta. The independence era in Nigeria has changed very little with respect to violence as an organizing principle. For instance, over a million lives were lost during the Nigerian civil war between 1967 and 1970. Nigerians have also witnessed decades of military dictatorships that led to bloodshed. Between January 1966 and May 1999, Nigeria experienced eight military

---

4   Interviewees 11, 15, 19, 20 and many other ex-insurgents who were interviewed.

dictatorships with a failed civilian government between 1979 and 1983 and an 88-day pseudo-civilian regime in 1993. This period was punctuated by a number of botched putsches including one led by predominantly Niger Delta officers against the General Ibrahim Babangida junta on April 22 1990. The regime of General Sani Abacha had a death squad dedicated to eliminating opponents of the regime. Journalists, human rights activists and dissidents of all kinds lived in fear of the state. The perpetual crisis of legitimacy besieging the Nigerian state has led to the use of the most atrocious means of manufacturing the consent of citizens to state authority (Ogundiya 2009).

The routine loss of human lives, flippant disregard for human rights as well as clampdown on peaceful protests have generated widespread use of violent forms of protests in Nigeria. While one does not presuppose a deterministic, unilinear or teleological relationship between everyday violence and equally volatile forms of protest in Nigeria, the reality is that where a repressive political culture exists, protesters can more readily turn to more violent repertoires and thus become radicalized (see della Porta 1995). Two examples may suffice to accentuate the influence of this atmosphere of repression and violence on the national psyche as well as the architecture of protest in Nigeria as a whole and the Delta in particular.

First, on Saturday, October 17, 1998 a major petrol pipeline ruptured at Atiegwo in Ethiope West Local Government Area of Delta State. Villagers converged on the scene to scoop fuel having been facing scarcity of petroleum products for some time. An ensuing explosion—called the *Jesse fire disaster*—killed over 1000 persons and injured hundreds. The government alleged that the pipeline was sabotaged while the Delta public insisted that the saboteurs were the oil corporations and the federal government.[5]

Second, the cataclysmic scale of violence that followed the annulment of the June 12, 1993 presidential election by the General Babangida regime caused Nigeria to teeter dangerously on the precipice of self-annihilation. Chief Moshood Abiola, a southerner, reportedly won the election. A year after the election, Abiola declared himself president. Abiola was jailed on charges of treason on June 16, 1994. Pro-democracy groups, activists and supporters of Abiola and those simply irked by the injustice meted to the president-elect began violent confrontations with the Abacha regime that had since usurped power from the lame Ernest Shonekan government installed by Babangida. The tensions were reminiscent of the buildup to the 1967–1970 Civil War. Ethno-religious clashes were rife. From peaceful demonstrations, the crisis degenerated into bomb detonations and Nigeria as a whole became ungovernable. These incidents among several others have punctuated Nigeria's socio-political landscape and provided fertile grounds for violent resistance.

---

5   See "Causes of the Idjerhe fire disaster: ERA's environmental testimonies No 1". URL: http://www.waado.org/Environment/IdjerheFire/CausesOfFireDisaster.html Accessed May 19 2010.

Constitutional reforms

Several changes in the Nigerian political configuration have contributed to the rise of kidnapping in the Delta. As is widely recognized, collective action is fundamentally shaped by variations in opportunities. While the variations in opportunity are a function of interactions of social movements with political and institutional actors (Koopmans 2009), the structure of the society shapes available opportunity. Therefore, political opportunities are not mere strategic initiatives of social movement organizations (Koopmans 1999; Noonan 1995).

What is presented here is a cursory explanation of relevant constitutional changes in Nigeria. Many of these changes are well-documented, albeit how they have contributed to kidnapping has yet to be fully acknowledged. First, the establishment of the Midwest state on 9 August 1963 was the first of such state-creation exercises in post-independence Nigeria. The Midwest state was formerly part of the Western region. Though a political masterstroke on the part of the federal coalition government led by Alhaji Abubakar Tafawa Balewa against the Western region's Action Group, the Midwest state was the culmination of several decades of yearnings and efforts of the minorities of the Delta region. This act was a concise delimitation of Delta minorities in Nigeria. The creation of states was intended to give voice to the aspirations of the Delta people, accelerate social development, and assuage minority clamor for autonomy from the dominant ethnic groups. However, state-creation by successive military regimes has further enabled the compartmentalization of Delta peoples into specific geo-political states even though some remained spread all over neighboring states and beyond.

State-creation means more revenue for Delta peoples as federal allocations are based on the population and number of states and local governments. Without state creation, minorities would have significantly limited platform to articulate their demands. The delimitation of Delta peoples into specific states in the federation has enabled the mobilization of geo-political identities and substruction of cultural identity. The result is the intensification of identity politics (see Ikelegbe 2005a).

However, state creation is janus-faced. It has also had the unintended consequence of accentuating differences among erstwhile neighbors. A "we" versus "them" orientation was exacerbated as Delta peoples (as well as many other Nigerians) were delimited. The idea of the "core" Niger Delta states—Bayelsa, Rivers and Delta—for instance, developed even though ethnic Ijaws, for instance, have a very visible presence in a state like Ondo, which is dominated by the Yorubas.

Second, the advent of "democracy"[6] on 29 May 1999 after nearly three decades of military rule has paradoxically catalyzed kidnapping. Nigeria's democracy has

---

6 The contradiction in analyzing the charade of elections that has dominated Nigeria's political landscape since 1999 as somehow democratic is noted. Nigeria's self-professed democracy is taken at face value to the extent that there has been continued civilian leadership.

opened more political space for civil society and many other actors in spite of its many flaws and contestability of its credentials. Ikelegbe (2005a: 251) calls this an "associational flowering". Several groups, associations and non-governmental organizations have developed in the Delta as a result of the political opportunity offered by democratic governance. By 2003, some such groups had become very militant in orientation. On the other hand, while law enforcement agencies largely retained their deserved reputation for insouciance and ruthlessness, Abacha's killer squad was gone, although assassination of key political figures continued to punctuate the political landscape. The Olusegun Obasanjo administration though repressive in its attempts to curb insurgency in the Delta could not eradicate kidnapping. Its actions such as the military invasion of Odi and Odiama only soiled the administration's reputation. By 29 May 2007, when Alhaji Shehu Musa Yar'Adua was sworn in as president, the ironic impact of the democratic process on kidnapping in the Delta was becoming clearer.

Generally perceived as simple, committed but not necessarily charismatic, Yar'Adua's presidency was no match for MEND and its crew whose tactics grew in brazenness. The patent weakness and impotence of the Nigerian state under the Yar'Adua administration—unfortunately embodied in the terminal illness of the president—contributed to the upsurge in kidnapping. By 2009, MEND's unabated campaigns—especially bombings, and kidnappings—and the government's realization that there would be no military solution to the Delta crisis, finally led to declaring amnesty for interested insurgents.

So far, structural factors such as, inattention to earlier forms of peaceful protest, routinization of violence and constitutional reforms as some of the issues providing a favorable environment for kidnapping of oil workers in the Delta have been examined. Other socio-political and economic factors that have made kidnapping possible are accentuated below.

Backfire on military "lesson" in Niger Delta communities

Several other factors in Nigeria's political process have contributed to fostering an atmosphere conducive for kidnapping. Two of these are the availability of influential allies for challengers and the extent to which a regime represses dissidents (see Tilly and Tarrow 2007: 57) or their constituency. The repressive actions of the Nigerian state generated sympathy for insurgents among important elites. For example, on November 10 1999, President Olusegun Obasanjo sent a letter to the governor of the oil-rich Bayelsa state, Diepreye Alamieyeseigha, in which he warned of the impending declaration of a state of emergency:

> Recent events of kidnapping and subsequent wilful murder of seven policemen are clear demonstrations that you have lost grip of the security situation in the State ... During Council deliberations, it was further reported that four soldiers had been kidnapped while four others had been decapitated. You assured members of Council that the perpetrators would definitely be arrested.

It is significant that after the National Security Council of 9th November 1999 had deliberated upon and condemned the killing of seven policemen in your State, you seemed to take no effective measure to arrest the culprits. Instead, reports have reached me that 3 other policemen and civilians have been killed. It is apparent from the foregoing that the security situation in your State is getting beyond your control. It seems to me that if those responsible for the maintenance of law and order are not safe in your State, there is little hope for the safety of private citizens ... I give you 14 (fourteen) days within which to restore law and order in your State and effect the arrest and prosecution of all those responsible for these killings, failing which I shall set in motion process to declare a state of emergency in Bayelsa State.

The letter from the president was a tall order considering the bewildering political system in Nigeria. While a governor is the Chief Security Officer of a state, in reality, the police establishment is a federal agency beyond the control of the governor. Alamieyeseigha thus had no legitimately armed organization that he could call on to restore order. Obasanjo declared a state of emergency in Bayelsa state and ordered troops unofficially estimated at 3,000 to 5,000 mobilized for the invasion of Odi five days before the ultimatum. About 2,483 civilians allegedly died as Odi was reduced to rubble at the end of the operation named HAKURI II (Courson 2006). Only a church and a bank stood as the relics of Odi. One John Agim of the Nigerian army boasted that: "The intention was just a show of force to let them (Odi people) know they cannot continue like that. I think that has been achieved ... No village will want to go through what that village went through. It has been taught a lesson."[7]

Matching violence with greater violence in Odi backfired on the Nigerian state. Not only did the Obasanjo administration lose credibility nationally and internationally, many political activists and some elites in Nigeria clearly rallied to the side of the Delta communities as demonstrated in their public display of sympathy for the Delta insurgents even though they did not necessarily support their tactics. The military invasions also generated more violence as such acts are wont to do (Ruggiero 2006). Alamieyeseigha publicly supported the invasion to save his political career. He lamented privately that the operation was tantamount to "overkill". A renowned human and environmental rights activist Oronto Douglas put it succinctly: "I think people will not want to take it quietly. They may want to act." Local community leaders like Isaac Osoka of the Ijaw Youth Council suggested that there would be more violence. Other prominent and highly respected elites like the Nobel Laureate Wole Soyinka, for instance, condemned the government's "revenge mission" and berated the president for "laying a human habitation to waste" and "unleashing the animalism of the military on Odi because

---

7 See 'Army teaches a lesson in Bayelsa state'. URL: http://www.waado.org/ environment/fedgovt_nigerdelta/bayelsainvasion/FederalGovernInvadesBayelsa/ MilitaryInOdi/ToTeachOdiALesson.html Accessed 25 May 2010.

a crime was committed".[8] Some prominent politicians like the Senate president Dr. Chuba Okadigbo offered no comments publicly after visiting Odi but the media interpreted their silence as a sign of their disappointment in the government.

Subsequent state acts of repression in Liama in 2001 and 2002, Okerenkoko and Gbaramatu in 2003 and Odiama in 2005 led to further loss of lives and property (Courson 2006; Human Rights Watch 2002) that further tarnished the government's image and generated sympathy for the insurgents. A pattern of wanton killings in the Delta by the Nigerian military had been firmly established by the time Agge community in the Ekeremor local government area of Bayelsa state was invaded by operatives of the Joint Task Force (JTF) in August 2008. In addition, the federal government's credibility had been depleted. Images of scores of dead bodies littering whole communities had become firmly entrenched in the minds of Deltans and those sympathetic to their cause. These images of the high-handedness of the government also succeeded in radicalizing even those who would not have joined any militia. Oyefusi's (2007: 2, 16) survey of 1,337 participants spread across 18 communities in the Delta reveals the damage done: while 5.12 percent of the subjects were "personally satisfied or undisturbed with the status quo", 80.84 percent *demonstrate a high grievance level against the State* and 36 percent demonstrate a *"willingness or propensity to take up arms against the state"* (emphasis added).

The repressive measures adopted by the Nigerian state have diminished support for the state (see Tilly and Tarrow 2007) and have backfired in a number of ways. First, such measures have radicalized more youths in the Delta as stated earlier. This is reflected in the youth willingness to take up arms against the Nigerian state (Oyefusi 2007), as tactics and strategies of protests depend on the social context (Meyer 2004). Second, military repression has generated greater feelings of marginalization and oppression among the Delta people. In this atmosphere, the government (and not the insurgents) has become the villain as those who would not necessarily participate in militancy, increasingly view the militants favorably. Third, the government alienated key human rights activists and political elites by the sheer enormity and inhumanity of its crackdown on Delta communities in the quest to flush out militants. For example, in an e-mail sent on 28 September 2009, MEND's spokesperson Jomo Gbomo announced the formation of the "Aaron Team":

> Some eminent Nigerians have graciously accepted to dialogue on behalf of the Movement for the Emancipation of the Niger Delta (MEND) with the Federal Government of Nigeria whenever the government realizes the need to adopt serious, meaningful dialogue as a means to halting the violent agitation in the Niger Delta. ... These eminent persons will be known as the Aaron Team and

---

8 See Nwaja, Osita. 1999. "Obasanjo condemned for the situation in Nigeria", URL: http://www.waado.org/environment/fedgovt_nigerdelta/bayelsainvasion/FederalGovern InvadesBayelsa/MilitaryInOdi/MilitaryMassacres.html Accessed 26 May 2010.

have our mandate to oversee a transparent and proper MEND disarmament process that conforms with international standards ... The Aaron Team is:

– Vice Admiral Okhai Mike Akhigbe (rtd)
– Professor Wole Soyinka (Observer)
– Major General Luke Kakadu Aprezi (rtd)
– Dr. Sabella Ogbobode Abidde, PhD

It is surprising that retired top military officials and academics accepted MEND's invitation to serve. Of all the persons named above, perhaps the most interesting and indicative of the level of support insurgents have been able to garner among elites is the inclusion of Professor Wole Soyinka. Soyinka is the only non-Deltan in the group, a Yoruba from South West Nigeria, and a member of one of the three major ethnic groups that have dominated Nigeria's socio-political and economic life. Soyinka's inclusion in the Aaron team also marks a departure from previous years when Delta activists did not actively engage the support of sympathetic elites outside the Delta. Third, Soyinka's acceptance to serve on the Aaron team also lends credence to the agitation of the Delta militants as he is highly respected nationally and internationally. This helps to confer legitimacy on MEND. Like many other activists, Soyinka became increasingly involved in the Delta struggle having been irked by the gruesome military invasion of Odi.[9]

Actions of oil corporations

Oil corporations in Nigeria also carry out certain acts that fuel kidnapping of their staff. First, they deploy private security that often violently represses protest by community members. Second, oil corporations actively collaborate with the state by providing logistical support for repression of legitimate concerns and gross abuse of human rights. For instance, in June 2009, Shell agreed to pay $15.5 million compensation to the families of Ken Saro-Wiwa and eight other Ogoni activists hanged by the General Sani Abacha regime in 1995. Shell denied any wrong doing but was facing charges for complicity in the hangings before the settlement was reached. Third, there are allegations of discrimination against oil corporations. Oil corporations foster nepotism within their rank and file in drawing the distinction between "expatriates" and "local" workers. There are cases of expatriates—meaning white workers—being flown to oil rigs while their Nigerian counterparts take a boat to work at the same location. Some of the local workers become alienated by these and other policies and provide intelligence for insurgents for monetary reasons and as a way to gain revenge against discriminatory organizational practices. The actions of oil corporations

---

9 The Aaron team had its first meeting with the federal government on Saturday, November 14, 2009 in Abuja. A former MEND overall field Commander Farah Dagogo, and Henry Okah attended the meeting as observers.

thus create an inadvertent alignment between human rights and environmental justice activists and insurgents.

In addition to these acts, the process of oil production is a harbinger of environmental devastation. All the stages of oil production involve potentially deleterious consequences for the environment (Omoweh 2005) even under the most ethical production regimen. The April 20 2010 British Petroleum (BP) Deepwater Horizon explosion in the Gulf of Mexico brought the catastrophic tendencies of oil production to the United States and invariably to a global stage. Eleven lives were lost in the explosion. Cable television and the Internet graphically displayed the real cost of oil. The incident has led to comparisons with oil spills in the Delta region of Nigeria. Many activists are convinced that the location of the spill made a huge difference in terms of response. Reacting to the efforts made by BP to clean up the spill, Nigerian environmental rights activist Nnimo Bassey argues that:

> (I)n Nigeria, oil companies largely ignore their spills, cover them up and destroy people's livelihood and environments. The Gulf spill can be seen as a metaphor for what is happening daily in the oilfields of Nigeria and other parts of Africa. This has gone on for 50 years in Nigeria. People depend completely on the environment for their drinking water and farming and fishing. They are amazed that the president of the US can be making speeches daily, because in Nigeria, people there would not hear a whimper. (Vidal 2010)

The Delta not only produces the highest quality oil in the world, it also suffers the worst form of environmental degradation (Vidal 2010). With over 7000 km of pipelines, 275 flow stations, 10 gas plants, 14 export terminals and four refineries as well as over 6,000 oil wells and 606 oil fields (Watts 2008b), the Delta is a workshop of transnational oil corporations. While a measure of environmental disasters is inevitable, the frequency, longevity and reaction to oil spills, gas flaring and other forms of hazards demonstrate oil corporations' lackadaisical orientation towards the welfare of the people of the Delta. Environmental pollution in the Delta is in a class of its own. The federal government of Nigeria estimates that over 7,000 spills occurred from 1970 to 2000. The government also officially recognizes over 2,000 major oil spill sites and thousands of minor ones that have not been cleaned up (Vidal 2010). A report produced by the WWF UK in collaboration with the World Conservation Union (WCU) and officials of the federal government of Nigeria as well as the Nigerian Conservation Foundation (NCF), estimates that in the last 50 years the Delta has witnessed the spillage of about 1.5m tons of oil (Vidal 2010). Considering that the well-publicized 2010 BP Macondo oil disaster in the United States spilled 4.9 million barrels, the Delta case becomes more troubling. Amnesty International determined that at least nine million barrels of oil was spilled in 2009 (Vidal 2010). Shell has admitted to spilling in 2009 14,000 tonnes of oil during 132 spillages (Vidal 2010). This was below the yearly average of 175 spills (Vidal 2010). The magnitude of pollution and environmental menace of the oil industry in the Delta is frightening, as there are other oil corporations in the Delta besides

Shell. Shell alone currently faces over 1000 oil spill related cases in the Delta (Vidal 2010).

The impact of the incessant oil spills in the Delta may never be fully known. For a people whose major livelihood is fishing and farming, oil spills further worsen the economic conditions of Deltans by throwing them out of work. There are cases of rivers and water wells serving whole communities and families rendered unusable because of oil spillage (Bassey 2009a, 2009c). Oil spills are poisonous for marine animals and plants. Acid rain is common as the weather also becomes unpredictable due to gases and other chemical substances regularly saturating the atmosphere. Ceaseless pipeline construction also ensures that homes and farmlands are often cleared to make way for sweet crude. The health of the people is also at stake as mysterious illnesses sporadically occur. There are documented cases of bronchial asthma, gastro-enteritis, cancer and several respiratory problems related to unethical oil production.[10]

None the less, even the worst critics of the oil industry will concede that oil corporations do not set out to spill oil or cause environmental problems. However, oil companies are believed to be culpable in environmental degradation in at least three ways. First, a company's production techniques, lack of safeguards, and the means of transportation of oil can engender spills. Second, oil spills can be a consequence of equipment failure, human error or sabotage. While no company would logically wish its equipment failure, an error of judgment by management and/or staff can prove disastrous. Third, when oil spills happen, as they often do, an oil corporation can choose how to respond. It is at the stage of reaction to spillage that oil corporations in the Delta have earned a reputation of being slow— if they ever act—lethargic and unscrupulous.

A spill caused by leaks from an ExxonMobil pipeline in Akwa Ibom, one of the Niger Delta states on 1 May 2010 amply demonstrates why people perceive oil corporations as entities that provoke violent protest in the Delta. At that location, over one million gallons of oil were spilled in one week while security guards of the corporation ensured that attempts by community members to protest were met with stiff resistance (Vidal 2010).[11]

Consequently, there is a belief in the Delta that the destructiveness of oil corporations' activities created opportunities for kidnapping. For instance, long before kidnapping became ubiquitous, Ken Saro-Wiwa was unequivocal in his belief that Shell, which controls over 70 percent of production in Nigeria (Omoweh 2005) would receive its recompense. Facing a certain death, he declared: "there is no doubt in my mind that the ecological war that the company has waged in the

---

10   See "Shell in Nigeria: What are the issues?" URL: http://www.essentialaction.org/shell/issues.html Accessed 2 June 2010.

11   The affected community in Akwa Ibom is seeking a $1 billion compensation for the effects of the spill including illness and economic damage (Vidal 2010). Gas flaring was routine and the stench in the area was literally sickening during visits to various oil sites at Ogboloma and environs.

Delta will be called to question sooner than later and the crimes of that war be duly punished".[12] A disproportionately large number of conflicts in the Delta are protests directly against the activities of oil corporations from the 1990s (Ikelegbe 2008). For environmental rights activist, Alagoa Morris, for instance, MEND's tactic of kidnapping oil workers "is part of the struggle"[13] for environmental justice and resource control. The degradation of the Delta environment helps in aligning human rights and environmental justice activists to the standpoint of insurgents even though the former may oppose violence in principle. The ranks of the political elites are fragmented as politicians from the Delta speak against the suffering of their people because of ecological damage. Therefore, kidnapping is a trajectory in the protest regime in the Delta.

Corruption

The character of the Nigerian rentier petro-state nourishes kidnapping. No other social malaise exemplifies the character of the Nigerian rentier petro-state than corruption (see Maier 2000). The pervasiveness of corruption and the enterprise of graft have become *sine qua non* for conducting business in everyday life at all levels of government and strata of society. Embezzlement of public funds designated for roads, electricity, schools and even workers' salaries is a national embarrassment. Transparency International (TI) ranks Nigeria 130th position out of 180 countries in the world in terms public sector corruption in its 2009 annual Corruption Perception Index. As this is a rather self-evident point to anyone with only a cursory understanding of events in Nigeria, only three examples are used to demonstrate how the corruption of the state fosters kidnapping in Nigeria.

The kidnapping of Professor Nimi Briggs (see *The Nation*, December 15, 2007), a former Vice Chancellor of the University of Port Harcourt and chair of the electoral commission in Rivers state symbolizes the intrinsic interconnection of seemingly disparate elements within and outside government circles in the production of kidnapping episodes. Benjamin Okaba, professor of sociology at the Niger Delta University, and Director, Centre for Niger Delta Studies, a neighbor of Professor Briggs argues that:

> When governor Amaechi (Rotimi Amaechi, Rivers state governor) visited the family, a call came from the kidnappers that they should give the phone to the governor that they wanted to talk to him. It was very clear that among the government functionaries, there was somebody that was monitoring

---

12   For a dedicated and critical appraisal of Shell's activities in Nigeria, see Okonta, Ike and Oronto Douglas. 2001. *Where Vultures Feast: Shell, Human Rights and Oil in the Niger Delta.* San Francisco: Sierra Book Club. Also see, Omoweh, Daniel. 2005. *Shell Petroleum Development Company, the State and Underdevelopment of Nigeria's Niger Delta: A Study in Environmental Degradation.* Trenton, New Jersey: Africa World Press.

13   Interview, 2009.

issues. Kidnappers have gone to the extent of asking for their slot in the local government elections. Kidnappers have gone ahead to demand that this person should be made a minister or not and in some cases, that was what happened. So, government has a way of legitimizing the functions of these militants. So, that is one point you have to stress: The nature, character of the Nigerian state and the legitimization of criminality. Government promotes them.[14]

Second, the prevalence of illegal oil bunkering and the operation of unlicensed refineries are other indications of the corrupt character of the Nigerian rentier petro-state. When news reports emerged that Brigadier General Wuyep Rimtip, commander of JTF in Delta state had been relocated to Bayelsa state, insurgents and miscellaneous illegal oil bunkerers in Delta state were ecstatic. One of the insurgents was quoted in the *Nigerian Tribune*: "That General gave us real hell. He was unlike others who occasionally cooperated with us" (16 March 2009). Such brazen public operations as oil theft require the connivance of a multiplicity of actors at all levels of society: militants, political, military and business elites, elders in the community and members. As this example demonstrates, illegal oil bunkerers could count on the cooperation of all but a few of state security agents given the responsibility to protect oil infrastructure. This relationship between non-state actors and state agents fosters insurgent acts because some of those responsible for security are active participants in illegal oil bunkering and not an effective check on insurgents.

Third, the level of corruption in the amnesty program for militants is another instance of the character of the Nigerian state. Declared by the federal government in 2009, the amnesty program offered a pathway to reconciliation between the government and the militants at the creeks. However, a short period after the program began, Jomo Gbomo, MEND spokesperson stated that:

> the government has been offering bribes to a number of militants who surrendered their birth rights under its amnesty program in the form of contracts. ... The group wants to make it abundantly clear that all those who have capitulated are of no significance to the continuation of the struggle.

At first, the statement would seem like a desperate attempt by MEND to malign the amnesty program, which a number of high-profile militants like Henry Okah had begun to embrace. In an e-mail on 5 September 2009, Jomo Gbomo alleged that:

> The Browning .50 Caliber Machine Guns (listed by government as **Brandy** Machine Guns) displayed on Saturday, August 22, 2009 in Yenagoa, Bayelsa state were identified by Cameroonian Military Intelligence as suspected weapons seized after an attack on November 12, 2007 in its territorial waters by unknown

---

14   Interview 3.

gun men from Nigeria believed to be men of the Nigerian army in which 21 Cameroonian gendarmes were killed.

We hope that the Nigerian military whom we accused recently of providing its weapons for display at that shameful disarmament ceremony will allow an independent international armament expert in the presence of both Cameroonian and Nigerian officials to examine the Browning weapons in question to determine their origin.

MEND has always called for a proper peace and disarmament process to avoid this sort of embarrassing situation where fraud, rent-a-crowd and monetary inducement is now a part of an amnesty charade. (highlight in original)

On 7 October 2009, Jomo Gbomo released another e-mail titled "Amnesty Scorecard". Jomo Gbomo argued that "(m)ost of those who participated in this fraud (amnesty program) were rented by the government in the hope that real militants would be persuaded to emerge".

The assertion that the amnesty program had become ridden with corruption assumed huge proportions early in 2010. On 25 April, *NEXT*,[15] a national daily reported the restructuring of the amnesty program by then acting President Goodluck Jonathan. The President appointed his special adviser on the Niger Delta to take charge of the program. Prior to the restructuring exercise, former insurgents had taken to the streets in Yenagoa and other states in the Delta to protest against corruption among government officials handling the program. The exact number of insurgents who surrendered and guns recovered on the 4 October 2009 deadline remains shrouded in secrecy or conflicting figures (Ebhuomhan 2010). While the amnesty committee reported having "about 10,000" ex-militants, President Jonathan stated on CNN that the figure was 20,191 (Ebhuomhan 2010). At the Obubra rehabilitation camp in Cross River state, the 20,191 figure is the official statistic. *NEXT*'s investigation, however, shows that the real figure could be no more than 12,000 (Ebhuomhan 2010). Allegations of diversion of funds are also rife. The program's 10 billion Naira budget approved by Nigeria's Senate is also excessive in spite of the disputable number of actual militants (Ebhuomhan 2010).

The rise of the Movement for the Survival of Ogoni People (MOSOP)

Mobilization of dissidents may remain elusive even when the political atmosphere is favorable and there are numerous resources (Diani 1996; Ferree and Miller 1985; McAdam 1982). Therefore, mobilization by SMOs is crucial (Bob 2002; Diani 1996; Gerhards and Rucht 1992; Snow, Rochford, Worden and Benford 1986; Ferree and Miller 1985; McCarthy and Zald 1977). Mobilization is a function of the internal dynamics of a group with a set of grievances (Oberschall 1973; Freeman

---

15   Publication of *NEXT* ended in September 2011.

1973). Protest of any kind can only occur to the extent that there are existing networks or associations to serve a catalytic role (Oberschall 1973; Freeman 1973). McAdam's (1982) *The Political Process and the Development of the Black Insurgency 1930–1970*, is a classic in the enterprise of mobilization and the political process framework generally. McAdam argues that a propitious political atmosphere can only be utilized through effective use of resources possessed by minority communities. This is the "conversion potential" of the community (Katz and Gurin 1969: 350, cited in McAdam 1982: 43–4). Such resources intrinsic to an aggrieved conglomeration of people include its membership, established structure of solidary incentives or interpersonal rewards, communication network, and leadership (McAdam 1982: 44–8). "Cognitive liberation" is also a basic prerequisite for insurgency (McAdam 1982: 48). This refers to the "subjective meanings" aggrieved people attach to their social conditions (McAdam 1982: 48). Cognitive liberation, for McAdam mediates between political opportunity and action. It is, however, dependent on both political opportunity and the presence of indigenous organizations (McAdam 1982, 1983). For African-Americans, three key institutions—the Southern Black Church, Black colleges and Southern chapters of the NAACP—played vital roles in mobilization during the Civil Rights struggle (McAdam 1982). The alignment of external supporters was also crucial during this period creating what may be characterized as a feedback loop (McAdam 1982). As the black insurgency demonstrates, the interplay of several actors in social movement ensures a complex process of negotiation, (re)alignment of forces, and sometimes conflicting roles.

Although the military regimes in Nigeria in the 1990s did not condone dissent, new actors (see Tilly and Tarrow 2007) managed to rise and challenge the Generals in power. This era was also marked by political instability. This served as an opportunity for challengers (see Tilly and Tarrow 2007). Coups were common in the 1990s. The government of Ernest Shonekan, for instance, was in power for only 88 days. His successor, General Sani Abacha, would prove to be more repressive. One of the new set of actors was the Movement for the Survival of Ogoni People (MOSOP) established in 1990, as stated earlier. Led by Ken Saro-Wiwa, the Ogoni struggle against environmental degradation, marginalization by the state and disregard of community welfare by oil corporations became the zenith of the Delta struggle in the 1990s (Okonta 2008). MOSOP popularized and internationalized the Ogoni (and by extension, the Delta) struggle by turning it into an environmental issue (Bob 2005, 2002).[16] Saro-Wiwa and his social movement organization used press releases, publications, conferences, symposia, lectures and public enlightenment to raise awareness about the marginalization of the Delta.

---

16 For Welch (1995: 644) the "Ogonis are not the most disadvantaged group in Nigeria". He argues that the high quality of MOSOP "globally-oriented" leadership, which spearheaded their course and the efficacy of turning what began as an ethnic marginalization issue in the Nigerian federation into an international environmental issue enabled MOSOP and the Ogonis to garner sufficient worldwide attention.

These tactics could not provide answers to state repression. About 80 persons were killed and 500 homes destroyed in Ogoniland by mobile police personnel working on behalf of the state and the oil corporations in October 1990 (Welch 1995). MOSOP reacted with a large demonstration of about 300,000 people.

Saro-Wiwa's era represented a period of non-violent protest. The extra-judicial conviction of Saro-Wiwa on charges of murder by a military tribunal and his hasty execution on November 10, 1995 by the regime of General Abacha before he could appeal the sentence was the anticlimax. The hanging of Saro-Wiwa and eight of his comrades remains the watershed of the checkered history of protest in the Delta (Okonta 2008; Bob 2005, 2002; Douglas, Kemedi, Okonta and Watts 2004; Ikelegbe 2001; Osaghae 1995). The ineffectiveness of peaceful means to fight for the rights of the Niger Delta people particularly for the Ogoni People under the leadership of the late Ken Saro-Wiwa contributed to propelling militants to resort to violence[17] (Osaghae 1995).

Socio-economic problems

The avalanche of socio-economic problems in Nigeria has also contributed to the rise of kidnapping for both political and economic purposes. The social conditions in the 1980s exacerbated an already difficult situation. The mid-1980s in Nigeria saw the beginning of World Bank and IMF inspired neo-liberal, Structural Adjustment Program (SAP) under the regime of General Ibrahim Babangida (famously known and hereafter referred to as IBB). This program led to enormous social problems. Some of the cardinal tenets of SAP in Nigeria included deregulation of the agricultural sector that had hitherto enjoyed incentives and price stabilization by marketing boards. Others were the privatization of public enterprises, relaxation of rules governing Foreign Direct Investment (FDI), reduction in public expenditure, devaluation of the Naira (Nigeria's currency) among other measures tellingly described in more recent times (based on evidence from Latin America) as the "shock doctrine" of "disaster capitalism" (Klein 2007). SAP was a monumental failure (Obi 2007) as it led to massive unemployment, skyrocketing prices of commodities and general social upheaval.

As Nigerians from different regions groaned under the juggernaut of SAP, there were widespread riots by the masses all over the country led by pro-democracy groups and human rights activists. In the Delta, the grievances and demands of the people rose beyond their communities to ethnic groups, federating units, and the entire region as civic activist groups increased in number and in the vociferousness of their demands in Nigeria (Ikelegbe 2001). Civil associations grew in number within this state of affairs in Nigeria generally and the Delta in particular. Politically, Nigeria was gasping for breath. The result of the presidential polls on June 12, 1993 was annulled by IBB. The aftermath was an iconic scale

---

17   For more on how MOSOP mobilized Ogoni people and garnered international NGO support during the Ogoni struggle in the 1990s, see Okonta (2008) and Bob (2005).

of nationwide protests that brought Nigeria to its knees. IBB would later "step aside" and appoint an Interim National Government (ING) headed by Ernest Shonekan. Alongside political instability, economic problems like unemployment have ensured that huge numbers of people are able and willing to get involved in kidnapping. Nigeria's economy literally over-produces potential kidnappers with an inflation rate of 11.5 percent as of 2009 and 70 percent of the population living below the poverty line.[18]

The Kaiama Declaration and its consequences

The Kaiama Declaration is one of the defining events in the trajectory of protest in the Delta. The community of Kaiama in Bayelsa state played host to an unusual event on 11 December 1998. Representatives of over 500 communities cutting across 40 clans of the Ijaw nation as well as 25 organizations concerned with the Niger Delta came together to discuss "the best way to ensure the continuous survival of the indigenous peoples of the Ijaw ethnic nationality of the Niger Delta within the Nigerian state".[19] The participants issued 10 resolutions christened the *Kaiama Declaration* after identifying 10 cognate root causes of the Delta problems including British colonization, corruption, and environmental degradation inter alia. These include an assertion that the Ijaws own their land and not the state, denunciation of military decrees and military operations in Ijawland, and demand for cessation of oil drilling and evacuation of oil company staff from Ijawland by 30 December 1998. More tellingly, the Ijaw Youth Council (IYC) was formed as part of the course of action of the declaration "to coordinate the struggle of Ijaw peoples for self-determination and justice".

The impact of the Kaiama Declaration on the Delta movement was instantaneous. First, the Kaiama Declaration raised the level of "consciousness" (see Taylor and Whittier 1992: 111) of Niger Deltans. Second, it was audacious as it confronted the government of General Abdulsalam Abubakar, who succeeded General Sani Abacha during a period of military rule, when brutal suppression of dissent was routine. The threat posed by the organizational prowess of the Ijaw youth after the declaration was arguably the first major threat to the Nigerian state from the Delta after the crescendo of the MOSOP uprising and the anti-climactic hanging of Ken Saro-Wiwa and eight others. Third, the Kaiama Declaration signaled a remarkable turn in the Delta struggle: Young people became more involved than ever before. The formation of the IYC was a major step in mobilizing the Delta youths. One of the most notable militants, Asari Dokubo, was IYC president from 2001 to 2004 before leaving to form the Niger Delta People's Volunteer Force (NDPVF). At least 20 other militant groups were formed after the declaration (Etekpe 2008).

---

18   See Nigeria's profile in the CIA World Fact Book. URL: https://www.cia.gov/library/publications/the-world-factbook/geos/ni.html Accessed 4 June 2010.

19   See "The Kaiama Declaration". URL: http://www.unitedijawstates.com/kaiama.html Accessed 7 June 2010.

Fourth, attempts by the Nigerian state to deal with the fall out of the Kaiama declaration further provided political opportunity for dissidents and ultimately culminated in the current spate of kidnappings. The IYC proclaimed "Operation Climate Change" beginning 28 December 1998 aimed at purging Ijawland of the vestiges of oil drilling. A demonstration in Yenagoa, capital of Bayelsa state heralding IYC's planned operations was attacked by soldiers. Some of the protesters died in the attacks. None the less, IYC's "Operation Climate Change" continued to impede oil production and eventually led to the Odi massacre (discussed above), perpetrated by the Nigerian military on the orders of President Olusegun Obasanjo in 1999. As discussed above, the Odi massacre as well as other supposed "military lessons" served to fuel the crisis and heralded the adoption of extremely violent architecture of protest by Delta youths including kidnapping.

Three key arrests and the liquidation of All States Trust Bank

Four distinct but inter-related events have also contributed to the political opportunities for kidnapping by militants in the Delta. The arrest of Diepreye Alamieyeseigha (popularly known as Alams), Governor of Bayelsa state by British authorities allegedly for money laundering and Alhaji Asari Dokubo, leader of the Niger Delta People's Volunteer Force (NDPVF) and former president of the Ijaw Youth Congress on charges of treason on 15 September 2005 and 21 September 2005 respectively was perceived as witch-hunting of political personalities from the Delta. The All States Trust Bank owned by Chief Ebitimi Banigo became the subject of investigation by the Economic and Financial Crimes Commission (EFCC) in October of the same year. The EFCC was an ascendant organization at the time but one that also earned a reputation for being used to persecute opponents of the Olusegun Obasanjo administration. The Niger Deltans were convinced that the federal government wanted to completely muzzle their business might, and political strength when the panic created by the EFCC's move against All States Trust Bank eventually led to the liquidation of the bank. Like Dokubo and Alamieyeseigha, Banigo was from the Delta region. The crisis was further complicated by the arrest of the leader of the Klansmen Konfraternity (KK), Olo, in November 2005 and led to rapprochement among multifarious insurgent leaders (see Asuni 2009).

MEND, an amalgam of militant groups in the Delta was formed to fight for the release of Dokubo and Alamieyeseigha in December 2005. The latter was rearrested in Yenagoa after allegedly jumping bail in London disguised as a woman to ensure his escape. Onengiya Erekosima, president of the Niger Delta Non-Violent Movement (NDNVM), an NGO concerned with brokering peace among rival militant factions and brokering truce between militants and the government puts the opinion of a lot of Deltans poignantly about the Alamieyeseigha imbroglio:

> Alams (the governor) was tricked into this so-called arrest because he was a
> threat for them in the election that was to return Obasanjo for the third term or

to make the plan for them to remain in power forever. They felt Alam's freedom as an Ijaw man, as a man who governs his people well will be a threat if they are thinking about who comes to the presidency or VP position. Alams was set up just to make sure people like him do not get to where there will be people who have voice in making decisions for this country ... They decided to silence him. So, he was set up. They designed a woman, put his face there and said he escaped as a woman. It was a computer job ... The government purposely rubbished him. He wanted transparency and good governance ...

Obasanjo was engaged in efforts to tinker with the constitution to secure an unconstitutional third term in office. Opponents of the third term project were being hounded by the EFCC on charges that had previously been known but were never brought up until they disagreed with the government. None the less, the statement above is truly remarkable coming from a peace activist because in reality, British police had incontrovertible evidence of millions of British pounds confiscated from Alamieyeseigha at the airport and at the expensive homes he had bought in cash. However, the credibility of his alleged escape disguised as a "woman" depends on what facts one chooses to believe. To the majority of the Delta people, Alamieyeseigha was only being persecuted by the federal government through its foreign allies. Indeed, when Alams returned to Yenagoa, the people trooped out in large numbers to welcome him as a hero.

Erekosima argues that "Asari Dokubo was arrested because the older generations had failed, so Dokubo was the "voice of the people" and 'they (the government) thought he was a threat. Asari was being outspoken. Asari was saying it the way it was'".[20] Kidnapping began when Asari Dokubo and Alams were arrested by the Nigerian state. The moment Asari Dokubo was arrested a second time, Erekosima argues, many Delta people believed that Nigeria "kidnapped our person. So, the boys started kidnapping." Erekosima said he had warned that:

if you don't release Asari this thing will get out of hand. I told them if you release Asari this thing will die a natural death. They did not listen to me; they delayed it until it became a full time business where companies were kidnapping their own persons setting up their own persons. Family members started kidnapping their own persons. It became a big time business.[21]

Erekosima points out that the delay in releasing Asari Dokubo led to several kidnappings that were not connected to the Delta struggle. Therefore, kidnapping became another type of commerce in Nigeria. Alagoa Morris, project officer of Environmental Rights Action and Bayelsa state secretary of Civil Liberties Organisation of Nigeria met with Asari Dokubo where "he said it was after his

---

20 Interviewee 1. Onengiya Erekosima, president Niger Delta Non-Violence Movement. Personal interview, Port Harcourt Rivers state, July 2009.

21 Interviewee 1.

arrest that MEND came into existence". MEND was unequivocal in its public demand for the release of Dokubo and Alams. Kidnapping increased at a frightening rapidity at this period to buttress the demands of the insurgents. Some insurgents kidnapped nine expatriate oil workers specifically to demand the release of their leader, Dokubo at this period.[22]

Foreign oil workers as the colonialist Other

There are emotive factors that have contributed to kidnapping of oil workers in addition to factors inherent in Nigeria's political process. Three of these factors are examined to accentuate the invention of a socio-cultural space imbued with favorable sedimented inter-generational emotions central to the kidnapping of oil workers in the Niger Delta. One of these is the perception of oil workers. As one insurgent points out:

> I see them personally as instruments of oppression. I look at them as agents of colonialism. These oil workers come to work in our community, impregnate our girls, do shady things with our money, dent the community and I'm jobless: You want me to be happy?[23]

Kidnapping in the Delta is dangerously but unsurprisingly catalyzed by the *othering* of foreign oil workers. The foreign oil worker represents the Other par excellence: a *colonialist* as well as *Other*; a *colonialist Other*. S/he is perceived by the people of the Niger Delta as a vulture that feeds on the people and an embodiment of all that has gone wrong in the Delta and other resource-rich regions of the developing world. To many, the palm oil trade, slave trade, colonialism, the banishment and eventual death of several traditional rulers, among other incidents (see Etekpe 2008) and on-going unequal relations between the West and the rest demonstrate that the "white man"—historically the British imperialist—likes reaping from where he did not sow. Expatriate oil workers become easy targets, as they are largely phenotypically distinct from the local populace. Hundreds of years of history are recalled because of what Western oil workers (arguably unwittingly) symbolize.

There are more immediate mundane but emotive reasons why some people loathe the presence of the expatriate oil worker. First, such workers live in gated communities with all imaginable amenities of life often in proximity to oil producing communities with no social infrastructure. While the latter wallow in darkness at night, they only have to look out the window to see foreigners living their dream. Community members see foreign oil workers in the day time being

---

22   Interviewee 4. Alagoa Morris.

23   Interviewee 20 (Militant 1. A man in his 40s with a degree in the arts, he worked as an oil contractor simultaneously as intelligence director of an insurgent group in the Niger Delta.). Personal interview August 2010, Obubra camp Cross River state.

chauffeured around by their Nigerian kith and kin in air-conditioned SUVs. The full impact of such bizarre contradictions on the grievances of the Delta can never be fully estimated.

Second, as stated earlier, oil expatriates also incur the ire of their Nigerian counterparts because of perceived preferential, if not discriminatory treatment. The atmosphere of favoritism in oil corporations manifests in differential earnings, emoluments and promotion between foreign oil workers and the local staff. The former typically earn more than their local colleagues for doing the same job. It is no surprise, therefore, that local oil workers sometimes supply information and expertise to militants in carrying out attacks.

Third, foreign oil workers, who are mostly males, are perceived as morally bankrupt persons, who destroy the values and fabric of society. It is believed that they corrupt young girls and lure them with money into prostitution (Okorie and Williams 2009). The increasing numbers of racially mixed children in Niger Delta cities like Port Harcourt is singled out as the evidence of transgression of imaginatively forbidden sexual liaisons between young Nigerian girls in the Delta and foreign oil workers.[24] Asari Dokubo points out, for instance, that "rather than create employment opportunities for Niger Delta youths, the oil companies through their staff had been infecting them with HIV/AIDS" (*The Punch*, August 7, 2007, page 7).

Fourth, oil workers are easy targets in the Delta because in many cases, oil companies are the only government presence in remote oil-bearing communities. Therefore, to get the attention of an absent Leviathan whose only presence is the array of oil infrastructure and oil workers, the latter become the sacrificial lamb. An insurgent argues that "(s)ince I can't get hold of the government, it's the oil workers I can see physically".[25]

Consequently, insurgents believe that kidnapping foreign oil workers is exploitation in reverse: the exploiter is now being exploited. One encounter in the course of the fieldwork for this book exemplifies this resentment. One of my gatekeepers and I were traveling in a car. He saw a number of soldiers and said they were guards for the white oil workers. He pointed to a foreign oil worker at a pipeline site and said to me: "dem be natural resources",[26] which means *they (oil workers) are natural resources*. With relish, he estimated how much the unsuspecting expatriate could be worth, if kidnapped by the "boys". His estimation was roughly $20,000 (CAN.). This encounter with an individual who was not involved in the kidnapping venture but somehow finds it exhilarating

---

24 The world-historical policing of gendered sexual boundaries, of course, knows no cultural bounds. Myrdal (1962), who was imported from Europe to diagnose the "American dilemma" shows that the worst fears about desegregation, was racial mixture between white women and black men, especially through sharing the same classrooms.

25 Interviewee 20 (Militant 1).

26 Interviewee 7 (A politician in the Delta). Personal interview and private tour of oil installations in July 2009.

demonstrates not only what the oil worker represents but also how they have become othered, and objectified. It also shows what little sympathy people have for kidnapped expatriates in the oil industry. Everyday people in the Delta need to construct the oil workers as the *colonialist Other* for kidnappings to take place regardless of who carries out the act. Kidnapping is supposedly their just dessert. It is noteworthy, however, that no oil worker has died in the custody of militants in the Delta (Okonta 2006).

The Abuja-Oloibiri nexus

The community of Oloibiri in Bayelsa state stands as a tragic relic of Nigeria's bullish days of oil ascendance. Oil was first discovered in Oloibiri on August 3, 1956, while exportation to the world market began in 1958. However, oil has since dried up in Oloibiri. The concomitant effect is that the community today is in a dire situation. The state of disrepair and devastation of this once vibrant oil-producing community stands as a metaphor for the level of underdevelopment in the Delta. It is also an algorithm for what will befall Delta communities when oil dries up (see Ehwarieme 2008). Ehwarieme (2008: 158, 161) coins the term "oloibirinization" to denote "decline in economic importance of a town, community or region (which) leads to its political oblivion, social obscurity and developmental neglect and decay ... because its economic glory has departed". Oil-producing communities run the risk of becoming Oloibirinized if oil flow ceases or becomes irrelevant in the world market (Ehwarieme 2008; Kaldor, Karl and Said 2007). The Delta public is not oblivious of this point. For instance, the signification of Oloibiri was not lost on those who crafted the Kaiama Declaration (discussed above). Article "f" of the Kaiama Declaration states in part that: "Oil and gas are exhaustible resources and the complete lack of concern for ecological rehabilitation, in the light of the Oloibiri experience, is a signal of impending doom for the peoples of Ijawland."[27]

Oloibiri has thus become significant and signifying. Oloibiri signposts and embodies the consequences of a state's oil inebriation. Oloibiri is the insignia of the suffering as well as the signature of the Delta peoples' historical subjugation within the Nigerian rentier state.

Abuja, on the other hand, stands in sharp contrast to Oloibiri. Built from scratch to replace the congested Lagos as the Federal Capital Territory, Abuja represents the unabashed pompous display of Nigeria's oil wealth. In fact, it is hard to imagine that Oloibiri and Abuja are located in the same country. While Oloibiri lacks everything from roads to potable water, well-equipped schools and constant electricity, Abuja, which produces virtually nothing is arguably a "modern" city. Abuja is deceptive as it presents the façade of a rich and flourishing petro-state.

---

27 See 'The Kaiama Declaration'. URL: http://www.unitedijawstates.com/kaiama. html Accessed 7 June 2010.

Paradoxically, the Abacha "One-million-Man-March", a spectacle organized by crony organizations such as Youths Earnestly Ask for Abacha (YEAA) led by one Daniel Kanu on March 27 1998, created one of a constellation of *transformative events* (see McAdam and Sewell 2001; Hess and Martin 2006) that have shaped the trajectory of the Delta struggle. At the time, maximum ruler, General Sani Abacha, was engaged in a plan to succeed himself in office as civilian president but needed public prodding and affirmation. The likes of YEAA and Youth Movement of Nigeria (YMN) mobilized youths from all over the federation to attend the event through generous funding from the government. Participants received cash gifts for their efforts. Several buses were hired to convey participants to Abuja. Among those youths were individuals from the oil-rich Delta region. The splendour and grandeur of Abuja was unbelievable to many of them. This was a transformative moment for a number of reasons.

First, Delta youths realized that not all parts of Nigeria were as underdeveloped as their own. Second, as the youths were aware that crude oil from the Delta was the largest source of revenue for the government, a sense of injustice (see Gamson et al. 1982) was palpable as they were mesmerized by the level of infrastructural development in Abuja. Third, it dawned on the youths that if Abacha could spend a lot of money to convey people from different parts of Nigeria to converge on Abuja, the country must have a lot more to spare. Fourth, the youths realized that their voices had not been heard and that they could change things if only they could mobilize themselves.

Oloibiri and Abuja represent the two ends of a fundamentally flawed social spectrum. That Oloibiri, the genesis of Nigeria's oil wealth, could remain in such a condition while a consumer and mere administrative city like Abuja glitters and basks in the euphoria of unearned oil revenue is not only a major source of grievance but endless consternation for the people of the Niger Delta. None of the people interviewed in the course of the research had come to terms with how a community that produced oil for many years could have no veneer of industrialization. To remember Abuja for the people of the Delta is to be concurrently cognizant of Oloibiri and other oil-producing communities suffering the brunt of decades of oil exploitation. Abuja for the people of the Delta is not simply the federal capital territory of Nigeria; it is a painful reminder of the systematic pillage and state brigandage they and their forbears have endured since at least 1956. Abuja, for Deltans, is the name of the insufferable symptom of an unfair system.

Ironically, Abuja enables the lucidity of the condition of the people of the Delta and its vivid juxtaposition with what is possible even in Nigeria. Consequently, Abuja is a very emotive social and physical space; the architectural expression of generational oppression. It is a space in which Deltans do not feel they belong because it conjures phantasmagorical images of the appurtenances of the good life which the Delta people have been perpetually deprived.

Specters of the Past: Isaac Adaka Boro and Ken Saro Wiwa

The past refuses to lie down quietly.

> Archbishop Desmond Tutu, Chair, South African Truth and
> Reconciliation Commission

On 23 February, 1966, a little known minority rights activist, Isaac Adaka Boro alongside his insurgent group, the Niger Delta Volunteer Force (NDVF) proclaimed the excision of the "Niger Delta Republic" from the Federal Republic of Nigeria. "Remember your 70-year-old grandmother who still farms before she eats; remember also your poverty-stricken people; remember, too, your petroleum which is being pumped out daily from your veins; and then fight for your freedom" Boro (1982) urged the Niger Delta people.

The Adaka Boro-led insurgency was quashed within 12 days by the might of the state forces (Boro 1982). Boro and his men were tried and convicted of treason. He would go on to fight on the federal side during the Nigerian Civil War (1967–1970) after being pardoned by the General Yakubu Gowon regime. Boro died in 1968 before the end of the war. In spite of Boro's failure to actualize the independence of minorities of the Delta from the Nigerian federation, his accomplishments provide a political opportunity in many ways to events in the Delta 42 years after his death.

First, Boro's insurgency was the first systematic use of violence to vociferously challenge the foundational contradictions of the Nigerian state. Delta leaders had used petitions and made representations before the state to ameliorate their conditions before Boro's emergence. Their efforts were often rebuffed. Second, Boro was arguably the first to awaken the consciousness of the Delta people. He did not mince words in asking Deltans to *fight* for their rights. Third, Boro embodies the beginning of a concatenation of Delta activists to use suave, persuasive words and actions as well as allegorical imageries of the Delta situation to mobilize the people and garner by-stander interest. The idea that oil was being pumped out from the veins of the Delta people daily carried the quintessential imprimatur of Adaka Boro. Lastly and more significantly, Adaka Boro has become an unprecedented transcendental figure and source of inspiration for many in the Delta. Activists who favor non-violence and those who use violent tactics alike have not hidden their admiration for, and intellectual debt to Adaka Boro[28].

Asari Dokubo, leader of the Niger Delta People's Volunteer Force (NDPVF) maintains an e-mail signature that reads:

> We must avoid falling into the throes of what Adaka Boro foresaw forty years ago. Let them call us terrorists, let them call us bandits but it is important and critical that we remain resolute in the pursuit of the ideals of our fallen heroes like Isaac Adaka Boro, Ken Saro Wiwa and a host of others.

---

28   Interviewees 24–36.

Clearly, for Dokubo and others engaged in armed struggle against the Nigerian state and its oil industry, Adaka Boro is emblematic of their insurrection. The similarity in the name of Adaka Boro's defunct group and that of Dokubo is striking. Boro is believed to be a reference point for the justness, humaneness and raison d'être of their actions. Being a young person, aged only 30 at his death, many young men in the Delta see treading the path charted by Boro as their destiny. Adaka Boro is akin to the ghost of Hamlet's father that shaped the plot of William Shakespeare's *Hamlet*. The restless specter of the past embodied in Boro: His audacious rebellion, imprisonment, decision to join the Nigerian army, participation in the liberation of the Delta from the Biafran insurgency and his calamitous death under controversial circumstances in Rivers state during the civil war remind Delta youths of the imperative of the struggle and justification for their actions.

The "evocative symbolism" of Saro Wiwa and Adaka Boro is extremely potent and incontrovertible in the mobilization of dissidents. Both men fought for the rights of Delta people and died in the process: Boro in the Nigerian civil war while Wiwa died by hanging in the hands of General Sani Abacha; all under questionable circumstances. Both were daring, outstanding speakers, whose vision for the Delta was social justice and enjoyment of their oil wealth. The twin-capacity of Boro and Wiwa's deaths in generating passions and evoking feelings of injustice among the Delta peoples is unprecedented. In particular, Boro fore-shadowed what could have been—a free and independent Niger Delta.

Boro is also critical to the violent struggle in another way: The lack of popular support for Boro during his insurgency is a neutralizing technique for today's militants. Today's insurgents are quick to explain that even Boro was not supported by his people.[29] Boro was called all manner of names in his lifetime, a trouble-maker, and militant, rebel and so on, but was undaunted. Many Delta people never quite understood why he took the dangerous expedition of confronting the federal government. This provides succor for today's militants.

On the other hand, Ken Saro-Wiwa remains the avatar of the failure of non-violent protest (Watts 2004; Bob 2005; Ikelegbe 2001). Wiwa was convinced of the significance of the treatment meted out to him in shaping the Delta struggle. He predicted that Shell would be "punished" for its "ecological crimes" in the Delta. The intensified disruption of oil production activities particularly against Shell and the kidnapping of predominantly foreign oil workers thus fulfill the apocryphal prophecy of Wiwa: "Whether the peaceful ways I have favored will prevail depends on what the oppressor decides: what signals it sends to the waiting public". Clearly, Wiwa's peaceful ways are no longer in vogue, as events in the Delta since January 2006 demonstrate. The deaths of both men perform the "emotion work" (Perry 2002: 111) for the insurgency and other-worldly call to fulfill destiny. The supreme sacrifice of Boro and Wiwa is central to the rise of a world view characterized by feelings of oppression and injustice in the Delta. This partly accounts for the rise of kidnapping oil workers in the Delta.

---

29   Interviewee 19.

In summary, this chapter analyzes the complexity of the phenomenon of kidnapping. Drawing on the political process paradigm, the major socio-political, economic and historical contours in Nigeria, particularly the Delta, serving to produce kidnapping episodes are interrogated. Factors such as inattention to earlier forms of protest, routinization of violence, constitutional reforms, backfire on military lesson in the Delta, actions of oil corporations; the Kaiama Declaration and the Niger Delta terrain among others are underscored. This chapter also enunciates three major emotive factors—othering of foreign oil workers, the Abuja-Oloibiri nexus and the specters of the past—in conducting the "emotion work" (see Perry 2002: 111) for kidnapping and other violent repertoires of protest. However, it is difficult to know which of the aforementioned factors played the most important role in bringing about the wave of insurgency in the Delta. The standpoint is that kidnapping of oil workers in the Delta is a phenomenon with several contributory factors. This chapter provides the socio-political context, historical background and economic conditions that have fostered kidnapping at the spaces of oil infrastructure in the Delta. This achieves one of the objectives of the book: how the political process of Nigeria helps to shape kidnapping of oil workers in the Delta.

Chapter 4

Car Bombing "with due respect": The *Idea* called MEND[1]

Introduction

FG battles mend with 7000 troops, 2 warships, 14 gunboats

The Punch, 16 May 2009.

With due respect to all invited guests, dignitaries and attendees of the 50th independence anniversary of Nigeria being held today, Friday, October 1, 2010 at the Eagle Square Abuja, the Movement for the Emancipation of the Niger Delta (MEND) is asking everyone to begin immediate evacuation of the entire area within the next 30 minutes ... Several explosive devices have been successfully planted in and around the venue by our operatives working inside the government security services ... There is nothing worth celebrating after 50 years of failure.

Jomo Gbomo MEND's spokesperson, 1 October 2010.[2]

An uber-insurgent movement "organization" was formed in late 2005. Christened the Movement for the Emancipation of the Niger Delta (MEND), it operates as an amorphous, multifaceted amalgam of insurgent groups with unprecedented devastatingly clinical precision in executing its intents. The explicit aim of MEND is to cripple the capacity of the Nigerian rentier petro-state to produce crude oil— its lifeblood. An anonymous group bombed two Shell pipelines in the Okirika and Andoni areas of Rivers state in December 2005 (Courson 2009). Kidnapping of foreign oil workers purportedly in protest against the marginalization of the oil producing communities of the Delta by the state and transnational oil corporations, particularly Shell assumed a frightening dimension very early in 2006. MEND issued its statement of intent on 11 January 2006, when its operatives engaged Nigerian military personnel in a shoot-out as four foreign oil workers were kidnapped (Courson 2009). MEND combatants destroyed two military boathouses and a flow station in Bayelsa state on 15 January 2006. MEND's insurgency had begun.

On 15 March 2010, MEND's spokesperson Jomo Gbomo announced a breach of security at the annex of the Delta state government house in Warri venue of a

---

1 This chapter was first published under the same title in *African Security* 6, 1, 2013 (with Kevin Haggerty and Andy Knight) and 'The Delta creeks, women's engagement, and Nigeria's oil insurgency,' *British Journal of Criminology*, 2012. 52, 3: 534–55.

2 Jomo Gbomo e-mail statement (number 27) Friday 1 October 2010.

post-amnesty dialogue organized by the *Vanguard* newspaper. Gbomo advised the public to avoid the venue and vicinity warning that the "deceit of endless dialogue and conferences will no longer be tolerated".[3] MEND proceeded to detonate a car bomb at exactly 11:30 hrs. as outlined in the e-mail. A second car bomb followed. Tragically, six people were injured and eight persons died in the incident. MEND decided not to detonate the third and "most powerful" bomb it had installed because "operatives noticed that the participants at this jamboree fled towards the direction of the last bomb" and they feared killing more people.[4]

Seven months later, MEND attacked again on the auspicious occasion of Nigeria's 50th Independence anniversary celebration in Abuja on 1 October. The event was pricey with a tab of US$109 million. Public condemnation ensured that the budget was cut to US$63 million only (*Afrique en ligne* 2010). Disgusted by the expensive spectacle, MEND released a statement asserting that there was "nothing worth celebrating after 50 years of failure" and that the injustice suffered by the Niger Delta people remained unaddressed.[5] The organization announced that several car bombs had been planted at the venue and warned the public to stay away. When the dust settled, at least 12 persons died and 66 sustained injuries in the attacks.

This chapter addresses three major issues. First, it interrogates the meta-phenomenon called MEND; the rise of MEND, its demands and mode of operation. Second, the significance of the social space represented by the creeks is analyzed using one of MEND's affiliates, the Niger Delta Freedom Fighters (NDFF) based in Edo state. Third, the role of women in the MEND insurgency is articulated. One of the major arguments here is that contrary to popular belief, women are active participants in the violent turn of the Delta movement.

The Rise of MEND

MEND has become the avatar of the insurgency of young people in the Niger Delta region against the Nigerian state and transnational oil corporations despite its fairly recent emergence. MEND's rise is a consequence of several historical incidents and loosely connected contemporary events. First, as every standard analysis of the insurgency in the Delta recognizes, the squalor and poverty of the Delta region certainly played a huge role in the emergence of insurgent groups (Courson 2007; Joab-Peterside 2007b; Watts 2009a, 2008c, 2004a, 2004b; Von Kemedi 2006; Oruwari 2006) including MEND (Courson 2009; Ukiwo 2007; Okonta 2006). This is further compounded by pervasive environmental degradation and destruction of the livelihood of the people (Watts 2009b, 2008a; Omoweh 2005). The origin of MEND is divided into two timelines for clarity.

---

3   Jomo Gbomo e-mail statement (number 20) Monday 15 March 2010.
4   Jomo Gbomo e-mail statement (number 21) Monday 15 March 2010.
5   Jomo Gbomo e-mail statement (number 27) Friday 1 October 2010.

Historical considerations

MEND draws its membership from the Ijaw-speaking peoples who have a history of strong resistance against domination (see Ukiwo 2007; Okonta 2006). Historically, the Ijaws have always been a minority among minorities. The Ijaws were dominated politically and economically in colonial times by their neighbors the Itsekiri and Urhobo, groups that were also minorities within the Western region (Ukiwo 2007; Willink Commission 1958). The Yoruba constituted the largest number of the population of the Western region and dominated the body politic of the region. The Western Ijaw, specifically in the Warri area in the present Delta state were geographically isolated and could not participate in trades with Europeans, a major source of economic empowerment at the time (Ukiwo 2007). The ensuing unrest between Itsekiris who served as middlemen in trade with Europeans in the Western Delta and Ijaws earned the Ijaws a reputation as "pirates" (Ukiwo 1963: 592).[6] For instance, Lloyd (1963: 221) argues that

> Ijoh (sic) pirates, based in the creeks to the south of Itsekiri county, had been a menace for centuries; almost every traveller describes an affray with them. In the early 1850s the English merchants had themselves fitted out war canoes to chastise the Ijoh, but with little permanent effect, for in 1856 the pirates were looting boats within sight of the factories and the consul was advising the Itsekiri always to send their canoes in convoy.

The Ijaw people feared that they would be further marginalized in the emerging country as Nigeria approached political independence from Britain. Alan Lennox-Boyd, British Secretary of State for the Colonies, appointed a four-member panel chaired by Henry Willink to "ascertain the facts about the fears of minorities in any part of Nigeria and to propose means of allaying those fears" in September 1957 (Willink Commission 1958: iii). The commission's report warns that the oil-rich minority region "should not be neglected or so badly treated or oppressed to rebel (sic) so that no troops will be needed to quell such rebellion" (see Nigeria 2008: 131). The committee failed to recommend creating separate political structures as the minorities clamored for (see Akinyele 1996).

Nigeria became a sovereign state on 1 October 1960 and the fears of the minorities became exacerbated as postcolonial leaders embarked on questionable state-creation drives (Akinyele 1996). Isaac Adaka Boro's insurrection as explained in the previous chapter remains a fundamental reference point in the struggle. It marked the first time a group within the federation would take up arms against

---

6   A detailed analysis of the history of the Ijaws is beyond the purview of this book. For more on the historical trajectory of Ijaw "pirates" and marginalization of the Ijaws within the Western Delta in colonial times, and the "social origins" of the Ijaws, see Ukiwo's (2007) brilliant piece. On the historically frosty relationship between the Itsekiris and the Ijaws, see Lloyd (1963) and Ikime (1967).

the Nigerian state. Leader of the Niger Delta People's Volunteer Force (NDPVF), Asari Dokubo, states succinctly that the "person we draw our inspiration from today is Isaac Adaka Boro and to us, he is the hero of the struggle".[7] Ken Saro Wiwa's non-violent approach and consequent hanging alongside eight of his comrades fundamentally altered the trajectory of protest in the Niger Delta. Both men are seen as heroes and champions of the people by the insurgents.[8]

The Warri crisis of March 1997 significantly contributed to the emergence of insurgent groups, including MEND. The ownership and control of the petro-City of Warri was at the center of the struggle among the Ijaws, Itsekiris and Urhobos (Imobighe 2002). The Ijaws (see Peretomode 2002), the Itsekiris (see Tonwe 2002) and Urhobos (see Akpotor 2002) have been embroiled in claims and counter claims over who "owns" Warri and thus should enjoy the accruing political patronage. Warri South-West local government was created by the General Sani Abacha administration with headquarters in Ogbeh-Ijaw in the Ijaw-dominated area of Warri. The headquarters was relocated to Ogidigben in the Itsekiri area of Warri allegedly because of political pressure from influential Itsekiris.[9] The relocation of the Warri South-West local government headquarters sparked violence in an already toxic situation.

The ensuing crisis in Warri spectacularly shaped the Ijaw-led insurgency in at least three crucial ways. First, Ijaw-speaking peoples in Bayelsa, Edo, Lagos and other states around the country volunteered or were recruited to support Ijaws in the armed struggle against the Itsekiris in Warri. Several unemployed young men from Lagos in particular felt obligated to fight for their people.[10] Therefore, the quest for ownership of Warri not only turned the city into a battleground that led to the death of hundreds of people, it also became an inadvertent recruitment drive and rehearsal for the violence to come. Therefore, the influx of volunteers of Ijaw origins to Warri during the crisis ensured that the city emerged as the bastion of the festering insurgency. Several MEND leaders live freely in Warri and are known to the people but remain elusive to the authorities (Okonta 2006).

The second way in which the crisis contributed to the emergence of the insurgency is that a major arms proliferation and arms race emerged in Warri. These arms would become readily available for insurgent purposes. Several ex-militants including the founder of the NDFF, the major insurgent camp in Edo responsible for kidnapping four (American) oil workers in 2007, Henry Bindodogha, point to

---

7   Interviewee 11. Personal interview, Abuja, July 2010.

8   Interviewee 24 (Militants 2). Personal interview, Obubra camp, Cross River state, August 2010.

9   Interviewee 38 [Oboko Bello, President, Federated Niger Delta Ijaw Communities]. Personal interview August 2010. The Warri South local government headquarters is now back to Ogbeh-Ijaw.

10   Interviewee 34 (Militant 12. A reggae artiste responsible for entertainment at one of the major militant camps). Personal interview, August 2010, Obubra camp Cross River state.

the Warri crisis as the avenue for garnering arms for the insurgency.[11] Different sides to the conflict used the crisis as a way to establish superiority in a manner that suggests mutual capacity for destruction. Arsenals were established in schools and churches to evade detection by authorities.[12]

Third, the reversal of the decision to relocate the headquarters of the Warri South local government confirmed what had been largely believed: the Nigerian state only understood violence. Ijaw combatants in the Warri crisis believe that if they had not engaged in the mayhem, the Itsekiris would have succeeded in permanently taking the local government headquarters and accompanying perks such as political appointments, civil service jobs, and contracts from them. While the impact of this realization is hard to measure, many activists and insurgents, agree that the Warri crisis was a landmark event in the Niger Delta insurgency.[13]

Immediate causes of MEND's birth

Several other factors provided political opportunity for the emergence of MEND. As explained in Chapter 3, the arrest of Diepreye Alamieyeseigha (popularly known as Alams), then Governor of Bayelsa state by British authorities allegedly for money laundering and Alhaji Asari Dokubo, leader of the NDPVF and former president of the Ijaw Youth Congress on charges of treason on 15 September 2005 and 21 September 2005 respectively was perceived as witch-hunting of political juggernauts from the Delta.

Asari Dokubo was arrested partly because he was the first to call for the use of violence against the Nigerian state, arguing that armed insurrection was the only language the state could understand.[14] The older generations had failed, so Dokubo became the "voice of the people" and the government "thought he was a threat", one activist argues.[15] Several activists and insurgents corroborate this assertion.[16]

Asari Dokubo also confirms that MEND was established to fight for his release from prison. During my interview with him, he stated that the "name MEND was used to bring me out of the prison by those who are too afraid to show their face". In its early days, therefore, MEND was unequivocal in its public demand for the release of Dokubo and Alams. Kidnapping increased at a frightening pace during

---

11   Interviewee 19 (He is now senior special assistant to the Edo state governor on surveillance and waterways security). Personal interview during a private tour of the NDFF camp). Edo state, August 2010.

12   Interviewee 20 (Militant 1).

13   Interviewees 38 and 39 (Bolou Custom, media coordinator of the Federated Niger Delta Ijaw Communities [FNDIC]). Personal interview, Warri Delta state, August 2010.

14   Interviewee 22 (Honourable Kingsley Kuku, member Presidential Amnesty Committee and former public relations officer of Ijaw Youth Congress [IYC]). Personal interview, Obubra camp, August 2010.

15   Interviewee 1 (Onengiya Erekosima, president Niger Delta Non-Violence Movement). Personal interview, Port Harcourt July 2009.

16   Interviewee 4.

this period to buttress the demands of the insurgents. Several oil workers were kidnapped to specifically demand the release of Dokubo and Alamieyeseigha, as stated earlier (Courson 2009; Ukiwo 2007; Okonta 2006).[17]

The Demands of MEND

MEND has fine-tuned its demands since its major objective in its early days, the release of two Deltans, Asari Dokubo and Governor Alamieyeseigha, from incarceration. There are four cardinal demands of MEND. These are convocation of a Sovereign National Conference, fiscal federalism, the socio-economic well-being of Niger Deltans, and the Delta environment. These demands are examined below.

Sovereign national conference

MEND demands a conference of all ethnic nationalities to determine the fate of Nigeria. This entails deciding whether or not the peoples of the Niger Delta, and any ethnic group, region or linguistically identifiable category wishes to continue to be part of Nigeria.[18] This demand concerns the precarious foundation of Nigeria as a British colonialist experiment conducted without regards to the aspirations of people constituting Nigeria. Asari Dokubo, for instance, argues that the

> most peaceful way, the only panacea to the Niger Delta problem is the convocation of a sovereign national conference where all the nations, all the tribes of what is called Nigeria will sit down. If they decide or some people decide they longer want to be Nigeria, these people should be allowed to go. It's a decision of their own.[19]

Besides the obvious possibility of Nigeria's balkanization, the national conference is also aimed at accomplishing "serious, meaningful dialogue as a means to halting the violent agitation in the Niger Delta".[20] MEND commissioned a four-member committee—the Aaron Team—in 2009 to signify its readiness for discussions. As stated earlier, the team comprises prominent Nigerians like Vice Admiral Okhai Mike Akhigbe (rtd), Professor Wole Soyinka, Major General Luke Kakadu Aprezi (rtd), and Dr. Sabella Ogbobode Adidde. The Aaron Team had its first meeting with President Shehu Musa Yar'Adua on Saturday 14 November 2009.

---

17   Interviewee 4.

18   The quest for a national conference predates MEND. Civil society organizations and the media called for a national dialogue in the 1990s following the annulment of the 12 June 1993 presidential election and the incarceration of the presumed winner Chief MKO Abiola. Abiola died in prison under murky circumstances.

19   Interviewee 11.

20   Jomo Gbomo e-mail statement (number 3) Tuesday 15 September 2009.

By 17 November 2009, cracks emerged in the peace process as the JTF carried out an operation in the Kula Community of Rivers state. The home of a MEND commander, Christian Don Pedro, was affected.[21]

MEND executed a "warning strike" on a Shell/Chevron pipeline in Abonemma, Rivers state[22] on 18 December 2009. MEND called off its unilateral ceasefire on 30 January 2010.[23] Three days later, MEND attacked the Shell Trans-Ramos pipeline.[24] An opportunity for dialogue was over.

Fiscal federalism

Nigeria's system of government has generated huge academic debates. While supposedly a "federal" political system, in reality, a unitary system—strong central government and weak units—prevails. This has serious implications in terms of distribution of state wealth and appurtenances of power in a country of at least 252 ethnic groups, all but three of whom are minorities. The centralization of power ensures that the police establishment and sundry organizations that federating units are entitled to in other parts of the world are exclusively controlled by the federal government of Nigeria. In addition, laws passed by various military administrations, such as the Land Use Act Decree of 1978 guarantee that ownership of all lands and resources therein are vested in the government. This leaves minorities at a huge disadvantage relative to the dominant ethnic groups. For instance, the current constitutional arrangement made by military rulers ensures that only 17 percent of oil revenue is provided oil producing states. MEND is concerned that the people of the Delta suffer marginalization in the current political and economic arrangement in Nigeria.

Consequently, MEND is committed to fiscal federalism or more specifically *resource control*. From MEND's perspective, the land of the people of the Delta has been "stolen for fifty years" by the Nigerian state.[25] MEND demands that the "control of the resources and land of the Niger Delta be reverted to the rightful owners, the people of the Niger Delta".[26] This will ensure that oil producing states in the Delta may agree terms and conditions with oil companies they elect to mine and refine the crude oil in the region. That way, the people of the Delta can use its resources to develop the region.

Socio-economic well-being of Niger Deltans

The widespread poverty, low level of education, poor health facilities, absence of other basic social amenities, militarization of the Delta, and low quality of

---

21   Jomo Gbomo e-mail statement (number 10) Tuesday 17 November 2009.

22   Jomo Gbomo e-mail statement (number 12) Friday 18 December 2009.

23   Jomo Gbomo e-mail statement (number 15) Friday 29 January 2010.

24   Jomo Gbomo e-mail statement (number 16) Tuesday 2 February 2010.

25   Jomo Gbomo e-mail statement (number 12) Friday 18 December 2009.

26   Jomo Gbomo e-mail statement (number 16) Friday 29 January 2009.

life of the people of the Niger Delta form the core of MEND's demands. MEND strongly believes that the degree of human suffering as a result of poverty and health complications arising from oil production in the Delta is morally wrong and unjustifiable in a region providing at least 85 percent of all state revenues.

In addition, MEND and other insurgent groups regard the high unemployment rate of young people in the Delta as an aberration in view of the number of oil and gas corporations working in the region. Therefore, employment of indigenes of the Delta by oil corporations is an important objective of the insurgency: "We have to let Nigerians know that unless the oil companies are compelled to recruit most of their staff from their host communities, I am sorry, there might be no peace in the area" (Asari Dokubo, in *The Punch*, August 7, 2007: 7).

The Delta environment

Mitigating the environmental degradation in the Niger Delta is a major demand of MEND. Insurgents point to ceaseless gas flaring, and oil spillage polluting rivers and land in the Delta as indicative of the systematic destruction of their environment. These environmentalist concerns were first brought to international prominence by Ken Saro-Wiwa during the ascendance of MOSOP in the 1990s (Saro-Wiwa 1992; see also Bob 2005). The prevalence of acid rain, lung problems and other health issues also necessitate demands that the Niger Delta environment must be a central focus of the Nigerian state.

A New War? The Mode of Operation of MEND

Many insightful and enlightening theoretical models have been used to explicate the rise of MEND and the Niger Delta crisis in general. These include the notion of "the oil complex" (Watts 2007: 643), the "economics of war thesis" (Ikelegbe 2005; see Collier and Hoeffler 1998), and the "resource curse thesis" (Courson 2009: 7), among others. These analyses fundamentally enrich a literature that remains overwhelmingly descriptive. Producing greater theoretical and empirical insights into the operational micro-mechanics of MEND is particularly important given the geopolitical significance of the oil-rich Niger Delta, and the speed with which developments are unfolding in that region.

This section draws on the new war thesis to offer several insights into the efficacy of MEND's operations based on interactions with 42 ex-militants, all but one (i.e Asari Dokubo) of whom acknowledged being former members of MEND. A combination of factors pertaining to the loose structure and secrecy, public sympathy, Niger Delta terrain, vast resources, technological savvy and media relations have fundamentally contributed to MEND's operations in the on-going insurgency. The selection of these factors is far from random. *Mao Tse-Tung* in his book, *On Guerrilla warfare* (Griffith 1978) identifies some of the major factors articulated below. The new wars share many fundamental principles with guerilla warfare (see Münkler 2005: 12).

Two of MEND's major operations in recent times revealed its organizational prowess. The bombing of the Delta state Government House Annex, in Warri on Monday 15 March 2010 and the Abuja bombing during Nigeria's 50th independence anniversary celebrations on Friday 1 October 2010 each demonstrate that MEND must be taken seriously. MEND gave prior notice of its intentions in defiance of state counter-insurgency.[27] The notice and attendant attacks underscore MEND's audacity and confidence in its operations and operatives. The analysis below demonstrates important ways in which the MEND-led oil insurgency aligns with tenets of the new war thesis. Important caveats to using this approach in the Niger Delta case study are also provided.

> It is not a conventional warfare; it is asymmetric. This is the first time that the Nigerian armed forces have been faced with this challenge and so it is a learning process. It has been quite hectic.[28]

Asymmetrical warfare pervades the new world order. Transnational non-state, para-state, private, militia groups, or extra-legal actors existing in the interstices of nation-states have rendered old paradigms of war obsolete. The new kind of war has no definite battlegrounds; it is everywhere but nowhere (Münkler 2005, Kaldor 1999). The "new war thesis" (Münkler 2005; Kaldor 1999) explicates this relatively new development. The new wars are marked by three fundamental characteristics. They are *de-statized* (see Kaldor 1999) in contradistinction to old wars that were fought between nation-states. The new wars are privatized, organized violence involving private military forces exhilarated by the cheapening of the cost of war (Münkler 2005; Kaldor 1999). In the new wars, opposing sides are never equally matched (Münkler 2005). This refers to the *asymmetry of military capacity*. In addition, while old wars had definite military systems with rules of engagement, new wars have none. Münkler (2005: 3) calls this the *autonomization* of violence.

MEND has been waging an insurgent campaign against the Nigerian state that fits the "new war" model. This is responsible for a large measure of its success. MEND operatives are largely anonymous, unconfined to any space, adept at using civilians as human shields—kidnapped oil workers and community members—for protection and are unbound by any conventional rules of engagement. The MEND project is also invigorated by an accident of geography—the difficult terrain of the Niger Delta region. The riverine Delta region guarantees that MEND insurgents remain unperturbed by JTF operatives, as it takes years of having fished or swam in the rivers and expansive tributaries and farmed in the mangrove marshy lands

---

27   Jomo Gbomo e-mail statement (number 20) Monday 15 March 2010 and number 27, Friday 1 October 2010.

28   Interviewee 10. JTF spokesperson, Lt. Col. Timothy Antigha. Personal interview, July 2010.

to *know* the area. Inaccessible areas such as mountains, trackless plains, creeks and waterways innervate banditry (Hobsbawm 1969). The JTF authorities confirm that riverine asymmetrical warfare is "something new" and an "emerging concept" to the Nigerian military.[29] They also see similarities in this regard with the US experience in Vietnam, Afghanistan and Iraq.[30]

The JTF confronts a bi-dimensional phenomenon that even the best armies in the world find almost insurmountable: *riverine asymmetrical warfare*. The decade-long war in Afghanistan demonstrates the elusiveness of insurgent groups in difficult mountainous regions. The creeks serve the same purpose in the Delta region of Nigeria. The insurgent campaign was so devastating to the state that at one point in its operations, the JTF was on the defensive. It resorted to aerial bombardment of suspected MEND hideouts like Gbaramatu Kingdom when in one instance the leader of Camp 5, Tom Polo, allegedly killed 18 soldiers.[31]

The difficulty the JTF has in navigating the harsh terrain is exacerbated by years of state neglect that ensures that physical infrastructure, such as roads and bridges, which could have made the mission less cumbersome, are absent. Consequently, the JTF operation is not merely a battle with insurgents; it is a war against Mother Nature, and human failure.

Loose "structure" and anonymity

Insurgent groups engaged in asymmetrical warfare seem to thrive on loose structures. For instance, in analyzing the Revolutionary United Front of Sierra Leone (RUF), Abdullah and Muana (1998: 177) argue that "(i)t could hardly be said that there was an organization" among the disparate alienated youths who formed the RUF. Conversely, partly due to its origins (see Asuni 2009; Okonto 2006), MEND conscientiously adopts a loose structure. "MEND is not an 'organisation' in the formal sense of the word. It is an idea, a general principle underlying the slew of communal, civic, and youth movements ... in the Niger Delta ... particularly in the Ijaw-speaking areas" (Okonta 2006: 10). Undoubtedly, MEND is not a definite, physically-bounded entity with a coherent hierarchical structure. MEND is everywhere but nowhere. There are reports, for instance, that e-mails from MEND have been traced to computers in South Africa (Junger 2007, cited in Ukiwo 2007: 607). MEND operates as a supra-organization within multifarious insurgent organizations and an extra-terrestrial insurgent collectivity. Within scores of insurgent groups, gangs, cults, and militias in the Niger Delta, MEND is *sui*

---

29   Interviewees 12 and 10. JTF Commander, General Bello and spokesperson, Lt. Col. Antigha respectively. General Bello compares the battle in the Delta with the US experience in Vietnam.

30   Interviewees 12 and 10.

31   Interviewee 12. General Bello showed me pictures of exhumed corpses of soldiers undergoing autopsy and DNA verification on his camera. The materials were restricted; hence, copies could not be obtained.

generis. Therefore, the suggestion that MEND is not an *organization* discursively euphemizes its devastating acumen and clinical precision in project execution.

Consequently, the notion that MEND is an "idea" (Okonta 2006) encapsulates the intricate mechanism and inherent genius of MEND. As sovereign of the creeks, whose members traverse major cities with impunity (Okonta 2006), MEND is a *thing* that eludes easy description or delineation. MEND operates in and through multiple insurgent groups. It is a product of a "multi-organizational field" (Curtis and Zurcher 1973: 53; Klandermans 1992). Top militant leaders such as Tom Polo, "Africa", Asari Dokubo, Egbema "1", Boyloff, etc. have at one time or the other been linked with MEND. Set up principally for maximum media impact, the insurgents "just want to make sure MEND takes the responsibility for their actions".[32] This means that MEND was established as an umbrella coalition to take the credit for various insurgent collective actions. Militant leaders endorsed a pact in late 2005 to credit various successful insurgent activities of their largely independent affiliates to MEND.[33]

MEND's lack of a coherent structure is a functional masterstroke. It is difficult to track MEND as there is no single recognized leader. For MEND, it is imperative that its leaders remain "unknown" and absolutely lack public identity. It is difficult for the army to combat MEND when they are largely unknown. This is a strategic initiative of MEND. In a statement released by Jomo Gbomo, Farah Dagogo, the overall field commander of MEND and other field commanders in Rivers state who accepted the Presidential offer of amnesty were declared to have "been ushered out by MEND. All commanders have been replaced by unknown commanders".[34] The said commanders acquired a public identity and thus ceased to be useful to MEND by accepting the amnesty offer. Their images had appeared in newspapers across the country contrary to the universally masked countenance of MEND fighters. The spokesperson for the military's Joint Task Force (JTF) points out that the army is

> fighting with groups that are almost anonymous ... Someone wants to pose as a defenceless civilian for 30 days of the month and on the last day, he appears, and you assume that he is that harmless civilian you have been seeing. He appears on the 31st of that month and attacks you. That is the nature of the crises.[35]

In addition, the sophisticated network of cliques and groups also serves MEND well. MEND is the livewire of the violent turn in the Niger Delta social movement. It has entrenched itself at the center of a conglomeration of nodal insurgent

---

32   Interviewee 1 (Onengiya Erekosima, founder Niger Delta Non-Violent Movement). Personal interview, Port Harcourt, June 2009.

33   Interviewees 11 and 19.

34   Jomo Gbomo e-mail statement (number 5) Saturday 3 October 2009.

35   Interviewee 10 (Lt. Col. Timothy Antigha, Coordinator of the Joint Media Campaign Centre [JMCC] of the JTF). Personal interview in Abuja July 2010.

groups with multifaceted organizational structures, commands, and loyalties. This is a significant feature of major social movement organizations generally (see McCarthy and Zald 1977). However, the capacity of MEND to sanction, de-sanction and re-sanction independent insurgent groups and their violent acts is astonishing. MEND's polymorphism and vast network present a conundrum to the Nigerian state. The 8 January 2010 attack on Chevron Makaraba pipeline, for instance, was "sanctioned by MEND but did not involve" MEND operatives.[36] One activist with expansive contacts with the insurgent explains that

> we have splinter organizations because you cannot trust the Nigerian situation. Ken Saro Wiwa was killed, Adaka Boro was killed, Asari (Dokubo) was almost killed. So, if there was only one group, it would have been easier going after the leader, get him executed. As they say, if you kill the head, the body will scatter.[37]

Each insurgent group can operate using MEND's name at will and may choose to act alone (Okonta 2006).

Also, MEND has embarked on a quasi-democratization of leadership portfolios partly owing to the presence of multiple independent insurgent groups. Therefore, MEND has a stupefying number of "Commanders" and "Generals" at any time. This further complicates matters for the JTF as there are many "leaders" of MEND to go after. MEND seems to have learned lessons from the insurgencies—peaceful and non-peaceful—of the past. Consequently, MEND shrouds its leadership in secrecy. Adaka Boro's 12-day insurgency in the 1960s was, by his own admission, a "much publicised revolution" (Boro 1982: 95). Ken Saro-Wiwa had a relatively significant public image in Nigeria prior to the Ogoni uprising and was a fine speaker. The tragic death of Boro during the Nigeria Civil War under contentious circumstances and the hanging of Wiwa are a testament to the more insidious methodology adopted by MEND. The two men had public identities that made them easy targets.

Fluid Membership

A corollary to the point above is that membership of MEND is extremely fluid to the consternation of the authorities. This is not necessarily a quality of MEND, but it is in fact, a fundamental characteristic of the entire insurgency in the Niger Delta. A few insurgent groups have become apprenticeship schemes for manufacturing more insurgent groups. The "parent" insurgent groups include the Niger Delta People's Volunteer Force (NDPVF) led by Asari Dokubo and Camp 5 established by Tom Polo. Also, members of one group often migrate to another with relative ease. This enables militants to learn different roles in the various groups or hone

---

36   Jomo Gbomo e-mail statement (number 14) Saturday 9 January 2010.

37   Interviewee 4 (Morris Alagoa, Project Officer, Niger Delta Resource Centre). Personal interview in Yenagoa Bayelsa state, July 2009.

their skills at a specific task. Individuals typically move around various groups based on reasons ranging from the fame of the group, leadership, and ambition.

The career of one major militant leader in the Delta may suffice to illustrate this point. Henry Bindodogha, founder of the NDFF was a trainee under the tutelage of the "masters" of four different groups in the struggle. He served Asari Dokubo's group in Rivers state. He left Dokubo's NDPVF for Commander Amadabo's camp and later worked with Prince Odolo. Tom Polo's Camp 5 in Gbaramatu Kingdom was his last apprenticeship centre before he founded his own insurgent group in Edo state which had almost been immune to the insurgencies in neighbouring Niger Delta states. Bindodogha was the Chief Priest in all of the four groups he worked with before establishing his own group. His role was to pour libations and seek spiritual protection from the ancestors (for example by giving each of the boys a bath) so they can return safely from their expeditions. At least four other insurgent groups were established by young men who trained under Bindodogha. These include one Ezekiel Apesibiri's group, Ogbudugbudu barracks and Adumaduma camp.

The impact of such a fluid membership cannot be overemphasized. At the height of the insurgency, most of the major militant leaders of independent camps knew one another and often communicated by mobile phones on first name basis. Therefore, they were able to share vital intelligence about such things as the strength of the JTF deployment in their areas, occasional personal contacts with JTF operatives who sometimes cooperated with the militants on the understanding that soldiers would not be attacked and where next to strike.[38] In addition, a militant group under attack from the Nigerian military could seek reinforcement from other militant groups. This symbiotic relationship was fostered because each camp had members who had worked with a different camp or knew persons at another camp. While not meaning to suggest that all the camps worked in unison (there were certainly elements of mistrust), the rapport among various leaders was solidified by the fluidity of insurgent membership.[39] This cooperative lineage precedes MEND and has worked to its advantage.

Enigmatic status

Another element of MEND is its unparalleled enigma. The scientific rigor of its major attacks on oil installations, hostage-taking and car bombings have deservedly earned MEND an image as the behemoth of the Delta insurgency. Four main factors underlying MEND's insurgent activities accentuate its status. These are *spectacle, performativity, symbolism and impact*. MEND revels in using spectacles in its insurgent activities. MEND's choice of where and whose oil workers are

---

38   Inteviewee 19.

39   Interviewee 19. Bindodogha points out that there was greater trust and cooperation among various leaders while the militants were in the trenches than after they had accepted the government's amnesty program.

kidnapped, what company's facilities are destroyed and sites of bomb detonation are a work of art. The choices suggest that the spaces and faces chosen by MEND are a priori designed performatively. The spectacle, performativity, symbolism and impact of MEND's insurgency are captured in three major insurgent acts.

MEND's first major spectacular act occurred in February 2006 when its operatives kidnapped nine foreign oil workers (Okonta 2006). The workers were hired by Willbros, a firm executing a contract on behalf of Shell. This particular incident sent shock waves around the world because the workers were kidnapped offshore. The incident demonstrated that contrary to widespread opinion, insurgents had developed the capacity to attack oil facilities that were not onshore. The dexterity with which the act took place and the ease with which the MEND operatives disappeared from the site demonstrated that a preternatural kind of insurgency had begun. In addition, all nine hostages were Westerners—a major symbolic act on the so-called "oppressors"—a recognition by MEND that several world powers would be drawn to the crisis when their citizens were kidnapped (see Okonta 2006). The impact was instantaneous as the attention of the US, UK and French governments was immediately drawn to the incident. The incident might not have garnered much attention if the kidnapped workers were Nigerians (Okaba 2009; Okonta 2006).

The Monday 15 March 2010 car bombing at the Delta state government house annex in Warri provides a second example. The *Vanguard* newspaper organized a post-amnesty dialogue intended to "Restore Hope in Niger Delta" (Amaize 2010).[40] Niger Delta governors, government officials at all levels, civil society representatives, militant leaders and several stakeholders attended. A number of activists including Ledum Mittee, leader of MOSOP and chair of the Niger Delta Technical Committee, endorsed the event. MEND made use of this conference for a spectacular performance. MEND gave notice of impending violence specifying the time and places of their attacks in an e-mail. MEND warned that the "deceit of endless dialogue and conferences will no longer be tolerated". MEND detonated two car bombs at the event. The blasts forced the dignitaries and everyone in attendance to run for safety.[41] The attacks were intended to persuade the governor of Delta state, Dr. Emmanuel Uduaghan, that MEND was not "a media creation" and that "we exist outside of cyberspace".[42]

The artistic contemplation of MEND is also evident in the 1 October 2010 bombing in Abuja noted in chapter 1. The attention of the world was beamed on Nigeria as it marked the 50th Independence Day anniversary. Heads of state, the *crème-de-la-crème* of the diplomatic corps, and dignitaries from all over the world

---

40   Amaize Emma. 2010 (March 15). Vanguard's Post-Amnesty Dialogue begins in Warri today—It's timely, stakeholders. URL: http://allafrica.com/stories/201003150063. html?viewall=1 Accessed 26 October 2010.

41   Some invited guests like the British and American delegations as well as former dictator General Ibrahim Babangida did not attend the event.

42   Jomo Gbomo e-mail statement (Number 20) Monday 15 March 2010.

gathered in Abuja. The celebration was rudely interrupted by car bombs at the nearby ministry of justice. At least 12 persons died and several others were injured in the incident (*Nigerian Compass*, 2010). This attack is significant for many reasons. It was the first time MEND's insurgency would reach the capital city. The symbolism of the attack was unmistakable as captured in MEND's official statement: "There is nothing worth celebrating after 50 years of failure".[43] It was also a spectacular performance: On one hand, MEND iterated its operational precision and on the other hand, portrayed the Nigerian state as patently weak, vacuous and incapable of protecting its political elites and masses. The timing of the attacks was spectacular. The impact of the attack was immediate and is still unfolding. For instance, the US Council on Foreign Relations (CFR) released an expert brief—"Nigeria's Pre-election Tensions"—in which it criticizes the Nigerian government for having "failed to take the appropriate steps" to prevent the attacks and mishandling the aftermath.[44]

These attacks were not only high profile but also marked a fundamental shift in tactics, impact, and targets between 2005 and 2010. The attacks also demonstrated the new waves of intensification of the crisis and focus on public spaces, rather than exclusively on oil production sites and infrastructure.

Public sympathy: "There are things that are worse than kidnapping"

Public support is a basic prerequisite in wars; particularly the new wars (see Griffiths 1978). Years of marginalization of the Niger Delta region affords MEND a level of public support that would be the envy of every populist group. People who identify or empathize with MEND's objectives abound in the Niger Delta (Okonta 2006). This core of public sympathy helps MEND operatives execute attacks and quickly return to society (Okonta 2006). None the less, supporters may not necessarily support kidnapping oil workers or detonating car bombs. However, the idea that the Nigerian state caused the unfolding violent confrontation and that the people of the Niger Delta have been forced to react through insurgent groups is not a radical one among the people.

During a focus group discussion with two women representing two NGOs in the Delta, one participant declared: "Mr. Man, I am a militant! Every Niger Deltan is a militant at heart because the people have been pushed to the wall". She assured me that the people of the Niger Delta were unapologetic about the rise of militancy. The second participant felt that kidnapping of oil workers had helped raise the profile of the Niger Delta, thus benefitting the people.[45] Non-violent

---

43   Jomo Gbomo e-mail statement (Numbers 27) Friday 1 October 2010.

44   Campbell, John. 2010 (October 18). "Nigeria's Pre-election Tensions", expert brief.   URL: http://www.cfr.org/publication/23176/nigerias_preelection_tensions.html Accessed 26 October 2010.

45   Focus Group 3 (Representatives of two women-focused NGOs). Yenagoa Bayelsa state, July 1 2009.

activists are also somewhat "militant" in their approach. Asked if he feared for his life, an environmental justice activist said he feared torture more than death: "As far as I can die with minimal suffering through one or two bullets, I am fine."[46]

The Federated Niger Delta Ijaw Communities (FNDIC) exemplifies the comingling of peace advocacy and violent agitation in the Delta which serves MEND. FNDIC was established in 1997 as a non-violent, prodemocracy organization to achieve equal political space for all Nigerians, particularly Ijaw-speaking peoples. The organization also advocates for resource control and federalism. FNDIC was involved in kidnapping oil workers in 2003 and 2006 in spite of its "non-violence" advocacy. FNDIC president, Dr. Oboko Bello, argues that "if there is any stain of colour" on the non-violent credentials of the organization, it is because its members "had to do a few things within the context of self-defence" as "there were threats to our lives".

FNDIC led members of the Okerenkoko community in a mass action against mapping out electoral constituencies in Warri South-West local government. Three gunboats were dispatched by the JTF on March 13 2003. One of them opened fire on community members who were on a boat following the protest at Escravos. The JTF operatives allegedly received logistical support from Chevron. Foreign oil workers were kidnapped in the FNDIC-led attack on Chevron facilities because the company provided the "springboard" of the attack on Okerenkoko.

The FNDIC leader argues that "(t)here was a war situation. Kidnapping is an act of war if it is used to prosecute a war situation. There are things that are worse than kidnapping … (like) military men dropping bombs". As noted in Chapter 2, the expatriates became "human shield" for the Okerenkoko people on the assumption that the government forces would not shoot foreigners and risk the ire of several Western powers.[47] Utilization of human shields is a routine tactic in new wars. Nevertheless, FNDIC has been at the vanguard of campaigns for peace in the Delta. FNDIC engages in public lectures, seminars and television programs to disseminate its non-violence advocacy. Its publication "Nonviolence Approach" reached its seventh series in 2010.

Public sympathy for MEND also reaches the corridors of power. Former IYC public relations officer and member of the Presidential Amnesty Committee, (now presidential adviser on the Niger Delta) Kingsley Kuku believes that "*MEND is every Ijaw man, MEND is every Ijaw community, MEND is every Niger Delta man* (sic) who feels that there's injustice and when injustice is seen anywhere, it is everywhere. So MEND is a platform, it is a spiritual platform that has come to

---

46 Interviewee 4.

47 Interviewee 38. Rather tellingly, the current edition of the "Non-violence Approach" publication is titled "One Man One Vote by any Means Necessary". See Bello, Oboko. 2010. "One Man One Vote by any Means Necessary". Federated Niger Delta Ijaw Communities Nonviolence Approach series 07. Warri: Eregha Publishers.

stay"[48] (emphasis added). The commandant of the federal government's amnesty camp in Obubra, retired Lt. Col. Larry Parkins, believes the "younger people thought that if they fold their hands they will continue to suffer as their fathers and their fore fathers suffered".[49]

Consequently, *disentangling violent agitators from non-violent protesters in the Niger Delta struggle is a fool's errand.* This is not to suggest that everyone bears arms against the state and its oil interests or wish to do so. However, the line between the militant and the non-militant is tenuous because of years of marginalization and the matured sense of injustice among the people. The JTF spokesperson, Lt. Col. Timothy Antigha describes the situation eloquently. He argues that "unofficially" Niger Deltans acknowledge the success of the JTF activities but in the open, because of the "fact that the people of the Niger Delta have felt marginalized for a long time, they appear to have given their support to illegalities that are being perpetrated by their sons and daughters in the name of militancy"[50]. Even the highest echelon of military authorities responsible for quelling insurgency in the region agrees that the Niger Delta people have not been treated fairly by the Nigerian state.[51]

There also seems to be a code of silence among the Niger Delta people regarding insurgent activities in the region. While some elites and everyday people privately criticize the militants for their excesses, very few people dare to criticize them publicly in order not be perceived as enemies of the people. For example, General Sarkin Yaki Bello, Commander of the JTF, narrates how at a meeting, a delegation of Niger Delta political and opinion leaders collectively expressed strong displeasure over the military operations in the region. An unnamed federal legislator sought a private audience with the General at the end of the meeting. He said "thank you very much for this operation, thank you very much General. You know I cannot express this outside, these people will kill me".[52] Consequently, Niger Delta elites who do not offer any support to the insurgents do not oppose them either—at least not publicly. This is because they fear reprisals by the masses of the Delta who generally support or tolerate the insurgency.

Three factors map out why violent and non-violent agitators are almost intertwined. First, there is symmetry between the overarching objectives of MEND and non-violent protesters. MEND has resource control as its most important objective. The same holds true for non-violent groups. As the objectives

---

48   Interviewee 22. Member Presidential Amnesty Committee. Personal interview at the militant rehabilitation camp in Obubra, Cross River state. Personal interview, August 2010.

49   Interviewee 16. Lt. Colonel Larry Parkins, Commandant of the militant rehabilitation camp in Obubra, Cross River state. Personal interview, August 2010.

50   Interviewee 10.

51   Interviewee 12. (General Sarkin Yaki Bello, Commander JTF). Personal interview, August 2010.

52   Interviewee 12.

are similar, one may reasonably expect the accompanying protests to occasionally be coterminous as both sides use what they know best to achieve a mutually recognized goal. One non-violent activist best exemplifies this problematic: "We appreciate the emergence of several groups to advance the cause of the struggle and that includes MEND".[53]

Second, there is a sense that Nigeria's exceptionalism is at play in the Niger Delta region and makes adhering to the tenets of non-violence difficult if not impossible. Major exponents of non-violence like Mahatma Ghandi and Martin Luther King (Jr.) would have found Nigeria particularly belligerent and frustrating as their peaceful methodology relied on the presence of a listening opposition and sympathetic bystanders. Besides, the Ogoni Nine paid the supreme price for adopting nonviolent repertoires of protest. Therefore, those who advocate peaceful repertoires of protest in the Delta are generally suspicious of the relevance of these tactics within the Nigerian context.

Third, due to the contradictions in the political economy of the Nigerian system, the Niger Delta crisis implicates everyone and blurs the line between non-violent advocacy and protesters who use violence. For instance, some insurgents like Asari Dokubo have family members who work for oil companies (Peel 2009). Yet, such persons openly advocate kidnapping oil workers as an act of war.[54] They are able to use their influence in the insurgency to secure the lives of their family members on the other side. The family members who work for oil companies in turn cannot report the whereabouts of their militant kith and kin to the authorities that have been repressing their people for so long. Government officials from the Niger Delta also tacitly support the insurgency or refuse to condemn it vehemently in public because they know they will be out of government someday and presumably return to their communities.[55]

MEND is not oblivious to the level of support it enjoys among the Delta people. In a statement MEND states: "We thank all patriotic and justice loving citizens of the Niger Delta and Nigeria for their unwavering support, overtly and covertly".[56]

The Niger Delta creeks

Research has yet to uncover the import of the social space represented by the creeks in the course of episodic kidnappings by insurgents in the Niger Delta. Hobsbawm (1969, 1959) it appears, was ahead of his time in articulating the functionality of certain spaces—mountainous regions, waterways, and creeks— for the rise and maturation of social banditry. In Italy where kidnapping is arguably an overdeveloped phenomenon (Jenkins 1985), it is worth reiterating that the geographical terrain of Sardinia in particular was a major driving

---

53   Interviewee 37.
54   Interviewee 11.
55   Interviewee 22.
56   Jomo Gbomo e-mail statement (number 15) Friday 29 January 2010.

force (Caramazza and Leone 1984). The creeks are not thus epiphenomenal to kidnapping but of first order significance. The creeks are theorized in an attempt to provide an understanding of their "symbolic transformation" (Lofland 1973: 140) from a public space—albeit a remote disattended one—into a conscientiously securitized space that serves an operational, socio-cultural, economic, religious and even psychological function for the insurgents.

Various spaces are imbued with seemingly unfettered powers to enthrone different types of belonging. By design, spaces can include or exclude certain kinds of people in a largely non-verbal but mutually intelligible way. Therefore, not all public spaces attract everyone to the same degree in spite of the liberal democratic guarantee of legal access to all (see Lofland 1973). Sicakkan (2005: 4–5) highlights four types of spaces and the character of belonging they create. First, there are *essentialized spaces* based on ethnic and religious forms of belonging. Second, *national spaces* derive their belonging from citizenship of a nation-state.[57] The relationship between essentialized and national spaces is symbiotic (Sicakkan 2005). This is hardly contestable, as the capacity of the rhetoric and sentiments of nationalism and commonality of ancestral homeland to generate non-inclusive orthodoxy requires no introduction. Third, there are *transnational spaces* that are unencumbered by any particular territory or socio-political organization. Transnational spaces are about people or humanity in general. Finally, there are *glocal spaces*, which welcome all modes of belongings. "Glocal spaces accommodate essentialized belongings, national and transnational modes of belonging, and new types of belonging which are inspired and informed by the idea of diverse society. Glocal spaces entail a variety of *local incipient forms of all-inclusive organizations*" (Sicakkan 2005: 5).

The space re-presented by the creeks is not a *glocal space*, where all belong and can participate; it is a fundamentally and unabashedly *essentialized space* based on ethnic, religious and linguistic forms of belonging and identity. Consequently, apart from serving as repository for kidnap victims, one of the primary functions of the creeks is dispensing a multilayered regimen of social sorting. Insurgents rely on *appearential ordering*, or the notion that people's identities are "written all over them" (Lofland 1973: 49). This is not simply an aesthetic consideration but a matter of life and death for insurgents as well as people who possess impressive ransom value. Therefore, a discriminatory regime of differences (see Sennett 2002) or *spatial segregation of persons* (Lofland 1973: 78) based on skin color, language and ethnicity is in effect in the creeks. Here, the non-lethal constellation of identities entails being black, Nigerian, Niger Deltan and Ijaw-speaking.[58] Therefore, being non-black in particular, means being "foreign" and belonging to the dangerous consignment referred to as "oyibo"—literally white person—but also discursively, "meddling alien". This category includes Americans, French, Canadians, British, Italians as well as the Chinese, Filipinos, Lebanese and Indians.

---

57   Not explicitly stated but implied by Sicakkan
58   In some cases, insurgents admit non-Ijaws like Urhobo into their groups.

This suggests a twisted form of multiculturalism and equal ethnic opportunity for "kidnappability".

As the Delta space has been designated highly inflammable for at least two decades (see Watts 2004), insurgents use their biophysical knowledge of what a Niger Deltan looks like or appeariential ordering and the order afforded by space (see Lofland 1973) to make a distinction between strangers who choose to remain in the Delta in spite of numerous warnings, thus possibly benefitting from the oil industry—foreign oil workers, and other non-Deltans—and Delta indigenes. For prospective insurgents at the NDFF creeks, for instance, a reference from someone in the echelons is required as well as a clear demonstration in a ritualized interview that the interested individual knows what the struggle is about and is ready to lose his or her life or limb for the cause.[59]

The character of the symbolic transformation of the creeks in the Niger Delta is significatory of what may be called, first, the Ìta èèwò or abominable space and second, the Ìta òmìnira or freedom space. This space is abominable to non-Nigerians, non-Deltans, and the uninitiated Deltans. Although there is no record of deaths of kidnap victims in the hands of insurgents, the level of human suffering they experience while in captivity is high. In addition, there is the risk of dying from stray bullets in the regular confrontations between the JTF and insurgents. One kidnap victim, for instance, died of gunshot wounds during JTF's bombardment of Gbaramatu kingdom in May 2009 which was designed to destroy Tom Polo's Camp 5. For the JTF, the creeks are no less of an èèwò space. As the home territory (see Lofland 1973) of insurgents, the JTF understands that the creeks have been effectively colonized by insurgents. The èèwò status of the creeks is intensified vis-à-vis the JTF by the fact that it is the fortress for repelling any attacks by outsiders, particularly the Nigerian state represented by the JTF. The creeks constitute an uncharted dangerous territory for the military.[60] The total number of soldiers who have lost their lives at the creeks or while guarding oil infrastructure is a closely-guarded secret in military circles. In one incident, when insurgents attacked two offshore oil wells owned by Agip at Forcados, 11 soldiers lost their lives (Technical Committee on the Niger Delta 2008). The creeks in contrast represent Ìta òmìnira or freedom space for the insurgents. The symbolic elasticity inherent in the social space represented by the creeks is overwhelmingly appealing to insurgents. Away from the intimidating presence of the JTF, the suffocating strictures of traditions guarded mostly by old men, the drudgery of unemployment and tedium of impecuniosity, insurgents transform the creeks to a citadel of refuge. It is a space that marks their rejection of domination and oppression, and asserts their masculinity, symbolically and in reality. The endless struggle of males, who believe they cannot be full men within the unequal conventional structures of the Nigerian society, finds momentary rest and a voice.

Besides, this space is a theatre of performativity. The creeks represent a social space for self-expression. It is the arena for rendering folkloric songs,

---

59 Interviewee 19.
60 Interviewee 10.

dances, savoring moments with peers of similar orientation, sharing feelings of brotherhood fabricated by having stared death in the face together and narrating panoramic hopes of a better future. The songs, dances and costumes transpose everyday young men from rural fishing and farming communities in the Delta to Èrùjèjè or fearsome personality. The performances instil fear and dread in the uninitiated public.

However, Òminira (freedom) at the creeks contains two antithetical forces Ìdera (comfort) and Ìnira (discomfort). Ìdera at the creeks manifests in the highest ideals and the vilest of vices. Ideals of a free Niger Delta and genuinely democratic Nigeria as well as railings against global capital exist side by side with unqualified access to kai-kai, ogogoro (local gin), relatively cheap money from insurgent exploits and consumption of banned substances like marijuana among others. Ironically, the creeks symbolize Ìnira (discomfort). The mosquito bites, poor water sources and inadequacy of several other supplies including food indicate that life at the creeks is challenging. Hostages are not intended to die and therefore, have to be securely kept and fed. It is not surprising that hostages often complain about the difficulty of life at the creeks. For insurgents, however, the discomfort is bearable because of the struggle.

The atmosphere at the creeks is awe-inspiring. I visited the Egbema 1 NDFF camp in Edo state on Friday August 27, 2010. We boarded the 6.7 million Naira Edo state government boat—one of Bindodogha's official vehicles as the special assistant on surveillance and waterways security to the governor. Knowing those parts requires making the creeks a playground. We traveled for over one hour on the waterways in addition to the nearly two hours of road travel. The atmosphere at the camp was intimidating. I wrote the following in my field notebook about my visit to the creeks:

> Finally, we entered the hallowed waterways. A guy right in front of Egbema 1 did libation: He touched the water and sprinkled some on us all three times. It was to show respect to the gods. The Egbema 1 creeks were before our eyes. We got in and saw many intriguing things. There was the burnt camp house and the jail house, where errant boys were kept for weeks until they confessed. There was the shrine, where Egbesu, the god of war was represented in symbols made of red cloth … We saw where the four hostages (kidnapped in 2007) that shot the Egbema 1 camp into limelight were kept … We stood where the hostages were kept. We saw the kitchen, playground, etc. of the boys. The eeriness of the place was numbing. This is not a place for the faint-hearted.

The camp was in a forest serviced by waterways that occasionally got blocked by debris. It was clear that a community of insurgents once lived there; that a counter-culture once thrived there in a manner similar to the urban studies of the famous Chicago School. While not meaning to establish a teleological or deterministic relationship between the similar background of many of the members and the activities of the NDFF, the idea that a delinquent subculture arises as a result of the formation of gangs dates back at least to 1927 when Frederic Thrasher's *The Gang* was published. As Shaw and McKay (1971: 252) point out, the "tendency of boys to organize themselves into some form of social group is more or less characteristic of the social life in the deteriorated and disorganized sections of the city". Such groups constitute an expression of longstanding "primary relationships" (Shaw and MacKay 1971: 253; see also Thrasher 1927). This suggests the type of relationship among gang members enunciated by Whyte (1943). In his study of the street corner society in an Italian slum, Whyte (1943) finds that the origins of most of the gangs can be traced to the fact that their members grew up in the same neighbourhood and the contacts and relationships they formed during their early socialization as young boys. The creeks represent the home of the NDFF members in the same way as the street corner was the home for the gang members studied by Whyte. They also take up nicknames that replace their given names. One insurgent, for instance, was given the nickname "OC brain". "OC" is the acronym for "Officer Commanding", a term borrowed from the Nigerian army. The said insurgent is believed to be the intellectual head of the insurgent camp and attracts tremendous respect from others as the intelligence officer and the most educated member of the group. His nickname is a sign of the overarching importance of the group in his daily activities (see Whyte 1943). His involvement in the group was such a consuming passion that it destroyed his marriage to an optometrist who he said "was beginning to see me as a failure".[61] Not surprisingly, his status in the conventional society diminished as his status in the group grew at the creeks because of the reversal of the standards of the former (see Shaw and McKay 1971).[62]

The creeks are symbolically transformed to a transcendental space. There are five major ways in which the creeks re-present an otherworldly space in the insurgency. First, the creeks are largely beyond the reach of the Nigerian state in whose jurisdiction they fall. The institutionalized legal system of the Nigerian state as well as its appurtenances like the criminal codes, the police, and the courts is effectively suspended, hence, not applicable at the creeks. At the NDFF creeks, a policeman serving as the security detail to Henry Bindodogha was confined to the fringes of the creeks though all other non-uniformed persons gained entry. It was interesting to note that the policeman's uniform still made him suspect and unwelcome at the creeks although he was Bindodogha's bodyguard and often spent long hours at his home outside the creeks ensuring he was well protected.[63]

---

61   Interviewee 20.

62   In spite of their relevance, one major limitation of using the findings of Thrasher (1927) and Shaw and McKay (1971) in analysing the activities of the NDFF members is that the former focused on gangs engaged in criminal activities and other social vices rather than groups constituting a form of protest apparatus against societal injustice. This is a fundamental distinction.

63   Another basis for the police officer's exclusion could have been that he was not from the Niger Delta but neither was I.

Suspending the laws and the entire criminal justice system of the Nigerian state may seem to connote lawlessness at the creeks. However, such a group "tends to develop its own standards of conduct by which it seeks to regulate and control the behavior of its members. It inflicts punishment upon those who violate its rules and rewards those who are loyal and conform" (Shaw and McKay 1971: 275). Anderson's (1999: 33) research on "the code of the street" exemplifies the salience of these informal rules, particularly in street culture and the incidence of interpersonal violence. Such rules typically evolve over time and space. They guide the activities of street gangs (see Brookman, Bennett, Hochstetler and Copes 2011; Adamson 1998), the mafia (Paoli 2003), inmate groups (Shoham 2010) and other criminal subcultures. A study of over a dozen memoirs of former Mafiosi, for instance, highlights the cultural roots of the Mafia, which promote solidarity, the pervasive code of silence or *omerta* and the dire consequences of breaking the code (Firestone 1993). For Russian inmates in Israel's prisons, tattoos are a fundamental part of the group life and are inscribed on the bodies of members to reflect class hierarchy, intransigence, opposition to mainstream authority and other values of the criminal subculture (Shoham 2010). The consequences for breaching the tattoo hierarchy or bearing a "stolen" tattoo may be death in the hands of the gang (Shoham 2010: 991).

Generally, these rules guide the activities of members; ensure loyalty, respect and honour. They define the boundaries of acceptable behavior, relations among members, and how to handle encounters with individuals from rival groups, security agents and the public. The insurgents have their own unique laws and regulatory framework. For instance, at the NDFF camp in the creeks, women, including insurgents' wives, are not allowed in the camps. This is one of the most serious laws and transgression has gruesome consequences. The refusal to allow women at the camp stems from several gendered factors. Insurgents believe that women may create unnecessary distraction as the boys may compete among themselves to get their attention. This has the potential to generate unnecessary rancor and negatively influence morale and camaraderie among the insurgents.

In addition, insurgents receive spiritual fortification to ensure that bullets do not penetrate their bodies when they are shot. Women are believed to neutralize this supernatural shield the gods put on the combatants. Therefore, should there be sexual interactions between a combatant and a woman while at the creeks; the former becomes highly vulnerable in any immediate battle. Consequently, only insurgents who are off-duty are allowed to have sexual encounters with women— wives or girlfriends. Before such off-duty and potentially sexually contaminated insurgents re-enter the camp at the creeks, an elaborate set of rituals including libations and ablution by menopausal (older) women would have to be done to restore the protective armor of the gods. In other words, they could not afford to be lawless bandits.

Other rules at the creeks regulate non-sexual behaviors like stealing, cheating, gambling, laziness, insubordination, and so on. Disobedience may mean appearing before the "Commander", his representative or anyone next in the hierarchy as a form of improvised judicial system. Anyone found guilty is sent to the prison at the camp made of bamboo trees, leaves and ropes. Such errant persons may also be sent out of the camp for a given period at which time they do not draw a salary. That way, the moral fabric is maintained at the creeks although it is beyond the gaze of the laws of society. Insurgents obey their rules in order to be effective at breaking the laws of the country. They obey the rules they make to break the laws of the Nigerian state. The creeks are thus an entity within an entity. It is paradoxical but it is rational. People who foment "lawlessness" actually follow a set of laws: a criminal code of their own; an insurgency legal or criminal code.

The NDFF camp at the creeks had an elaborate division of labor before being abandoned. Some insurgents served as cooks, gunmen, drivers, engineers, artistes, religious priests and spies. The organizational finesse in the insurgent group, the painstaking work that goes into running the camps, planning the minutiae of every operation is herculean. A considerable level of lawfulness rather than lawlessness is required to do all of these even though they are lawless persons in the eyes of the laws of the larger society.

Second, the creeks represent an extraordinary hallowed space as the gods constitute its surveillance architecture and paraphernalia. At the NDFF camp in the creeks, Egbesu, the Ijaw god of war, is proudly displayed in a shrine erected at a sacrosanct space. The Ijaw people of Nigeria believe that Egbesu is a just deity that helps to implement order and fight against injustice (see Omeje 2005). In Ijaw mythology, those who beckon on Egbesu must not engage in any act of evil (Omeje 2005). Therefore, elaborate spiritual ceremonies are conducted to purify insurgents before invoking the powers of Egbesu. In this space, there is no room for those who have not been purified by the persons who bear the sceptre of Egbesu. At the NDFF camp, Bindodogha performs the necessary spiritual rites, including baths, sprinkling water, incantations, long periods of silent meditation and placement of extraordinary objects or charms on his group members. Asari Dokubo's NDPVF uses an elderly woman for the same purpose. For reasons explained below, it is important that the woman is past reproductive age.

Third, the creeks constitute a supra-space as it is persistently in the minds of the powers that be: the political elite, the JTF, oil companies, private security companies, and the general public. It is not hyperbolic to suggest that the militants live in the creeks, while the creeks live in the minds of several other actors. Activities in this space affect global oil prices, as MEND suggests. Therefore, the impact of this space is felt beyond sub-Saharan Africa. Everyone dependent on fossil fuels experienced the creeks from the global south to the global north. Such persons might not have lived it like the militants but saw glimpses of it in fluctuating gas prices.

Fourth, the creeks represent an ideational space and locus of strategic initiatives for planning insurgent activities: how to generate revenue, sphere of influence of each insurgent group, political consciousness, and so on. Included in this category are operational activities like mapping out specific oil infrastructure as targets of attacks. While this seems rather straight-forward, it is in fact an endeavor that requires putting many factors into consideration. These include what company owns the facility (a foreign-owned one is preferred for maximum publicity), how many workers are present (this must be the right number depending on the capacity of the insurgents), where the oil workers are from (again foreigners are preferred) and the presence and number of JTF operatives. In addition, this space is used to cross-fertilize ideas, disseminate information, and words conducive to giving rank and file insurgents the needed motivation to fight against the state, oil corporations, and global capitalism.

Fifth, an air of invincibility pervades the atmosphere in the creeks. Insurgents are the Lords of the creeks with increasingly significant social capital and symbolic capital. Several young men, many of who have little education, have suddenly become celebrities overnight. They are sought after by the local and international media, the elite seeking political power among others. The creeks constitute the space that has made these young men powerful. They are no mere mortals anymore. Apart from an air of invincibility, the creeks offer an atmosphere of significance beyond the backgrounds of the young men, their level of education, their exposure and other disadvantages of the social demographic they belong. Well-sought for interviews as a kind of *nouveau* local cognoscenti with international appeal, insurgents know that the oil-thirsty world leans on every word they utter. Insurgents ensure that they *perform* for their audience who brave the odds to go to the creeks.

Also, the creeks constitute the space that affords insurgents the luxury of using force to get whatever they want. Insurgents who have accepted amnesty rue their inability to use force as "things get done faster when you have a gun".[64] Thus, leaving this space requires reorientation. Finally, the creeks embody the site of the (mis)appropriation of every facet of the Nigerian society. For instance, some Pentecostal pastors visit the creeks regularly to pray for the insurgents and collect handsome stipends for their efforts. This practice was routine at the NDFF camp in Edo state.[65] It is also common in Delta and Bayelsa states, where insurgents are keen to garner any spiritual protection they could afford. Politicians also strike deals with insurgents to win elections, particularly in Delta state, where the younger brother of a major insurgent leader has been elected chair of a local council. Everyone seems (in)directly connected to the creeks. Families of insurgents, traditional rulers, community elders, community members, the oil industry in general and the Nigerian state are all performatively positioned at the creeks through indirect participation, patronage, inertia, or complicity.

---

64   Interviewee 44. A commander from the NDFF, personal interview, Benin City, August 2010.

65   Interviewee 20. This interviewee refused to disclose the sums of money involved.

A well-oiled machinery: Funding the (MEND) insurgency

As insurgent groups rarely have the support of legitimate states that may thrive on taxes, and international trade (Münkler 2005: 17), the former must device means to generate adequate funds for their activities. Failure to do so may spell death for such an insurgency. Paucity of funds plagued the first post-colonial insurgency in the Niger Delta. Adaka Boro's 12-day revolution began with a capital of £150 (Boro 1982). Boro's troops resorted to extortionist strategies on ordinary citizens in order to support their group (Boro 1982). This led to a loss of public confidence and contributed to the failure of the insurgency 12 days after it began. The MEND insurgency, however, is very well-lubricated financially through funds from expropriated oil. The science of illegal oil bunkering is routinized in several remote oil-producing Delta communities, as stated in chapter 3. Illegal oil bunkering in such communities is not the exclusive preserve of a few individuals; it is a survival imperative for the young and old. This practice of refining illegally bunkered oil represents a fraction of sedimented survival knowledges in the Niger Delta handed down from previous generations. Numerous containers of varying capacities littered the streets in one of the communities visited while conducting research for this book. A bus was being loaded with locally refined diesel close to a river in the community. The conspicuous presence and calm mien of the persons in one of the illegal refineries visited demonstrate that the people do not see the act as deviant in any way.

Between 2008 and 2009, over 400 illegal refineries were discovered and destroyed by the JTF. On March 26, 2009, for instance, JTF's Brig. Gen. Wuyep Rimtip led soldiers to Oginibo community situated in Ughelli South local government in Delta state. Over 100 such refineries were set ablaze in that single raid (*The Punch* 27 March 2009: 9). The illegal refineries were supplied crude oil from ruptured pipelines of oil corporations. Suffice to state that the major source of funding for the insurgency is the commodity under contention—crude oil.

An insider account of one of MEND's affiliates provides a glimpse of this rich source of funding available to the insurgents. Insurgents have adopted a peculiar price mechanism for oil in the creeks. This is called the "Bush Price". For instance, a tanker of crude oil or 33,000 litres has a market value of 1.3–1.5 million Naira but is sold for 500,000 Naira in the creeks.[66] I had the following conversation with the said operative:

Interviewer: During this period, how much did you make to fund your activities?

Respondent: Yes, sometimes may be I got four badges of oil

Interviewer: What's the equivalent to what we can easily … (cuts in)

---

66   In cases where munitions are offered, the bush price of a tanker of oil could be as low as 200,000 Naira in the bullets for oil trade.

Respondent: A 1000 tonnes badges can take 40 tankers of oil

Interviewer: 40 tankers?

Respondent: Yeah and that's like ahmm 20 million Naira cash.[67]

Second, some affiliates of MEND fund the insurgency through ransom paid by oil companies for their kidnapped staff. Former Inspector General of Police Mike Okiro (as stated in chapter 2) estimates that militants collected at least $100 million or 1.5 billion Naira between 2006 and 2008 in ransom (*This Day*, April 1 2009).

Third, some insurgents have developed less complicated contrivances for raising funds. These include demanding "protection money" for securing oil facilities, banks, major supermarkets, hotels, and other business organizations in the Niger Delta. Tom Polo, the founder of Camp 5, perfected this art before the amnesty program was introduced in 2009. In turn, he ploughed the profits into several hotels in the Refinery Road area of Warri Delta state. Authorities in Delta state were reluctant to bring him to order as he was an indispensable political tool.[68] For instance, there were at least two commissioners nominated by Tom Polo in the 2010 cabinet of Delta state.[69] His younger brother, George Ekpemupolo, (as stated earlier) is the elected chair of the Warri South local government in the predominantly Ijaw area of Delta state. The patronage system in Nigeria dictates that political appointees and elected persons pay certain honoraria to their god-fathers. Therefore, Tom Polo can reasonably be expected to make more money through his nominees and political protégés.

Fourth, in cases where a different group kidnaps oil workers, some insurgents unconnected with the kidnapping often serve as middlemen for the release of the hostages. Investigations demonstrate that Tom Polo is once again the major player in this enterprise largely due to his political reach. Four oil workers were kidnapped in May 2007 by the NDFF in Edo state in one instance (*Vanguard*, 19 May 2007). The leader of the group, Henry Bindodogha, was once the Chief Priest at Tom Polo's Camp 5 before becoming independent. Tom Polo contacted Bindodogha stating that the Delta state governor asked him to give the Edo group 50 million Naira in exchange for the hostages. After protracted negotiations, Bindodogha collected 9 million Naira of the 50 million from Tom Polo's emissaries as the total logistical cost for kidnapping and feeding the expatriates, so as not to give the impression that all he wanted was money.[70] No one is sure of the exact amount

---

67   Interviewee 20.

68   Interviewee 20.

69   Interviewee 2. (A professor and activist in the Niger Delta). Persona interview July 2009. The activist did not name the militant but I found out the name of the insurgent and names of those nominated (which I have withheld) during the 2010 field trip.

70   Multiple sources but notably Henry Bindodogha (Interviewee 19). Personal interview, August 2010. Also, interviewee 20.

the Delta state governor paid for freeing the oil workers or what happened to the outstanding balance of 41 million Naira.

Finally, several insurgents mention receiving funding from fellow Niger Deltans at home and in the Diaspora. Asari Dokubo, for instance, claims that he receives funding for his activities from concerned Niger Deltans in the US (Peel 2009). No other insurgent corroborated this claim. None the less, some business elites and members of the political class of Niger Delta origins surreptitiously provide funding for the insurgency. Everyday folks also occasionally contribute by providing food and discreet temporary shelter for insurgents.[71]

Clearly, the funding of this insurgency in the Niger Delta exhibits a number of features now present in new wars: funds are drawn from the illegal control of resources; funds are secured by demanding protection money from businesses; funds are attained through ransoms of kidnapped victims; and funds are contributed by local supporters and sympathizers (including some government officials) and from the diaspora (see Mello 2010; Berdal 2003).

Media relations

> In conflicts of this nature, there is always propaganda. The first casualty is the truth … in the conflict in the Niger Delta; the militants have had the upper hand in propaganda. (General Sarkin Yaki Bello, JTF Commander)

The media plays a central role in warfare of any kind. This is particularly salient in asymmetrical warfare. As Mao Se-Tung points out: "Guerrilla leaders spend a great deal more time in organization, instruction, agitation and propaganda work that they do fighting, for their most important job is to win over the people" (Griffiths 1978: 27). MEND appears to understand the operational mechanics of the media, and anticipatorily manipulates the media for its purposes (Okonta 2006) while also ensuring that shock and awe trail its advertised activities or threats. The magnitude of its ability to manipulate the media compelled a governor in the Delta region to describe MEND as a "media creation".

MEND benefits tremendously from having an articulate spokesperson, Jomo Gbomo. Gbomo strategically releases press statements in the form of e-mails to select media organizations and scholars around the world. Media organizations like South African Broadcasting Corporation, Bloomberg News, Al-Jazeera, the *Financial Times* of London and the *New York Times* among others are part of an elite group on MEND's listserv. Proprietors of new media platforms like Omoyele Sowore of Sahara Reporters and scholars like Michael Watts of the University of California, Berkeley are part of this group of 50. Generally, MEND notifies those on its listserv before carrying out an attack, especially bombings.

Having such an elite listserv serves several purposes. First, the exclusivity of the listserv makes it highly coveted by media organizations, journalists, scholars

---

71   Multiple sources. Interviewees 15, 24–37.

and researchers. Its non-inclusivity ensures that those on the list have access to privileged information which becomes available to the global publics after MEND carries out its acts. Second, informing subscribers to the listserv of impending acts increases the awe with which MEND is viewed, particularly when those acts are carried out at the stated time and date.

MEND's official statements entail lucid prose laced with contrasting metaphors, sharp diction, coherent and convincing arguments and a command of English indicative of a formal education. The degree of articulation in MEND's e-mails has received widespread admiration even from people who fundamentally disagree with MEND's mode of operation, giving a veneer of intellectualism to an otherwise essentially violent struggle.

The almost fairy-tale example of Government Ekpemupolo or Tom Polo may suffice in explaining how MEND uses the media. Tom Polo is arguably the foremost militant in the Niger Delta. Among other crimes, the JTF holds Tom Polo responsible for the death of 18 soldiers in one attack conducted before the amnesty program. As of August 2010, the remains of some of the soldiers were still being exhumed for verification.[72] Although barely literate, Tom Polo worked with FNDIC as the mobilization officer. FNDIC's media coordinator, Bulou Custom, asserts that "we created Tom Polo".[73] Custom wrote many newspaper articles in Tom Polo's name and ensured adequate syndication in the media through his network. Alongside others in FNDIC, "a very purposeful" and "cool headed boy"[74] was transformed into a cult figure. This was a deliberate and calculated exercise by FNDIC. Many militant groups were established after some training at Tom Polo's notorious "Camp 5". Many ex-militants speak of drawing inspiration from a certain Tom Polo they have never met. Although FNDIC dissociates itself from the violence perpetrated by Tom polo, FNDIC president and spokesperson agree that they manufactured the Tom Polo brand through relentless press releases that bolstered his image, and publicized his activities.[75]

Furthermore, MEND has a regular cyber presence and participates in global flows of information. Jomo Gbomo issued 29 official statements (or just over two e-mails per month) on behalf of MEND between September 5 2009 and 19 October 2010. This figure does not include private correspondence with journalists and researchers seeking information or clarification.[76] As stated earlier, computers used to send MEND's e-mails have been traced to South Africa (Ukiwo 2007). Nevertheless, MEND has managed to be more technologically savvy than

---

72   Interviewee 12. JTF Commander, General Bello.

73   Interviewee 37. (FNDIC media coordinator Bolou Custom). Personal interview, August 2010, Warri Delta state.

74   Interviewee 38.

75   Interviewees 38 and 37.

76   I received a private e-mail from Jomo Gbomo on Monday 24 August 2009 in response to my request for inclusion in the MEND listserv having been introduced by an activist in the Niger Delta.

multiple security agencies in Nigeria tracking its Internet use and attempting to access its e-mail. The impunity with which MEND issues warnings about attacks, communicates with journalists and researchers while shielding the largely apparitional "Jomo Gbomo" from being arrested, is an indication that they know a few technological things the Nigerian authorities do not.

Multiple sources of weapons

One of the major strengths of MEND is the flow of arms to insurgents. This speaks to the growing "commercialization of military force" (Münkler 2005: 16) in new wars. As stated earlier, the evidence suggesting that the Warri crisis led to a proliferation of arms in the Niger Delta is incontrovertible. A number of insurgent groups, like MEND affiliate NDFF in Edo, acquired their first major consignment of arms during the Warri crisis. In addition, arms and ammunitions flow into the Niger Delta through local and international sources. The sources of arms and ammunition in the insurgency are divided into four major categorizes for analytical purposes.

First, insurgents buy arms from well-placed military sources in Nigeria.[77] For instance, on February 11 2008, five army officers,[78] a sergeant, two corporals, six lance-corporals and one private were court marshaled for stealing arms and ammunitions from army depots in the country and selling them to criminal gangs in neighboring countries and insurgent groups in the Niger Delta (*Nigerian Daily News* 2008).[79] Over 7,000 military assault rifles, sub-machine guns and rocket-propelled grenades were stolen between 2003 and 2007. MEND insurgents benefitted from the arms sale through a civilian middleman, Sunny Okah, brother of Henry Okah believed to be the leader of a faction of MEND. Six soldiers were sentenced to life imprisonment for their role in the arms theft at the end of the trial.[80]

Sahara Reporters, an Internet-based news organization, leaked a secret report on arms theft in the Nigerian Army on October 30 2010. The report titled "Investigation Report into the Theft and Sale of Arms to Niger Delta Gunrunner by an Officer and some Soldiers of the 1 Base Ordnance Depot Kaduna" was completed in 2007. It alleges that National Security Adviser, Gen Andrew Azazi (rtd), former Governors James Ibori and DSP Alamieyeseigha, and former

---

77   Interviewee 12. General Bello, JTF Commander.

78   These are Colonels R.O. Yusuf, Gadgere, Lieutenant Colonel Wesley, Majors M.K. Ahmed and A. S. Akubo.

79   *Nigerian Daily News* (11 February) 2008. "Gun deal: 5 Army officers, 10 others face court martial", URL: http://ndn.nigeriadailynews.com/templates/default. aspx?a=6160&template=print-article.htm Accessed 2 November 2010.

80   See "Nigerian troops jailed over arms sales to militants", *Daily Mail*, 18 November 2008. URL: http://www.dailymail.co.uk/news/worldnews/article-1087038/Nigerian-troops-jailed-arms-sales-militants.html Accessed 2 November 2010.

Director-General of the State Security Service, Lt. Col Kayode Are (rtd) were part of arms sale and purchase ring.[81]

Second, MEND affiliates generate arms and ammunitions from attacks on police officers and soldiers. Police and army personnel bearing arms in public are sometimes stabbed on the streets, so that their weapons can be stolen.[82] In addition, insurgents execute occasional raids on police stations to cart away arms and ammunition. Some MEND affiliates are good at identifying "vulnerable" police stations in the Niger Delta. This has led to a situation where police commissioners in the Niger Delta have stopped keeping arms in some police stations for fear of militant attacks.[83]

Third, a significant proportion of arms used in the insurgency comes from numerous local and foreign arms merchants. There are several creeks in the Niger Delta that lead to the Atlantic Ocean. Military authorities confirm that Nigeria's huge territorial waters and land borders are very rarely effectively patrolled. This makes such creeks and borders extremely pervious to illegal arms transportation.[84] The pervasive illegal oil bunkering in the Delta helps in arms proliferation.[85] In the creeks, for instance, shipments often arrive in the form of a lethal modern trade by barter—arms for oil.

Two major sets of actors are involved. The first are non-Nigerians or international arms merchants found in all conflict-prone regions of the world.[86] For instance, Nigerian Port security agents in Lagos confiscated an Iranian vessel for shipping 13 containers of arms disguised as "building materials" to Nigeria on Tuesday October 26, 2010.[87] Some of the impounded items included mortar shells, 107 mm artillery rockets, grenades as well as rocket-launchers. The second set of actors includes local merchants with established sophisticated networks of arms procurement in countries as far away as China. They include largely unknown business men and women. One prominent Nigerian involved in illegal arms business at a global level—operating in South Africa, China and Nigeria—is

---

81   See Sahara Reporters. 2010. "Secret Army Report Implicates NSA Azazi, Ibori, Alamieyeseigha, Henry And Sunny Okah In Sale Of Military Weapons To Niger Delta Militants", URL: http://saharareporters.com/report/secret-army-report-implicates-nsa-azazi-ibori-alamieyeseigha-henry-and-sunny-okah-sale-milita Accessed 2 November 2010. See a copy of the leaked report at http://www.saharareporters.com/sites/default/files/uploads/Azazi.pdf

82   Interviewee 12. General Bello, JTF Commander.

83   Interviewee 12. General Bello, JTF Commander.

84   Interviewee 12. General Bello, JTF Commander.

85   Interviewees 12 and 10.

86   Interviewee 37.

87   See *Afrik News* 2010 (2 November). "Nigeria: Iran remains quiet over seized arms ship", URL: http://www.afrik-news.com/article18430.html Accessed 2 November 2010. There are conflicting reports over the intended destination of the shipment. The Israeli government believes the arms were for Hamas, a group generally regarded as a terrorist organization by the US and its allies. Hamas denies the Israeli government claim.

factional leader of MEND, Henry Okah. As stated earlier, Henry Okah's brother was indicted in the illegal looting and sale of the Nigerian Army's arsenal. Asari Dokubo confirms purchasing large consignments of arms from Henry Okah, the "Master of Arms".[88] This category of local arms merchants also includes some women in Nigeria who supply bullets, referred to as "groundnuts" to the insurgents at prohibitive prices.[89]

Finally, there is a thriving illegal arms manufacturing industry in Nigeria. Local blacksmiths have manufactured guns for hunting and the security of communities and kingdoms since the earliest available records. Today, arms manufactured in Aba, Abia state and Onitsha, Anambra state in South East Nigeria are very effective and important tools in the insurgency.[90] The relative propinquity of the South East to the Niger Delta region ensures that when foreign arms merchandize falters, local entrepreneurs fill the void.

Nigeria's Oil Insurgency and the New War Model

There are at least six major ways in which the MEND-led oil insurgency in Nigeria demonstrates characteristics of the new war model. First, new wars thrive on the erosion of the state's monopoly of the use of force (Mello 2010: 298). The Delta insurgency is no exception. MEND insurgents and other groups have liberalized the state's monopoly on the use of force in Nigeria's Delta region. As this chapter indicates, insurgents rely on a plethora of means for acquiring sophisticated weapons, including private entities and corrupt state agents. Consequently, it is difficult to distinguish combatants and non-combatants in the Delta, as agents of the Nigerian state responsible for maintaining security readily admit. This key quality of new wars has been invigorated in the Delta by the well-documented decline in the legitimacy of the Nigerian state.

Second, the Delta insurgency contains elements that are congruent with the notion of the political economy of new wars (see Ikelegbe 2005b; Collier and Hoeffler 2005). These include the participation of a concatenation of actors: some ruling elites, top military brass, traditional rulers, and foreign merchants, among others, embroiled in the insurgency as an end in itself—in a Mertonian sense, an innovative method of economic survival. Third, the riverine asymmetrical warfare in the Niger Delta speaks volumes about how new wars are being conducted, and how these wars differ from traditional warfare. The MEND operation is a destatized war (see Münkler 2005; Kaldor 1999) involving well-armed government forces against a coalition of non-state actors, which has a loose structure and anonymity of

---

88   See "Asari Dokubo: Me, Henry Okah 'Jomo Gbomo', Judith Asuni and the Niger Delta Insurgency", URL: http://saharareporters.com/interview/asari-dokubo-me-henry-okahjomo-gbomo-judith-asuni-and-niger-delta-insurgency Accessed 2 November 2010.

89   Interviewee 20.

90   Interviewee 12. JTF Commander, General Bello.

leadership, and is not bound by traditional rules of engagement on the battlefields. The plurality of battlefields—oil infrastructure in the Delta region, targets in Abuja, Lagos and several other cities—help the insurgents to bring some balance to the asymmetry of the war. The major battlefield is located in an inhospitable and difficult Niger Delta terrain which, more often than not, gives the insurgents an advantage over the government's military forces. It is a physical and social space in which insurgents can simultaneously be kidnappers, illegal oil bunkerers, and terminators, as well as suppliers of social goods, such as scholarships, roads and electricity. This blurring of the distinction between wars, organized crime, major violations of human rights and philanthropy is an important feature of the new wars model.

Fourth, as is the case with many of the new wars, the battle is being fought over natural resources and insurgents have a level of control—albeit illegal. The conflict in the Niger Delta illuminates the issue of resource curse (Ghazvinian 2007; Sala-i-Martin and Subramanian 2003). Nigeria exhibits the bewildering paradox of plenty: despite the abundance of oil, the country is not experiencing the level of development that should be probable. It is worth reiterating that the wealth of the Niger Delta has not trickled down to the people of the region and has led to major grievances against the state and oil corporations. The focus that the Nigerian government has placed on oil revenues has meant that other economic and social sectors are neglected. This issue, combined with the volatility of the global commodity markets, the mismanagement of the economy by the Nigerian government and the systemic corruption that prevails at every level of governance, lends further fodder to the notion of the resource curse.

Fifth, many non-state actors in new wars benefit from closer ideational, economic, and cultural integration associated with globalization (Berdal 2003). As stated earlier, MEND has a regular cyber presence and participates in the global flows inherent in information technology. This enhances its propaganda machinery. Propaganda has always been a tool of warfare. But the new wars, such as the one being fought in the Niger Delta, rely heavily on the utilization and manipulation of the media – particularly new media. The impact that cyber-presence and technological savvy and sophistication of MEND have had in terms of the success of the insurgency against the Nigerian government is something that ought to be studied in more detail. The literature currently focuses on the economic angle, especially electronic transfer of funds to non-state actors across the world (see Berdal 2003).

Sixth, the oil insurgency in the Delta lends credence to the import of identity politics (Kaldor's 1999) in new wars. For Kaldor (1999: 6), identity politics—the "claim to power on the basis of a particular identity"—is a defining feature of new wars. Kaldor (1999) argues that such identities may be based on clan, national origin, religion or linguistic affiliation based on her research in Bosnia-

Herzegovina.[91] There is ample evidence suggesting that identity politics have played a role in the Delta insurgency. The delimitation of Delta peoples into specific states in the federation beginning from the establishment of the Midwest state on 9 August 1963 has enabled the mobilization of geo-political identities and substruction of cultural identity. The result is the intensification of identity politics (see Ikelegbe 2005a), as stated in Chapter 3. Combined with significant political, religious and socio-economic problems and inequitable distribution of resources in a manner that disproportionately favors the three major ethnic groups, the consequence has been the "supertribalization" (Osaghae 2003: 55) of young people in Nigeria.

The Warri crisis of March 1997 is one of several ethnic clashes among minorities in the Delta. However, a new form of collective identity—*the Niger Delta people*—has since emerged in a region of approximately 40 ethnic groups who speak over 250 languages and dialects in 13, 329 settlements (Watts 2008b). Insurgents now believe that conflict among the ethnic groups in the Delta region was not the struggle: "Before we formed MEND, our people were fighting, but it was a war between Ijaw and Itsekiri; that was not the Niger Delta struggle".[92] The real struggle appears to be against oil corporations, the Nigerian state and the Hausa-Fulani of Northern Nigeria, which MEND equates with the Nigerian state. This is significant because Adaka Boro, who led the first post-independence insurgency against the Nigerian state considered the assassinated Prime Minister, Sir Tafawa Balewa, a Fulani, and his party, the Northern People's Congress (NPC), as the "only protector of the Ijaws" (Boro 1982: 94–95). However MEND has since taken a different trajectory in framing its activities, as discussed in the next chapter. Nonetheless, MEND generally kidnaps expatriate oil workers, rather than Nigerians and targets oil infrastructure. In addition, although MEND purports to fight for the people of the Niger Delta, most of its members are from the Ijaw-speaking peoples (see Ukiwo 2007; Okonta 2006).

Important caveats

In spite of the relevance of the new war thesis in analyzing the MEND-led oil insurgency in Nigeria, there are four important areas, which suggest that this approach must be applied to the Delta insurgency with caution. First, unlike many new wars in which the use of child soldiers is endemic—estimated at 300,000 on a global scale (see Mello 2010: 299)—there does not appear to be any widespread recruitment, forced or voluntary, of children-fighters in the Delta insurgency.

---

91   The import of ethno-religious loyalties and identity politics generally constitutes a major point of divergence between Kaldor (1999) and Münkler (2005). Kaldor considers identity politics fundamental to new wars. Münkler (2005) however argues that although such factors are significant, focusing on them paints a romantic picture of new wars and shrouds the inherent economic motives of major players.

92   Cited in Courson (2009: 18) in an interview with Sunday Vanguard, May 25 2008.

Of the 42 insurgents who participated in this study, only one claimed to have *voluntarily*[93] joined an insurgent camp at the age of 17. Others stated that they were over 18 years old at the time of joining different groups.

Second, the "barbarism thesis" in new wars (see Mello 2010: 299; Kaplan 2000) seems to have little empirical validity in the Delta crisis. The barbarism thesis proposes that new wars create avenues for indiscriminate violence against the civilian population and widespread sexual violence against women. To be sure, MEND's activities have led to civilian deaths in cities like Warri and Abuja. However, there seems to be a relatively more cautious approach to civilian casualties in MEND's insurgency than the new wars literature suggests. MEND often issues what may be considered proactive warnings to civilians against going to specific locations marked for bombings, so as not to lose their lives or limbs.[94]

Third, as discussed below, several insurgent groups explicitly prohibit the presence of women at their camps while also forbidding sexual interactions with women in order not to nullify the ostensible spiritual fortification conferred on fighters during ritualistic ceremonies superintended mostly by post-menopausal women. The consequence is that *systematic* sexual violence by insurgents against women in the Delta has rarely come up in academic or lay analysis (see Oriola 2012: 549). This is not to suggest that there has been no incidence of sexual violence against women. Rather, it is submitted that this cannot be construed as a feature of the Delta insurgency. Paradoxically, those accused of sexual violence by victims, oil-producing communities, the media, human rights organizations and scholars studying the Delta crisis have often been government security agents (see Oriola 2012; Omotola 2009; Lenning and Brightman 2009; Ukeje 2004; Human Rights Watch 1999). Therefore, sexual violence against women by non-state actors is not necessarily universal (see Mazurana et al. 2002: 111) contrary to the presupposition of much of the new wars literature. Therefore, the Delta insurgency suggests an important caveat to the notion of "*autonomization* of violence" (see Münkler 2005: 3).

The apparent non-use of child soldiers, absence of indiscriminate violence against the civilian population and arguable rarity of sexual violence against women by insurgents perhaps speak to the geographical location of the creeks, where most insurgent activities take place. The creeks are located in the Delta region, which is predominantly populated by the people whom insurgents claim they are fighting for. Consequently, it is conceivable that insurgents are careful not to be seen as perpetrating violence against their own people. This is fundamental to retaining the tacit and explicit support of the people (see Hobsbawm 1969, 1959).

Fourth, the Delta insurgency also demonstrates that a wholesale presupposition that new wars are driven solely or principally by economic motives (see Kaldor 1999) or symbolize the "continuation of economics by other means" (Keen 1998:

---

93   The contestedness of the notion of voluntariness in participating in an armed conflict is acknowledged.

94   See Jomo Gbomo e-mail statement (number 20) Monday 15 March 2010.

11) is a misleading overstatement. This book aligns with the growing number of research suggesting the need to be cautious about the greed-grievance theoretical juxtaposition (see Collier and Hoeffler 2004). A multi-factorial approach that considers the historical context, political power struggle, and the role of religion, and culture, among others, (Berdal 2003: 490) provides a more nuanced explanation of the Delta situation.

Finally, MEND is not only the inheritor of over 50 years of widespread grievances of the people in the Ijaw-speaking areas of the Niger Delta (Okonta 2006), it has been bequeathed a wealthy legacy of resistance against constituted authority. Consequently, the phenomenon called MEND and its insurgent acts may be regarded as "tributaries of a more general stream of agitation" (Snow and Benford 1992: 133). MEND is the maturation of the oft violent historical struggle of the Ijaws against British colonialists, dominant groups such as Itsekiris, and Urhobos and the neo-colonial Nigerian state. MEND's loose structure and secrecy, the sympathy it enjoys from the masses of the Delta, the enablement of asymmetrical warfare by the difficult Niger Delta terrain have contributed to enhancing MEND's operations, making it intractable to the authorities. In addition, the vast resources available to MEND, its media relations and steady flows of arms have combined to produce an unprecedented insurgency machine.

The Role of Women in the Insurgency[95]

A brief analysis (and incomplete picture) of the role of women in the kidnapping episodes in particular and the insurgency in general is presented in this section. The role of women in the (MEND) insurgency undoubtedly deserves a book of its own, as stated earlier. Therefore, what follows offers only a glimpse of the level of women's involvement in kidnapping episodes.

The historical engagement of Nigerian women in struggles against perceived injustice is well-documented (Ikelegbe 2005a; Mba 1982; Van Allen 1971). For instance, women performed numerous pivotal roles when the Eastern region carried out a violent secessionist campaign from Nigeria. This culminated in the Nigerian Civil War (1967–1970) between the federal government and the breakaway Biafra Republic. An estimated one million lives were lost. Achebe (2010) provides an interesting account of the role of Biafran women in support of the war efforts. Women like Flowa Nwapa performed literary roles documenting the lived experience of Biafrans for posterity. Biafran women were also involved in children's welfare and education. Other women, including the author, Achebe, participated in the political struggles and demonstrations before the war. Several Biafran women were engaged in potentially lethal cross-border farming and

---

95   This section was first published under the title 'The Delta creeks, women's engagement and Nigeria's oil insurgency'. *British Journal of Criminology*, 2012; 52(3), 534–555. Reproduced by permission.

entered into enemy territory to procure food in the market at the risk of life and limb, as food supplies ran low during the war (Achebe 2010).

More fundamental for the purposes of this book, the Biafran women were a major part of the Organization of Freedom Fighters (BOFF), "an elaborately organized and carefully structured military organ set up to operate mainly behind enemy lines and to supplement the effort of the regular Biafran army" (Achebe 2010: 800). This was a vastly important war machine containing units such as Anti-Aircraft and Rocket, Anti-War Head and Rocket, Rocket Fuel, Hand Grenade, Telecommunication Equipment Modification, Training, Logistics, Intelligence, Agitation, and Propaganda, among others (Achebe 2010: 800–801). Their subversive tendency is accentuated by the fact that members moved around unarmed but provided training for fighters on how to use weapons and helped the Biafran army destroy the supply lines of the enemy (Achebe 2010). Several women with a high school diploma received training in weapon use and how to penetrate enemy camps (Achebe 2010). Women were part of the "Ogbunigwe group" responsible for Biafra's bombing expeditions (Achebe 2010) at an historical moment when women in Nigeria were largely excluded from the major socio-economic institutions of the Nigerian society. Two Biafran women were also part of the team that produced the impressive "piompion", a long-range antiaircraft missile (Achebe 2010: 802). In more recent times, the women of the Niger Delta mobilized against transnational oil corporations by attacking oil facilities during the Ogharefe revolt in 1984 and 1986 in the Ekpan women's uprising, all in Warri, Delta state (Ukeje 2004; Turner and Oshare 1994).

However, academic narratives on the engagement of women in the Delta struggle overwhelmingly center on how women encourage their husbands and children to fight or as non-violent protesters (Ukeje 2004). This creates the false impression that women in the Delta are not involved in using violent repertoires of protest or that they have largely been the "silent ones" who support others (George 2008a: 1195). The role of women in the movement goes beyond traditional issues like food production (see Okorie and Williams 2009; George 2008b), peaceful quest for economic empowerment (see Agboola 2008; Okafor 2008) and domestic duties such as performing sexual functions as wives or girlfriends and taking care of the children and the home when men are in the trenches.[96]

The areas highlighted above are some of the crucial roles of the Delta women. None the less, restricting academic analysis to these roles does no justice to the magnitude and inherent bravery of women's involvement in the explicitly violent turn of the movement since the late 1990s. Thus, this constitutes a reductionist portrayal of the agency of the Delta women. Besides, focusing on the role of women in the domestic domain inadvertently feeds into the patriarchal ideological underpinnings of the Nigerian society. Key areas in which women participate in the Delta insurgency are examined to demonstrate that women are an essential

---

96 Interviewees 19 and 29.

part of the violent forms of protest just as they have been active participants in non-violent protest.

Ammunition merchandizing and gun-running

Women play a critical role in ensuring the flow of arms and ammunition to insurgents in the creeks. Two categories of women are involved here. First, there are business women, particularly from the port City of Lagos, who specialize in buying oil from insurgents and paying in guns and/or "groundnuts" or bullets:

> if your assignment is like go get some "ground nuts", they call bullets groundnuts … the easiest way to get it is through women. You know women flock around guys with cash and because we do the oil business. Some who come (to the creeks) to buy oil are from Lagos since they know we use bullets, sometimes they pay us with bullets.[97]

The elevation of arms and ammunitions to the status of a major currency underscores their salience in the insurgency. Second, there are sisters or girlfriends of insurgents, who help procure arms from merchants in Lagos and other major cities.[98] This category of women is not directly involved in profiteering but none the less constitutes an important source of arms shipment from source cities to the Delta. A former insurgent explains in this conversation:

> *Respondent*: You know there are some women who see us, they know us to be … let me use the word militants and they even want to come close to you because of who you are, you understand. They even ask, "What can I do for you?"

> *Interviewer*: Hmmm

> *Respondent*: Some of these people know what we are fighting for, some of them are our sisters, blood sisters, you understand. Like let's say, I want to carry a carton full of bullets from Bayelsa State to Edo State, all I need do is call one of my big sisters, "Sister I beg come, carry this thing, buy garri put, carry am go give Solo (Solomon),". She might not even know what is inside, you understand?

> *Interviewer*: Yeah?

> *Respondent*: But she would deliver it. She takes it as foodstuff going to that camp. She does that, willingly.

---

97   Interviewee 20.
98   Interviewee 20.

Interviewer: So were you in any way terrified that you might be doing something that puts her in harm's way

Respondent: They were willing to do it.

Interviewer: In other words, they knew the risks involved?

Respondent: Of course, they will even tell you "Don't do it. I will do for you; if they (the JTF) see you your appearance is even suspicious". They are willing to do it.

As argued below, both groups of women benefit from the facticity of femininity and occupation of a socio-cultural space that construes the Delta woman as somehow less dangerous than the Delta man.

Mediating between insurgent groups, the Nigerian state and the oil corporations

When MEND announced the formation of the four-member, "Aaron Team" on 28 September 2009, it "nominated Ms Annkio Briggs to liaise on behalf of the group".[99] This is a significant achievement as the Aaron Team was established to represent the interest of MEND in the negotiations with the federal government. Briggs' nomination was a consequence of her active involvement at the front lines of the struggle in the Niger Delta. Briggs had become a household name and important voice in the Delta struggle in Nigeria and around the world prior to her nomination as liaison officer between the all-male Aaron Team and MEND. She had effectively become the "mother" of the struggle.[100] For reasons yet unclear, Briggs was relieved of her appointment by "mutual consent" on 25 October 2009 and replaced by Amagbe Denzel Kentebe.[101] In spite of the brevity of her appointment, it was a clear demonstration of trust and confidence in her prowess and level of engagement by the ultra-clandestine MEND. It also symbolizes how far women have come in the Delta struggle.

Many other women serve as peace activists in less prominent capacities. Women are actively involved in negotiations designed to secure the release of kidnapped oil workers. Many women are involved in NGOs that serve as negotiators, emissaries and go-betweens for various sides in kidnapping episodes. Some represent the oil corporations while others deliver the missive and demands of insurgents to the government and oil corporations.[102]

---

99   Jomo Gbomo e-mail statement (number 4) "Aaron Team", 28 September 2009.

100   Interviewee 4.

101   Jomo Gbomo e-mail statement (number 8) "Indefinite Ceasefire", 25 October 2009.

102   Focus Group Discussion 3; two women representing NGO groups, Yenagoa, Bayelsa state, July 2009.

Nudity as a form of protest

The view of African women as generally oppressed apolitical actors is largely a Eurocentric standpoint that has become a favorite pastime in some circles. The idea of non-agentic womenfolk on the African continent bears scant semblance to reality as women command considerable political power (Stevens 2006). One of the ways that women exercise their political power is through their "sexual power" (Stevens 2006: 596). The sexual power may be exercised through denial of sex to the menfolk or the exposure of the breasts and vaginas of large numbers of post-menopausal women (Stevens 2006; Turner and Brownhill 2004; Prince 1961). This public performance of nudity constitutes a "dangerous genital power" (Stevens 2006: 593). More than any coterie of experts, anthropologists recognize the cultural significance of the genitalia and its power to symbolically pollute anyone exposed to it as a form of protest by women (Stevens 2006; Prince 1961, cited in Stevens 2006). Anyone subjected to such "genital cursing" (Bastian 2005) may become mad or experience misfortune.

In November to December 1929 in colonial Eastern Nigeria, the women of Aba waged a war against several unfavorable policies: the poor economic climate and impending taxation of women that men failed to stifle (Afigbo 1966). Women sang, danced and used the sheer force of their sexual power, organizational discipline and determination for mobilization (Bastian 2005; Ifeka-Moller 1975; Afigbo 1966). Symbols of colonialism like the Barclays Bank, and prisons were attacked in the war (Van Allen 1971). The colonialists abandoned the plan to tax women, and reduced the powers of the warrant chiefs in the end (Mba 1982; Van Allen 1971)—two of the core demands of the women.

A similar incident occurred in Abeokuta on November 29 1947 at the palace of the traditional ruler, the Alake (Ukeje 2004). The women camped overnight at the palace singing songs with lyrics like:

> Idowu [Alake], for a long time you have used your penis as a mark of authority that you are our husband. Today we shall reverse the order and use our vagina to play the role of husband on you ... O you men, vagina's head will seek vengeance.[103]

The women "brandished their menstruation cloths" (Prince 1961, cited in Stevens 2006: 595) as the police attempted to stop the demonstration. The policemen ran away because of the belief that a lifetime of misfortune awaits any male who gets hit by a woman's menstrual cloth (Prince 1961, cited in Stevens 2006: 595). This act of political power through sexual power is not peculiar to women in Nigeria (Goheen 2000; Ardener 1975).

---

103 See "The Abeokuta Women's Revolt", URL: http://www.worldpulse.com/ node/19635 Accessed 14 December 2010.

This act is also used by women in the Niger Delta as a form of protest. This is a major contribution to the insurgency. For instance, about 600 Itsekiri women protested against Chevron/Texaco on 8 July 2002. The occupation of the oil facility lasted for 10 days (Ukeje 2004). The women "exposed their naked bodies, and most particularly their vaginas, to impose on oil company male dealers "social death" through ostracization, which was widely believed to lead to actual demise" (Turner and Brownhill 2004: 67). While this public performance may seem to provide another gendered spectacle for the entertainment of men and predominantly male journalists in the Delta, it allowed the women to enter into a rigorous negotiation process with the management of the oil company. The negotiation involved at least 26 demands (Turner and Brownhill 2004). These include construction of social amenities, jobs, monthly allowance for the elderly in the community, employment and so on. This was no mean achievement considering that the local women were fighting against the might of global capital (Turner and Brownhill 2004). Also, Niger Delta women succeeded in furnishing other movements around the world, particularly anti-war movements, with a new repertoire of protest—nudity (Turner and Brownhill 2004).

This type of protest by Niger Delta women abounds (Ukeje 2004) and enhances the urgency of the insurgency and the framing narrative of insurgents. Such protests often escalate the insurgency as militants are enraged about the treatment of their mothers, wives, sisters, friends and community members by the police. In one instance, a woman died in the hands of Shell police while participating in the 2002 protest (Turner and Brownhill 2004). This encourages insurgents in no small measure. They point to police brutality on unarmed women as evidence of the need to use violent tactics against the Nigerian state and big oil. The death of women and children in Gbaramatu Kingdom during the incessant bombing campaigns by JTF, for instance, is a major recruitment tool of the Camp 5 insurgent commander, Tom Polo.[104]

Women as combatants

Young women are also involved as "gunmen" in the insurgency, presumably participating in potentially lethal confrontations with security agencies. Interestingly, of all insurgents interviewed during the course of this study, only those from the NDPVF confirmed that women participate in active combat and also live at the creeks with male insurgents.[105] As other male-only creeks require, such women do not cook for insurgents and must have no sexual liaison with insurgents who are not off-duty. Anecdotal evidence suggests that such women are required to leave the camp as their menstruation approaches. As may be expected, insurgents offer very terse explanations for this and seem uncomfortable discussing it.

---

104   Interviewees 34, 35, 36. Ex-militants from Camp 5. Personal interviews, Obubra, Cross River state, August 2010.

105   Interviewee 15.

Women as emissaries

Women perform important roles as emissaries in the insurgency. Such women have varying relationships with insurgents. They may be insurgents' wives, girlfriends, sisters or mothers. Women's role as emissaries include dispatching messages, including oral and written messages as well as money from the creeks to insurgents' families and loved ones at home.

Second, women serve as informants to insurgents in the creeks. Insurgent groups deploy women to strategic locations such as oil infrastructure and JTF stations as spies. In this regards insurgents make use of women they "play with"[106] for these purposes. This suggests a soft form of prostitution, albeit a constructive one for which monetary gain is tangential. Such women deliberately befriend security guards, oil workers and JTF operatives for instrumental reasons. They are able to assess the number of personnel at the oil facility and JTF stations. They ascertain other vital intelligence such as what weapons or equipment the soldiers possess, their combat-readiness, how they run shifts and so on.

Third, women occasionally provide security for insurgents by accompanying them on the waterways when they are off duty or are on operations that do not require going in large groups or being armed. This provides easy passage on the waterways as the JTF operatives are aware that insurgents rarely allow women in their midst. Hence, as I learned during my fieldwork in Agge community, having a woman on board the boat was important to escape or minimize JTF scrutiny. This suggests that being in women's company makes men apparently appear harmless and not up-to-no-good.

Women's ability to perform these roles is enhanced by the security operatives' use of a gendered appeariential ordering (see Lofland 1973) or what Sacks (1972: 282–3) calls the "incongruity procedure", concerned with determining who looks suspicious or dangerous through a subjective assessment of individuals and matching of facial characteristics with public spaces.

Spiritual fortification

Women's role as the "power-house" in times of war is not a new phenomenon in the Delta. When King Koko led the Nembe-Brass people in the Akassa war against the Royal Niger Company and its nefarious trade policy, his "principal wife came out and showered brown chalk on him, completing the action by throwing the remainder on the canoe as a blessing" (Alagoa 1964: 98). The women were also customarily required to sleep in the yards and not the homes until the men returned from battle (Alagoa 1964). As demonstrated, for many insurgents at the creeks, women constitute Èèwò—abomination. Having sexual interactions with women is believed to destroy the protective cover offered by the gods. Hence, sexual acts with women at the creeks are considered Àgbedò—a forbidden act—as the charms

---

106   Interviewee 20.

insurgents adorn themselves with become impotent. Insurgents also believe that women's menstruation has a deleterious effect on their otherworldly charms.

Women are fundamental to the insurgency in this same area of spiritual fortification. In this regard, insurgents rely on post-menopausal or older women to perform religious rituals on them for protection against their enemies—security agents of the Nigerian state and oil corporations. As is applicable to nude protests, genital power is invoked by the women (Stevens 2006). In particular, women are believed to have a very efficacious "personal power" or *ashe* "explicitly associated with menstrual blood ... (which) intensifies as women mature, into and through childbearing—and beyond" (Stevens 2006: 594). Older women help insurgents to consecrate the physical and spiritual space of the creeks.[107] This is intended to ward off evil and ensure that the ground—a living being in many African communities' cosmologies—on which the creeks stand accepts the purpose for which it is being used: as an insurgent base. The elderly women pour libation on the creek grounds to appease the earth and the ancestors on behalf of their "sons", the insurgents. All elements of the weather are also entreated to cooperate with the insurgents.

The older women also bathe insurgents in spiritual concoction—varieties of liquids and gels—to make insurgents' bodies impenetrable to bullets and other dangers. In this case, both the women and insurgents become one in nudity. The older women perform this sacred exercise while nude just as the insurgents appear nude for the event. Insurgents occasionally receive lacerations on their heads, backs and below their eyes to make them spiritually agile and able to perceive and see things that are invisible to mere mortals.

Once these rituals are concluded, women become Èèwò at the creeks and to the insurgents. No woman experiencing menstruation or within the reproductive age bracket is allowed at the creeks. Her presence or more specifically her menstrual blood is believed to defile the grounds at the creeks and renders the fortification exercise null and void. Insurgents are not only prohibited from having sexual relationships with women, they are also barred from eating food cooked by women within the reproductive age.[108] Therefore, insurgents have designated cooks at the creeks who must be males.

One major insurgent commander, who has gone into retirement from active service, for instance, lives with an older woman who accompanies him everywhere he goes to ensure his protection. She tastes the food prepared by his wife before he eats it, as part of her duty. The insurgent leader had to request that the older woman leave the bedroom to allow him to speak alone with an interviewer. A few male insurgents, like Henry Bindodogha, come from Egbesu priestly backgrounds that guarantee that they have the requisite socialization and the spiritual fortitude to carry out these supposedly supernatural rituals.[109] The rarity of Bindodogha's spiritual prowess manifests in his having performed this role in at least four

---

107   Interviewee 19.
108   Interviewees 24 and 26.
109   Interviewee 19.

independent insurgent camps (including Camp 5 and NDPVF) before establishing the NDFF in Edo state.

Women's involvement in the insurgency functions on a number of micro and macro factors. At a macro level, women benefit from the patriarchal ideational infrastructure of the wider society about the "place" of women. This ideology constructs women as the "authentic inner country whose purity, sexuality, and traditional roles must be secured" (Baines 2003: 483). Therefore, their traditional roles do not extend to the trenches, as they are often construed as "natural peacemakers" (see Alison 2009: 212) or *victims* in armed conflicts, rather than rational actors and perpetrators of violence (see Meintjes 2007; Moser and Clark 2011; Mazurana, McKay, Carlson and Kasper 2002).

Consequently, patriarchy has had an unintended consequence of helping women who transgress societally enforced gender boundaries. Second, women's engagement with the insurgency receives considerable boost from the transgressiveness of femininity and womanhood. The idea of appearing "harmless" or "innocuous" is only one obvious example with a definite social constructionist but realistic underpinning. Third, insurgent women benefit from the chivalry displayed by security operatives. Security operatives' presupposition that somehow women are less dangerous than men helps the assignments of the women. Women can thus conceal weapons and bullets in food items without much scrutiny from security agents who often find the mere presence of the women titillating. Fourth, insurgent women also display incredible genius in executing their assignment. The sheer ingenuity, guile and cunning of the women help to deceive security operatives or divert their attention from performing their assigned duties.

A corollary to the point above is the use of sexual power by women. There are two major ways in which women's sexual power is used in the Delta insurgency. First, there is a soft form of prostitution, which entails sending women who are not enlisted in the insurgency to befriend oil workers and security operatives in order to gather vital information. Such women are encouraged to establish significant rapport with the targets beyond the supplier-client relationship. Greater emphasis is placed on building trust with the target than collecting valuables, such as money. It is difficult for male insurgents to perform these reconnaissance roles, as heterosexual orientation is still the norm among oil workers and JTF operatives as well as the wider society. This type of sexual power is well documented in several armed conflicts in Africa (Lahai 2010), Asia (McKay and Mazurana 2004) and South America (Ibanez 2001). Mazurana et al. (2001: 110) quote a Refugees International report (2002: 2) in which a 16 year old girl who participated in the conflict in the Democratic Republic of Congo (DRC) stated that:

> My sister and I joined the army because our parents were dead, and we had no jobs, I went to the front line many times, and my sister was sent to the enemy to be a spy. Girls were sent to be prostitutes and get information from the enemy. This is how my sister was used.

There seems to be an obfuscation of roles of female insurgents in the DRC case: some perform combat roles, while others serve as prostitutes to aid the insurgency. It is not clear if the roles are mutually exclusive. In the Delta insurgency, however, female insurgents do not serve as prostitutes. The services of non-insurgent women—for instance, professional prostitutes and girlfriends or sex partners of male insurgents—who are not part of the insurgency are engaged for spying, which often involves sexual services. This category of women—like all others within the reproductive age—is discouraged from visiting the creeks and has to rely on off-duty insurgents to pass on whatever information they may have.

The second type of sexual power exhibited by women in the Delta insurgency focuses on the spiritual fortification of insurgents as stated earlier. Apart from a handful of insurgents from Egbesu priestly backgrounds, this is the exclusive preserve of post-menopausal women.

Women also benefit from what may be called the *geographical excess* of Nigeria. With thousands of kilometers of land and waterways borders, policing the nooks and crannies of Nigeria is a gigantic task even under the maximum security state fostered during the years of military dictatorship. The Republic of Benin, Chad, Cameroon and Niger—all economically struggling states with tenuous adherence to the rule of law—share land borders with Nigeria. Incidents of illegal arms shipments occur at alarming rates. One of such was intercepted in the port City of Lagos in 2010, as stated earlier.[110] The propinquity of the Niger Delta to the Atlantic Ocean is a source of consternation to the JTF but logistic encouragement to the insurgents. As a corollary to the point above, the sheer ineptitude of the Nigerian state, demonstrated in the porous borders and multifarious governmental failures provide opportunities for insurgents. Finally, as demonstrated above, contrary to Ukeje (2004), women's involvement in the insurgency is neither indicative of nor contingent on the failure of men. Rather, it is an essential component in the insurgency spearheaded by men.

Women's participation in the insurgency comes at a huge cost. There is a growing body of evidence suggesting that although insurgent groups offer women greater opportunities for participation than conventional armies, the stereotypical roles often return when the conflict is over (Parasher 2009). Violent female actors challenge the patriarchal ideology of society yet the reality of such women in liberation struggles as Rajasingham-Senanayake (2004) suggests oscillates between victimhood and agency or "ambivalent empowerment" (Rajasingham-Senanayake 2001: 113). In the case of the Delta insurgency, female insurgents perform influential roles than the mainstream society accords them. However, the young women are perceived as wayward and unsuitable as wives and mothers. Their participation is also largely marginalized. When the federal government of Nigeria granted amnesty to all interested insurgents, for instance, women were among the last set of participants to go through the process of rehabilitation because male insurgents received priority

---

110   See "Arms importation—UN takes action", *Vanguard*, 6 December 2010. URL: http://allafrica.com/stories/201012060657.html Accessed 14 December 2010.

attention. Women's participation in the insurgency and the rehabilitation exercise seems devalued and relegated to the fringes.

This chapter provides an analysis of the metaphenomenon called MEND, the clearing house of the insurgency in the Delta. It focuses on the factors that have MEND a potent insurgency machine drawing on the new wars theoretical prism. These factors include its loose structure, widespread public sympathy, media relations, and the Delta terrain, among other factors. This chapter also theorizes and interrogates the creeks as the home territory of insurgents. It analyzes the social sorting taking place at the creeks and the operational significance and symbolism of the creeks. The role of women in the insurgency is also explicated in this chapter. Although scholarly attention has been overwhelmingly concerned with the supportive roles and non-violent protests of women, the Delta women are actively engaged in the on-going violent repertoires of protest in various capacities as gun-runners, combatants, mediators, emissaries of insurgents, source of spiritual fortification, among others.

Chapter 5
Framing the MEND Insurgency[1]

Introduction

The introduction of the framing approach as both a theoretical achievement and empirical imperative as well as response to criticisms of structuralist bias and negation of human agency gives considerable latitude to the political process framework. The rise of and attention to framing (see Snow and Byrd 2007; Westby 2002; Davenport and Eads 2001; Benford and Snow 2000; Snow and Benford 2000; Oliver and Johnston 2000; Johnston and Oliver 2000; Kubal 1998; Steinberg 1998; Skillington 1997; Nepstad 1997; Carroll and Ratner 1996; Mooney and Hunt 1996; Gamson and Meyer 1996; Diani 1996; Swart 1995; Čapek 1993; Gerhards and Rucht 1992; Snow, et al. 1986) is a major development in the political process framework in spite of its critics (see Benford 1997; Goodwin and Jasper 1999).

Frame analysis within the broader rubric of the political process paradigm is the maturation and intellectual distillation of several generations of work in the fields of cognitive psychology, hermeneutics, philosophy and phenomenology. Gregory Bateson (1972) first used the concept of *frame* in a manner consistent with its subsequent refinement by Ervin Goffman (1974) in his paper, "A theory of Play and Phantasy" in 1955. In his landmark *Frame Analysis*, Goffman (1974) explicates the notion of *frame* and maps out the model of frame analysis drawing on the likes of William James, W.I. Thomas, Alfred Schutz, Harold Garfinkel, John Austin, D.S. Schwayder, and Gregory Bateson among others.

A frame refers to a definition of a situation based on the principles of organization of the social and how an individual subjectively experiences events (cf. Goffman 1974: 10–11). Snow and Benford (1992: 137) describe a frame as "an interpretive schemata that simplifies and condenses the 'world out there' by selectively punctuating and encoding objects, situations, events, experiences, and sequences of actions within one's present or past environment". Implicit in the idea of frame is the recognition that societies are organized in certain ways[2]—as against many other possibilities—and the social world is experienced differentially by individuals. Consequently, individuals attend to the world in ways that are not totally their own making. Frame analysis, therefore, is an attempt to understand

---

1   A shorter version of this chapter was presented under the title "When 'Youth' *Take Over*: Oil Insurgency in Nigeria's Delta" at the XVII International Sociological Association (ISA) World Congress of Sociology, Gothenburg, Sweden, July 11–17, 2010.

2   Rather bizarrely, Goffman (1974) does not take up the contours of class or social inequality generally in his theoretical schemata, a fact he readily admits.

how the human experience is rendered intelligible at the actor level. It is an examination of how experience is organized (Goffman 1974: 11).

Social scientists in disciplines like psychology, communication and media studies, and political science among others have adopted the concept of frame (Benford and Snow 2000). Social movement scholars have also taken on the concept of frame to produce an increasingly sophisticated body of work, marking a refreshing upsurge of interest in the "cultural and ideational process" (Johnston 1995: 217) and the alchemy between social structure and agency. Frame analysis, in conjunction with resource mobilization and political opportunity—a theoretical trinity borne out of scholastic eclecticism and necessity—has become cardinal to analyzing the micromechanics of social movements and rudiments of mobilization by dissidents. Framing involves competing assessments, definitions and understandings of a given situation by political actors —activists, state agents, elites, journalists, media pundits and so on. Thus, a frame is *contentious* because it may not only challenge existing frames, but also radically differ from them (Benford and Snow 2000). These collective action frames (Benford and Snow 2000: 614) make participation in collective action meaningful (Klandermans 1997; Gamson 1992b).

This chapter draws on the framing literature to analyze how MEND frames its insurgent activities. It demonstrates how MEND portrays itself as part of a wider movement for social justice for the people of the Niger Delta compelled to adopt violent repertoires of protest. The framing strategies of MEND are analyzed cognizant that these strategies are not fixed but constitute on-going interactions between MEND on one hand and the Nigerian state as well as oil corporations on the other. MEND's engagement with the audience, which comprises Delta communities, the Nigerian populace, the media and international observers, is palpable throughout the analysis. The allegory of conscientiousness that the term *framing strategies* connotes is noted. However, the analysis does not mean to imply that all of the framing strategies discussed below were consciously fabricated by MEND. The analysis begins with the factors intrinsic to MEND's framing strategies to foreshadow how the frames resonate with the audience. Following Snow and Benford (1988), it demonstrates how MEND attends to the three core framing tasks in its struggle against the Nigerian petro-state and transnational oil corporations. MEND's *diagnostic framing* aimed at identifying the problem in the Delta and assigning blame and second, *prognostic framing*, which helps in suggesting solutions and mechanisms for solving the problem are interrogated. In addition, how MEND attends to the third core framing task *motivational framing*, which accomplishes the dyadic purpose of providing the raison d'être for the peremptoriness of action is explicated (see Snow and Benford 1988).

Factors Intrinsic to MEND's Framing Apparatus

This section examines aspects of MEND's framing that have contributed to ensure that MEND's collective action frames resonate with bystanders, allies, the public, and the media. While MEND makes efforts at laying out its framing strategies in a manner that would produce desired results, not all of the factors intrinsic to MEND's framing strategies were deliberately formulated. None the less, the following factors have furnished MEND's collective action frames with the requisite credibility and salience, which are fundamental to the resonance of collective action frames (see Benford and Snow 2000).

Religious overtones

The use of religious metaphors, symbols, references and parallels by insurgent groups is not uncommon in social movement mobilization (see McAdam 1982). MEND's collective action frames have strong religious overtones. Nigeria is a highly religious country with Christianity, Islam and many African Traditional religions (Iwuchukwu 2003). Thus, the country has several "religious publics" (Oha 2005: 21). Fundamentalist Christianity and militant Islam exist side by side in Nigeria. The human condition, in particular, has reconstructed the role of religion leading to what Oha (2005: 21) calls the "spiritualization of national issues". This concerns attempts at seeking otherworldly solutions to national malaise.

MEND has latched on to the fundamentalist Christian religious fervour in Nigeria. For instance, while announcing the formation of the Aaron Team on Monday 28 September 2009, Jomo Gbomo quoted the following passage of the Bible as a prelude to his e-mail message:

> *I have seen the way the Egyptians are oppressing them. So now, go. I am sending you to Pharaoh to bring my people the Israelites out of Egypt.* (Exodus 3: 9–10, italics in original)

The metaphorical reference to Pharaoh and the oppression of the children of Israel in Egypt is particularly striking. As those familiar with the Bible may know, the Israelites were slaves of Egyptians for over 400 years and attempts at allowing the people of Israel to go to the Promised Land were rebuffed by Pharaoh. Pharaoh and his army in the end perished in the Red Sea while in pursuit of the people of Israel.

By drawing on the tenets of the Bible, MEND constructs the Niger Delta people as a *Spiritual Jewish Nation,* a standard feature of the Judeo-Christian religion. They are also a numerically small people denied basic human/minority rights. This finds resonance particularly in Southern Nigeria. These religious overtones harp on the rough and totally misleading ethno-religious geographic delineation in Nigeria: North for Muslims, South for Christians. This works to MEND's advantage as the Muslim dominated Northern Nigeria is often perceived by many Southerners as benefitting from the prevailing political system in Nigeria.

Humanizing the insurgency

MEND's framing strategies resonate with the public because of its efforts at *humanizing* the insurgency even while carrying out its most violent repertoires. There are several ways in which MEND humanizes the insurgency. First, MEND presents its operatives as "normal" everyday people who detonate car bombs, kidnap oil workers and vandalize pipelines at great personal cost for the good of the people. For instance, after the March 15 2010 Warri bomb blast, MEND released a statement assuring that "all who participated in this operation, safely returned to their respective bases".[3] The said operation claimed eight lives, yet MEND considered it important to assure the public that its operatives—human beings like everyone else—were safe after the potentially dangerous mission they were given. Such a statement hails bystanders and allies to be aware that MEND's actions involve tremendous risks and human toil and blood.

Second, MEND positions itself as a compassionate revolutionary group rather than a collection of blood-thirsty political renegades. To this end, MEND ensures the safety of its kidnap victims. As stated earlier, no kidnap victims have died in MEND's custody to date (Okonta 2006). In the case of three abducted French nationals and another individual, whose nationality was not ascertained, MEND claimed that they were

> in negotiations with the abductors towards effecting a transfer of the men to the custody of MEND. When this is done, we will be in a better position to give further information about their state of health and the duration of their stay with us.[4]

The concern over the "state of health" of the victims is rather intriguing but quintessentially MEND.

Third, MEND quickly counters any suggestion that it demands ransom to release kidnap victims. Two Russian sailors Captain Boris Tersintsev and Chief Engineer Igor Shumik were kidnapped in Cameroon on 16 May, 2010 in one instance. MEND "categorically" denied that it was responsible for the kidnapping or that it demanded $1.5 million ransom. MEND said that it "can only prevail on the gang not to harm them in any way".[5] For MEND, it is important to differentiate itself from the "pirate gang" in Duala Cameroon and use this episode to demonstrate that it neither harms kidnapped persons nor makes monetary demands to release them. Doing any of these would be seen to damage its self-professed stance as a struggle against injustice even though it uses violent repertoires of protest. MEND

---

3   Jomo Gbomo e-mail statement (number 21) "Bomb blast Update", Monday 15 March 2010.

4   Jomo Gbomo e-mail statement (number 26) "Kidnapped French Citizens", Wednesday 22 September 2010.

5   Jomo Gbomo e-mail statement (number 23) "Two Russian Hostages", Saturday 12 June 2010.

also releases kidnap victims selectively on "humanitarian grounds". These actions are intended to preserve the credibility of MEND.

In addition, although many have died in the course of MEND's actions, including 12 people on 1 October 2010 in Abuja, MEND gives prior notice before any bomb blasts that may involve loss of lives. It is always quick to express remorse over the loss of lives. Before the Warri bomb blast, for example, MEND issued a statement: "In our usual effort to prevent the loss of innocent life, the Movement for the Emancipation of the Niger Delta advises the immediate evacuation of the Government House annex Warri and its immediate surroundings up to the Delta state Broadcasting Corporation." Furthermore, after the Abuja bomb blast, MEND stated that it "deeply regrets the avoidable loss of lives during our bomb attack" and said "our hearts go to the families of those killed who we know were sympathetic to our cause".[6] Not surprisingly, MEND blamed the "irresponsible attitude of the government security forces" for the loss of lives arguing that it had given a five-day notice.

Ridicule and Irony

MEND ridicules the Nigerian political establishment as a way of narrating its framing strategies. In one instance, MEND explains why it conducted a "warning strike" on 18 December 2009:

> While the Nigerian government has conveniently tied the advancement of talks on the demands of this group to a sick president, it has not tied the repair of pipelines, exploitation of oil and gas as well as the deployment and re-tooling of troops in the region to the presidents ill health. (Jomo Gbomo)[7]

The reference to a "sick president" stands out and strongly resonates among the public. Yar'Adua's state of health was a major issue during the presidential campaign. He was in fact rumored to have died in a German hospital before the elections. Yar'Adua earned the nickname "Baba-go-slow" among the Nigerian masses because of his perceived ineptitude, lack of vigor and poor health early in his administration (BBC 2008). President Umar Yar'Adua met with MEND's Aaron Team for dialogue on Saturday 14 November 2009. Yar'Adua's frail health deteriorated and he flew to Saudi Arabia for medical attention late in 2009 shortly after the meeting. The talks Yar'Adua initiated stalled as a result. MEND sarcastically wished the president "a speedy recovery" but warned that a "situation where the future of the Niger Delta is tied to the health and well-being of one man is unacceptable". This speech act ridicules the person of the president yet

---

6 Jomo Gbomo e-mail statement (number 28) "Abuja Bomb Attack", Saturday 2 October 2010.

7 Jomo Gbomo e-mail statement (number 12) "Warning Strike", Friday 18 December 2009.

highlights the need to de-privatize political power and decision-making in Nigeria. It is also tied to a popular joke among Nigerians about the political and biophysical vigor of the President.

Second, MEND reiterates the Nigerian state's penchant for corruption to buttress its framing strategies. The Nigerian state has earned a global image as an excessively corrupt and inept bureaucracy. MEND's framing strategies align with the cynicism of the public about the state and its agencies. Another opportunity to ridicule the Nigerian state emerged after a disarmament ceremony in Yenagoa on 22 August 2009. MEND alleged that the arms supposedly submitted by ex-militants belonged to the Cameroonian military. MEND called for an "independent international armament expert" and adherence to the "UN disarmament and weapons destruction protocol" to ascertain the origin of the weapons. "MEND has always called for a proper peace and disarmament process to avoid this sort of embarrassing situation where fraud, rent-a-crowd and monetary inducement is now a part of an amnesty charade".[8] The public requires little evidence to believe any of these allegations because the government lacks credibility. This is elaborated in Chapter 7.

Symmetry of MEND's demands and those of non-violent agitators

It is worth reiterating that some of MEND's demands such as, convocation of a sovereign national conference, and fiscal federalism or resource control, are not radical ideas in Nigeria. Several ethno-cultural groups like Afenifere in the South West and Ohaneze Ndigbo in the South East have also canvassed these objectives. Other progressive civil society organizations like human rights and environmental justice groups share many of MEND's concerns about the degradation of the Niger Delta ecology (Oboko 2010; Bassey 2009a, 2009b; Okaba 2005). Consequently, the symmetry of MEND's demands with those of non-violent actors aligns MEND's framing strategies with those of such legitimate organizations and the wider public. In particular, MEND's environmental justice frame (discussed in Chapter 6) receives considerable but unwitting support from groups like the Environmental Rights Action (ERA) (see Bassey 2009c, 2008). ERA, a non-violent, environmental justice SMO, that fights the "litany of Shell ecological violence" (Bassey 2009c: 98) in various communities in the Niger Delta.

For instance, in a series of oil spill incidents at the Diebiri-Batan community in Warri South local government, ERA's report "Shell pollutes (the) environment and harasses local people with military personnel" (Bassey 2009a: 63) is not fundamentally different from statements by MEND on similar incidents. ERA condemns the "extensive ecological damage" caused by "Shell's rusty and ill-maintained pipelines" while it is "spewing considerable quantity of crude oil into the surrounding environment" (Bassey 2009a: 63). For MEND, oil-producing

---

8   Jomo Gbomo E-mail statement (number 2) "Cameroon Army Weapons at Disarmament Ceremony", 5 September 2009.

communities as well as areas in the Niger Delta "without (oil) installations suffer the effects of gas flaring, spillages amongst others".[9] Like MEND, ERA also demands compensations for Niger Delta communities affected by environmental hazards produced by oil corporations (Bassey 2009c). Consequently, MEND's discursive construction of the environmental damage in the Niger Delta communities and its environmental justice frame align with those of non-violent SMOs.

The role of Jomo Gbomo in MEND's framing strategies

Social movement scholarship recognizes the importance of leadership in articulating an SMO's goals and strategies because it is an "agentic, interactive and discursive" process (Snow and Byrd 2007: 130). Saro-Wiwa was someone who combined intellect, significant personal wealth, and oratory with unqualified grassroots organizational finesse (Bob 2005) in articulating the frames of his SMO. MEND has recorded astounding success in articulating its frames. The elusive yet ubiquitous "Jomo Gbomo" is at the zenith of articulation of MEND's frames (see Courson 2009; Watts 2008a; Okonta 2006). Jomo Gbomo's agency is public relations coordination at its finest. Jomo Gbomo provides an intellectually engaging coherence to MEND's narrative practices through targeted, systematic, and propitious e-mail statements, press releases, occasional online question and answer sessions with journalists and a methodical intractable persona.

MEND discursively connects several ostensibly disparate events, historical moments and experiences to facilitate a strong narrative on the conditions of the people of the Niger Delta through Jomo Gbomo. This is a major objective of frame articulation (Snow and Byrd 2007). Included in this narrative is the British colonial experiment amalgamating the Northern and Southern Protectorates in 1914 that led to the formation of Nigeria, the socio-genesis of the oil industry in Nigeria, activities of neo-colonial rulers at the federal and state levels and the nature of the Nigerian rentier petro-state. Jomo Gbomo's statement "Bomb Alert in Abuja" on 1 October 2010 is a coercive study in frame articulation:

> Several explosive devices have been successfully planted in and around the venue by our operatives working inside the government security services ... There is nothing worth celebrating after 50 years of failure. For 50 years, the people of the Niger Delta have had their land and resources stolen from them. The constitution before independence which offered resource control was mutilated by illegal military governments and this injustice is yet to be addressed.[10]

This statement is inventive in several ways. First, the occasion was auspicious: the 50th Independence Day anniversary of Nigeria. The world was watching what spectacle the expensive event would highlight. Therefore, any insurgent act would

---

9   Jomo Gbomo (number 15).
10   Jomo Gbomo statement (number 27).

garner maximum attention globally. Second, the statement connects Nigeria's independence 50 years earlier to the appropriation of the lands of the peoples of the Niger Delta by the Nigerian state. It also underscores the questionable legitimacy of promulgators of the laws that vested resource control in the Nigerian state— "illegal governments"—and re-presents Niger Deltans as victims whose land has been "stolen". The statement also highlights state incompetence. More importantly, a very graphic picture of the injustice suffered by the Niger Delta people (injustice frame), loss of control over land and resources (environmental justice frame), tinkering of the Nigerian constitution by successive military administrations without redress (return to true democracy frame) and a willingness and capacity to plant "explosive devices" (imperative of violence frame) is painted.[11]

MEND's official statements are replete with words and phrases that elaborate its framing strategies as well as course of action. These include "slavery", "oppression", "injustice", "crime against humanity", "lawless governments in Nigeria", "hostilities", and "retaliatory actions", among others. These words accentuate MEND's goals and beliefs and are emblematic of the struggle (see Benford and Snow 2000). MEND purports to "end 50 years of slavery of the people of the Niger Delta by the Nigerian government, a few individuals and the western oil companies", and "burn down all attacked installations and no longer limit our attacks to the destruction of pipelines". It is also determined to "fight for our land with the last drop of our blood regardless of how many people the government of Nigeria and the oil companies are successful in bribing".[12]

This makes MEND's framing an important speech act. The role of speech acts—written and oral—in movement mobilization is fundamental to the success or failure of not only the framing strategies of an SMO's activities but also the entire cause (Lichbach 1995). Speech acts are important in generating interest in individuals otherwise unconcerned about a situation and ensuring that such persons remain committed to the cause (Davenport and Eads 2001; Lichbach 1995). Dissident rhetoric is *sine qua non* to explaining contentious politics (Snow and Benford 1992). Performatively sophisticated speech acts have contributed to the success of MEND's framing strategies. Jomo Gbomo's use of elegant prose, fine-grain metaphorical references and allegorical punctuations in issuing threats, conveying the standpoint of MEND, castigating its opponents and mobilizing dissidents appears persuasive. One example may suffice:

> The same government that is unable to maintain or repair the death traps called roads or the archaic rail facilities in Nigeria, is promising to build super highways and modern rail lines through the Niger Delta using funds it hopes to realise from divesting 19% of its shares in the joint ventures partnerships ... The Nigerian government in all its wisdom defines an oil producing community as

---

11   These master frames are expatiated in the next chapter.
12   Jomo Gbomo statement (number 6).

one where oil installations are sited; where oil is drilled or where flow stations and other facilities relevant to the continued bleeding of the Niger Delta ...

By this crude definition, the government will consider Kaduna state and other Northern states where pipelines pass through to the refinery in Kaduna, oil producing states. What gives this government the right to share the resources of the Niger Delta between its cronies in ceding this suggested 19 percent? The Nigerian government claims ownership of the Niger Delta where it dares not do so in the North. The land in the North belongs to Northerners while the Niger Delta belongs to the North as well. Communities in the Niger Delta without installations suffer the effects of gas flaring, spillages amongst others so why does the Nigerian government not consider these communities in all its planning? The answer is simple. This government is hoping it can divide the people of the Delta in order to govern and plunder the Niger Delta.[13]

Through this speech act, Jomo Gbomo performatively achieves many discursive goals. First, the speech act construes the Nigerian state as a failure. The "death traps called roads and archaic rail facilities" clearly conjures images of a failed state. This requires no introduction among the Nigerian public; it is an experiential reality. Second, the ridicule in Gbomo's tone is obvious with the mocking of the idea of "super highways". Third, this statement also diagnoses the problem of the Niger Delta. In fact, three of the loci of problems—oil corporations, Northern Nigeria and the Nigerian state—come to the fore in this statement. Blaming Northern Nigeria arguably leaves the South unscathed or untainted in the furtherance of the struggle. Hence, a line is drawn between those considered opponents and perceived allies.

In addition, the notion of the "bleeding of the Niger Delta" presents a graphic imagery of the conditions of the Niger Delta people in the mind's eye of the reader. The audience is vividly beckoned to take a glimpse at and share in the problems of the Niger Delta people: "the effects of gas flaring and spillages". Lastly, the speech act is also a direct call for unity among the peoples of the Niger Delta: the government can only "govern and plunder the Niger Delta" if it succeeds in creating division among the people. This suggests a homogeneous and monolithic ethnic collectivity in the Niger Delta which is, as is clear by now, non-existent.

Diagnosing the Problem with the Niger Delta

MEND has left little to the imagination in terms of its diagnosis of the problem in the Delta and assignment of blame. Blame assignment is a fundamental element of problem diagnosis that helps to identify the cause of a problem (Snow and Benford 1992). MEND and its subsidiaries situate the locus of the problem in the Delta and

---

13   Jomo Gbomo e-mail statement (number 15). "Ceasefire called off", Friday 29 January 2010.

blame on four major entities. These are the *British colonialist expansionism* and its offspring the *Nigerian state, Northern Nigeria, transnational oil corporations* and the *political elite in the Delta*. These four entities are examined to understand how MEND holds them responsible for the problem in the Niger Delta.

British colonial expansionism and its offspring the Nigerian state

> There was a mistake in 1914, a crime against all the nations when we were all forced, conscripted to become what is called Nigeria, and in terms of International Conventions in accordance with the law of Treaties, there is no such thing as Nigeria. (Leader of the NDPVF, Asari Dokubo in Aliu and Akpan-Nsoh 2009)[14]

British imperialist overlords amalgamated the Northern and Southern Protectorates to form Nigeria in 1914. Independence was granted to the fledgling state in 1960. Many militants, activists and political elites believe that the establishment of the Nigerian state without the explicit consent of its constitutive part is responsible for the trouble in the Delta. Similarly, the manner in which the Nigerian state has been managed over the years makes many to question its legitimacy. The marginalization in the polity is seen as inherent in the foundation of the country. For instance, Asari Dokubo whose former lieutenants populate the echelon of MEND argues that 'Ijaw leaders never signed any agreement to be part of Nigeria', therefore, "there would be no peace until the mistake of 1914 is corrected" (see Aliu and Akpan-Nsoh 2009). Dokubo restates this view in a personal interview. Asari Dokubo calls for "total dismantling of Nigeria". He argues that "Nigeria must be destroyed at all cost because it is evil, it is fraudulent. It was brought into being by fraud … Nigeria is not a country, it should be dismantled, it is a fraud".[15]

Official statements issued by Jomo Gbomo also indicate where MEND ensconces the locus of blame. MEND has persistently aimed to "end 50 years of slavery of the people of the Niger Delta by the Nigerian government, a few individuals and the western oil companies once and for all".[16] The number of years given for the "slavery" of the Niger Delta people is exactly the number of years of Nigeria's independence from Britain.

Transnational oil corporations

Why oil corporations receive blame for the Delta's problem requires little iteration. One major case may suffice. A 13-year law suit was settled out of court in June 2009 when Shell Petroleum Development Corporation (SPDC) agreed

---

14   Aliu, Alemma-Ozioruva and Inem Akpan-Nsoh. 2009. "Panel visits disarmament centre, Asari Dokubo faults amnesty", URL: http://news.onlinenigeria.com/ templates/?a=5516&z=12 Accessed 9 June 2010.

15   Interviewee 11.

16   Jomo Gbomo e-mail statement (number 6) Wednesday 7 October 2009.

to pay a compensation of $15.5 million (US) to the families of the Ogoni Nine; environmental and minority rights activists hanged by the General Sani Abacha regime in 1995.[17] Shell had faced charges of complicity in the deaths of the activists for allegedly providing weapons and other logistical support to military squads that killed protesting civilians.[18]

Oil corporations operating in the Niger Delta are generally seen as extensions of or at a minimum, partners of the Nigerian state in the problems of the Delta region (Saro-Wiwa 1992). Oil majors enjoy state protection, are perceived as "government's eyes", and since the Nigerian "government is like a spirit ... (and) the only presence of the government you see are the oil companies",[19] therefore, such companies are blamed as well. Oil corporations and their staff are believed to "breathe life" to the Nigerian state.[20]

Beyond perceptions, issues of environmental degradation in the Delta directly implicate oil corporations. As of 14 June 2010, for example, Shell had 268 oil spill sites it was planning to clean up (Ezigbo 2010). In addition, oil corporations are blamed for the high level of unemployment in the Delta. Insurgents and activists believe that oil workers are brought in from overseas or major cities like Lagos and Abuja rather than employing Niger Delta people. Practices such as "ghosting" work slots—paying bribes to influential persons rather than hiring actual human beings—in connivance with corrupt community leaders also contribute to unemployment and poverty in the Delta.[21]

For MEND, oil companies are allies of the Nigerian state who are "interested in buying off" the lands of the people of the Delta without due consultation.[22] Therefore, apart from assigning blame to oil corporations, MEND explicitly identifies the "Nigerian oil industry, the Nigerian armed forces and its collaborators" as targets of its guerrilla-style attacks.[23]

In particular, MEND insurgents treat the presence of Shell in oil producing communities in the Delta as problematic. The Nigerian state was forced to ask Shell to leave Ogoniland following the 1995 executions.

It is no exaggeration to suggest that insurgent actions against the oil industry in Nigeria are a war principally against Shell. Other oil companies like Total and Chevron are blamed for the same reasons as Shell, but attacks on them are almost an afterthought. For instance, while promising more attacks on oil facilities after the Warri bomb blast on 15 March 2010, MEND states that it "will spread out to

---

17   See BBC. 2009. "Shell settles Nigeria death cases", URL: http://news.bbc.co.uk/2/hi/africa/8090493.stm Accessed 3 November 2010. Shell did not accept any liability for the executions.

18   Interviewee 14. Ken Saro Wiwa (Jr.).

19   Interviewee 20.

20   Interviewee 11.

21   Interviewee 20.

22   Jomo Gbomo e-mail statement (number 6) Wednesday 7 October 2009.

23   Jomo Gbomo e-mail statement (number 7). Thursday 15 October 2009.

companies such as Total which have been spared in the past".[24] A few speculations can be made about the almost singular focus on Shell. First, Shell is the oldest oil company in Nigeria. Shell D'Arcy made the first discovery of oil in Nigeria in August 1956. Second, Shell continues to dominate oil production in Nigeria. Therefore, any disruption in Shell's production capacity will be significant on the economy by default. Third, Shell has somehow earned a reputation as a parallel government in Nigeria. On one hand, Shell sometimes provides social facilities for oil producing communities, as part of its social responsibility. In Agge community, Bayelsa state, for example, Shell built a block of classrooms and a town hall. On the other hand, the Nigerian government is believed to represent the whims of Shell. Therefore, the government is perceived as kowtowing to Shell. The fact that well-armed military personnel and/or stern mobile police officers heavily guard Shell offices only serves to confirm the widespread opinion. The rest of the argument rests on the corruption level in not only government circles but also the oil industry.

Fourth, leadership failure ensures that the only semblance of "government" that people in several oil producing communities see are oil facilities of Shell. Fifth, as a corollary to the previous point, Shell's attempts to provide basic amenities, such as clean water and electricity to its staff in their gated official quarters alienates communities who lack these services. Lastly, insurgents find the foreign ownership of Shell problematic. While indeed most oil corporations in Nigeria are foreign-owned, what insurgents find most appalling about Shell is that it is partly British-owned.[25] For Deltans, this worsens the situation, as the British largely denied them access to legitimate trade in the colonial times (Alagoa 1964) and were responsible for conscripting the Niger Delta into the Nigerian project in 1914. Thus, Shell is seen as the beneficiary of the injustice of its British forebears.

Northern Nigeria

The Niger Delta Volunteer Force (NDVF) formed in 1966 was the first insurgency by people from the Niger Delta against the Nigerian state as stated earlier. Present-day insurgents draw inspiration from the NDVF as may be obvious by now. It is quite remarkable that the assassination of Nigeria's Prime Minister Sir Abubakar Tafawa Balewa on January 15 1966 was one of the major reasons why Adaka Boro hastened to form a secessionist group. This is interesting because Sir Balewa was a politician of Northern extraction and alongside Northern region Premier, Ahmadu Bello, was the leader in the Northern People's Congress, which had the majority in parliament. When news of Balewa's demise became public knowledge, Adaka Boro states:

---

24   Jomo Gbomo e-mail statement (number 20). Monday 15 March 2010.
25   Interviewee 11.

I knew the day had dawned on the Niger Delta. If we did not move then, we would throw ourselves into perpetual slavery. *The only protector of the Ijaws, Sir Balewa was gone.* He and his party were the only people that had consideration for our presence in Nigeria. (Boro 1982: 94–5, emphasis added)

Boro (1982) believed that the North was the best ally of the Niger Delta in the ethnically organized political era of the 1960s. Ijaw peoples were minorities in the Western and Eastern regions. Adaka Boro held the Eastern region populated by the Igbos and the Western region dominated by Yorubas in suspicion, if not outright disdain (see Boro 1982). This was due to several structural issues such as inequitable distribution of employment and personal experiences, particularly in an Eastern university where he lost the student union presidential elections.

However, the diagnosis of the problem in the Niger Delta by today's insurgents takes a fundamentally different trajectory from the insurgency led by Adaka Boro. MEND bifurcates Nigeria into an essentialized dichotomy in its framing—a parasitic north and a plundered south. MEND's official statements are unequivocal in asserting that Northern Nigeria is responsible for the region's trouble. Two examples provide ample evidence that MEND blames the northern part of Nigeria for the woes of the Delta.

First, following the failed Christmas day (2009) attempted bombing of Delta flight 253 by Umar Farouk Abdulmutallab, a 23-year-old man from a wealthy family in the northern part of Nigeria, Jomo Gbomo released a statement two days later claiming that:

It should by now be evident that the threat to world peace will not emerge from the Niger Delta, a region agitating for justice as is acknowledged by every right thinking human being, but from the *Islamic extremist northern part of Nigeria covertly supported by its elite who assume leadership of Nigeria to be the birthright of this region.*

This attempted act of terrorism by this northern Islamic extremist does not come as a surprise to any Nigerian. *For decades, Christians have been murdered and raped in the north of Nigeria with impunity. No northern Muslim has ever been brought to book for the thousands of Christians killed in this region.* Northern Nigeria is fertile ground for international terrorism.

The Nigerian government has persistently turned a blind eye to Islamic extremists coming from Northern Nigeria, choosing instead to focus and waste its resources on military hardware and troop deployment in the Niger Delta.

The government of Nigeria which unfortunately has been dominated by the north since independence has bred such undesirable elements under false pretexts with the hope of creating a reserve army to counter agitation in the south and other parts of Nigeria.

In spite of this embarrassment to the nation, the government will not re-direct its
military to the North, neither will the rights of these violent people be trampled
as is the case in the Niger Delta.[26] (emphasis added)

Capitalizing on the failed bombing incident by a Northerner, Jomo Gbomo's use
of terms such as "Islamic extremist Northern part of Nigeria", "Northern Nigeria
is a fertile ground for international terrorism" (hence, the Niger Delta does not
breed terrorists), "undesirable elements", "these violent people", "embarrassment
to the nation" among others is a major speech act. These terms purport to delineate
MEND's opposition from its allies. It is worth noting that MEND equates the
Nigerian state with Northern rulership. Similarly, MEND equates Northern Nigeria
with Islamic fundamentalism—a major source of global concern post-9/11.

Second, in another official statement on Monday 15 March 2010 warning
of imminent detonation of bombs at the Delta state government House annex in
Warri, Jomo Gbomo was particularly emphatic in identifying *oil corporations,
northerners* and *governors of the Niger Delta states* as those responsible for the
woes of the peoples of the Delta:

> *The lands of the people of the Niger Delta was stolen by the oil companies and
> Northern Nigeria with the stroke of a pen ... The Niger Delta has been partitioned
> into oil blocks which have been distributed amongst mostly Northerners while
> indigenes of the Niger Delta can barely survive.* One such example being
> General T.Y. Danjuma.
>
> It is common knowledge that no southerner can lay claim to an inch of land
> in the North so *why should we continue to talk as the occupation of our land
> and theft of our reources (sic) by the oil companies and Northern Nigeria
> persists?*[27] (emphasis added)

The blame directed at Northern Nigerians like General T.Y Danjuma deserves
further elucidation. Former Chief of Army Staff, General Danjuma, served as
minister of defence during the government of Chief Olusegun Obasanjo, his
colleague in the army and fellow retired General. Danjuma announced at a meeting
in February 2010 the formation of the T.Y Danjuma Foundation with a personal
donation of $100 million in order to help the poor (Editorial, *Daily Champion* 25
February 2010).[28] He stated that his oil block allocation in Rivers state had fetched
him a major fortune:

---

26   Jomo Gbomo e-mail statement (number 13). Sunday 27 December 2009.

27   Jomo Gbomo e-mail statement (number 20). Monday 15 March 2010.

28   *Daily Champion.* 2010 (Editorial, Feb. 25). Danjuma's $500 million largesse',
URL: http://allafrica.com/stories/201002260528.html Accessed 9 June 2010.

At my age, I am 72 years now, what will I be doing with such money, $500million? ... If I put it in the bank, these people will steal it and I don't want my children to start fighting over money when I die, so I decided to commit 100 million dollars of the money to philanthropic activities that will help lift Nigerian society.

General Danjuma's unusually matter-of-fact comment drew both commendations and criticisms from many Nigerians. More importantly, it was another consciousness-raising moment about the fabulous wealth non-Deltans were making in the region. Danjuma's remarks only fuelled the suspicions Delta insurgents have often emphasized about the disproportionate benefits Northerners receive from the federation. Asari Dokubo, for example, shares Gbomo's view arguing that all key positions in President Yar'Adua's cabinet were given to the North. For Dokubo, the blame is reposed in the "arrogance" of the Nigerian rulers "as represented by those who were the direct beneficiaries of the stolen sovereignty of the people by the British, the Hausa–Fulani ruling Oligarchy in the North".[29]

As articulated in the case of the Nigerian National Petroleum Corporation (NNPC) appointments below, the commandeering of coveted positions in government establishments to officials of northern origin creates serious disaffection in other parts of the country. Blaming "northerners" is not simply a strategic framing device superficially adopted by MEND for instrumental purposes; minorities in the Delta strongly hold this as a self-evident fact. This makes it an effective framing device for MEND. Although other major ethnic groups have been beneficiaries of Nigeria's precarious winner-take-all political game, as argued below, MEND largely de-emphasizes this important caveat.

However, in spite of its resonance among many people in the Delta and southern Nigeria, blaming a supposedly monolithic entity called the "North" or "Northerners" is reductionist at the very least. While indeed military men and civilians of Northern extraction have ruled for nearly 40 of Nigeria's 52 years of independence and have arguably ensured a skewed distribution of patronage among their families and friends from different parts of the country in a neo-patrimonial atmosphere, the reality is that Northern Nigeria is a major victim of the mismanagement of the country by northerners and southerners. From all available social indicators—education, healthcare, industrialization to name a few—Northern Nigeria lags behind the South and the *talakawa* (the poor) of the north are dangerously deprived. The north has the highest incidence of poverty among all the poorest 10 states (out of Nigeria's 36 states). On the other hand, all the 10 states with the lowest incidence of poverty are southern states (Mohammed 2010).[30] This fact was reiterated in 2007 by former governor of the Central Bank,

---

29 Interviewee 11.

30 Mohammed, Sani. 2010 (21 January). "Why are we so poor in Northern Nigeria?" URL: http://www.leadershipnigeria.com/columns/views/issues/11080-why-are-we-so-poor-in-northern-nigeria Accessed 9 June 2010.

Professor Charles Soludo.[31] A Northern Senator[32] describes the situation in vivid terms:

> There are a lot of crises in the North today. There have been Boko Haram, Kala Kato, and the present Jos crisis. *The north is becoming the problem of the country* and it is the north that should come together and solve the problem. Apart from the issue of begging, there are other problems that are hitherto not known or associated with the North, but kidnapping is even here in the North. Our education has not only gone done (sic) but has also deteriorated; there is unemployment everywhere and no sign of improvement. (Awolusi 2010, emphasis added)[33]

Political elites in the Niger Delta

The political class in the Delta is blamed for the region's problem for several reasons. These include mismanagement of federal allocations, perceived pandering to the federal government's whims and caprices rather than constituting a unified force, and failure to develop the region. For instance, MEND's statement issued on Monday 15 March 2010 states that the "governors of the Niger Delta are shameless and visionless stooges who are more concerned with looting their state treasuries and seeking a second term in office, even against the wishes of their people".[34]

In 1999, Niger Delta states received N15.8 billion, in the year 2000, N108.6 billion, 2001, N168 billion and 2007, N564.4 billion (*Saturday Tribune*, 5 July 2008 p. 5). There is very little in the Delta to show for these sums of money. For instance, houses were yet to have a proper numbering system as of 2009 in Yenagoa, the capital of Bayelsa state. Some of the leaders from the region, such as former governors of Delta and Bayelsa states, James Ibori and Depreiye Alamieyeseigha respectively, have faced (or have been convicted of) charges of corruption involving huge sums of money.

---

31   As might be expected, Soludo's comments—uncharacteristic of such a well-placed government official—attracted political firestorm and there were widespread concerns that they might have contributed to the refusal of the Yar'Adua administration to grant him a second term in office.

32   Ladan Shuni, Vice Chairman of the Board of Trustees of Arewa Consultative Forum (ACF), a Northern socio-cultural group.

33   Awolusi, Bunmi. 2010 (Jan. 28). "North is becoming Nigeria's problem, says Arewa", URL: http://nigerianbulletin.com/2010/01/28/north-is-becoming-nigeria%E2%80%99s-problem-says-arewa-the-nation/ Accessed 9 June 2010.

34   Jomo Gbomo e-mail statement (number 20). Monday 15 March 2010.

MEND's Prognostic Framing

MEND's diagnosis of the Niger Delta problem comes with suggestions of mechanisms for solving the Delta problem. The convocation of a sovereign national conference, control of resources by the Delta people, and cleaning up oil spills to ensure reduction of environmental degradation are some of MEND's proffered solutions, as stated in the section on the demands of MEND. MEND also wants payment of compensation to the Niger Delta people for damage done to their health, environment, livelihood and quality of life. While these panaceas have become standard since at least Adaka Boro, how MEND aims to make these solutions possible is the main issue at stake. For instance, Asari Dokubo, leader of NDPVF asserts that the

> message the Nigerian state will understand is *the message of power*. The message of the people on the street and the creeks that will *take over our oil installations* that will take over our oil pipelines. That is the message the Nigerian state will understand. That is the message we can't compromise. And Shell will understand.[35] (emphasis added)

The "message of power" refers to the use of force or violence to jolt the state into listening to the people's grievances and help ensure self-determination for the Delta people. On its part, MEND has been ruthlessly efficient in implementing its proposed solution to the Delta problem—violence-induced incapacitation of the petroleum industry in Nigeria—owing to the failure of the state to ensure equitable distribution of resources to those on whose land crude oil flows. MEND has also demonstrated a willingness to engage in dialogue as shown at the meeting in Abuja of MEND's representative, the Aaron Team, with the federal government on 14 November 2009.

Nevertheless, MEND is not oblivious to its operating environment. MEND released a statement warning against the "harassment and intimidation of ex-fighters and innocent communities" three days after the Aaron Team met the federal government. MEND alleged that the JTF had gone in search of illegal weapons at Kula community in Akuku-Toru Local Government Area of Rivers state. Jomo Gbomo condemned the targeting of the home of a former MEND commander, Christian don Pedro that was "extensively destroyed" in the military action. MEND carried out a "warning strike" on a Shell/Chevron crude pipeline in Abonemma, Rivers state on 19 November 2009. MEND went back to the trenches on Friday, January 8, 2010 by attacking the Chevron Makaraba pipeline in Delta state. The use of violence by MEND is examined in greater detail shortly.

---

35   Nigeria's Oil War, 2005. Video documentary produced by Mark Corcoran for the Australian Broadcasting Corporation.

MEND's Motivational Framing and Mobilization of Insurgents

Insurgents do not merely elect tactics; they also provide motivational framing devices for inspiring their constituents to action and self-sacrifice. MEND's motivational framing is an extremely emotive set of speech performances. MEND motivates insurgents in several ways. First, the mundane, everyday lived experiences of the people constitute the tools for insurgent mobilization. Consequently, MEND emphasizes the poverty of the Niger Delta people, the environmental degradation in their communities and its consequences—the destruction of the people's livelihood like fishing and farming. MEND emphasizes that the Niger Delta people "suffer the effects of gas flaring, spillages amongst others",[36] a condition that is believed not to be part of the life world of many of those enjoying the Niger Delta wealth.

Second, MEND motivates insurgents by references to the sacrifice of revered heroes of the people like Adaka Boro and Ken Saro-Wiwa. This is an emotive but widely appealing issue. Third, MEND urges its constituency that they have the right to be angry about their social conditions and take action over "stealing" of crude oil in the Niger Delta by the Nigerian state, which they argue has been "acting like a victor over a conquered people".[37] Insurgents and supporters are informed that they are not criminals by taking what belongs to them. They are encouraged to believe that the real thief is the federal government of Nigeria and the oil corporations. Therefore, MEND encourages rebellion, sabotaging oil infrastructure, and illegal oil bunkering. One of MEND's commanders, Boyloaf (Victor Ben Ebikabowei) provides the rationale behind targeting of the economic power—oil infrastructure—of Nigeria:

> I believe the economy is the power. Like you may have known, I don't believe in fighting human beings, I believe in crumbling the economy. On my way crumbling the economy, if any military man comes across me and tries to stop me, I mean those people will kiss their graves. My bullet, nozzle is always targeted at flow stations, pipelines, etc. I don't believe in fighting human beings. *Before we formed MEND, our people were fighting, but it was a war between Ijaw and Itsekiri, that was not the Niger Delta struggle.*[38] (emphasis added)

Shifting the struggle from internecine conflicts between Ijaws and their neighbors the Itsekiris and Urhobos is a major accomplishment of the MEND insurgency. Although the Warri crisis led to arms proliferation and provided the first major installment of arsenal for the current trajectory of the struggle as discussed earlier,[39] MEND insurgents encourage their supporters to focus on crippling Nigeria's oil

---

36   Jomo Gbomo e-mail statement (number 15) Friday 29 January 2010.
37   Jomo Gbomo e-mail statement (number 15) Friday 29 January 2010.
38   Cited in Courson (2009: 18) in an interview with Sunday Vanguard, May 25 2008.
39   Interviewees 15, 19, 20 and 24–38, 41–2.

infrastructure rather than attacking fellow marginalized peoples in the Delta. The effect of this is that an Urhobo man, for instance, serves as intelligence director of a predominantly Ijaw insurgent group, the NDFF, an affiliate of MEND.[40] While animosities and mistrust persist among these linguistically divergent groups, MEND has been able to fabricate a marriage of necessity akin to the famous aphorism—the enemy of my enemy is my friend. Although MEND is essentially an Ijaw-led insurgency, the newfound sense of unison and collective struggle—albeit precarious—among the Ijaws and their neighbors harnesses the human power, resources and effervescence of violence they once directed against themselves to the Nigerian state.

This chapter examines the factors intrinsic to MEND's framing strategies such as its religious overtones, which creates an essentialized division between the Muslim North and Christian South and the use of speech acts to ridicule the Nigerian state and its key officials among others. These factors demonstrate how MEND strategically construes itself and its audience in the struggle. They also indicate the various constituencies MEND designates as either allies or opponents. In addition, the chapter draws on Snow and Benford (1992) to explicate how MEND conducts its diagnostic, prognostic and motivational framing. The analysis indicates that MEND blames four major entities for the problem of the Delta. These are the British colonial expansionist project that led to the creation of the Nigerian state, transnational oil corporations, Northern Nigeria and Niger Delta political elites. MEND externalizes the causal factors in assigning blame for the human and environmental crisis in the Delta, while simultaneously ensuring that long-standing ethnic feuds among Delta minorities are de-emphasized in favor of concerted action against the Nigerian state and oil corporations. Overall, this chapter foreshadows the master frames of MEND. The next chapter explains how MEND's diagnostic, and prognostic framing of the Delta malaise coalesce into a number of *master frames*. These master frames serve as a discursive strategy as well as a potent mobilization apparatus for MEND.

---

40   Interviewee 20.

Chapter 6

Master Frames in the MEND Insurgency

Introduction

Collective action frames purport to achieve a number of goals (Snow and Benford 1988: 198). First, challengers manufacture a simplistic (and sometimes caricatured)[1] depiction of a complex social reality. This is indispensable in order for the audience to make sense of the situation the way the framers desire. Second, collective action frames help to mobilize aggrieved or concerned people to a cause. Third, they help to draw the attention and ultimately gain the support of bystanders, who could otherwise be no more engaged than epicurean pedestrians. Fourth, collective action frames are designed to work against opponents of a movement (Snow and Benford 1988: 198; see Benford and Snow 2000).

The framing architecture that MEND employs to provide the motivation necessary not only for the raison d'être of its cause but also the peremptoriness of action is of sociological and practical concern. MEND's master frames are accentuated with a view to engaging with the minutiae of how MEND mobilizes dissidents for spectacular insurgent acts and how it "markets" its rebellion (see Bob 2005). As Snow and Benford (1992: 138) argue, "master frames are to movement-specific collective action frames as paradigms are to finely tuned theories". Master frames provide the "grammar" to identify and arrange disparate situations into an intelligible form (Snow and Benford 1992: 138).

It is imperative to state a fundamental caveat to this part of the analysis: explicating how MEND's master frames are directly used to mobilize dissidents is challenging because their activities are considered illegal by the state and thus, shrouded in secrecy. For instance, there have been cases where representatives of MEND even deny the existence of MEND. Ike Okonta (2006: 10) had an

---

1   The right-wing TEA party movement in the US, which gained acclaim in the summer of 2009 and 2010, readily comes to mind. In opposing a proposed healthcare legislation, the movement claimed that if passed the bill would ensure that health care insurance premiums would increase, seniors would be made to face a death panel when sick, and bureaucrats would select doctors for the people. The movement also argued that the bill signified a government take-over of the lives of the people and the end of freedom as Americans knew it. Of course, none of these was correct, but certainly effectual in ratcheting support for the movement and making the legislation politically toxic. The bill was passed on March 21 2010 by a slim majority of 219 to 212 votes. While not presupposing that an acerbic disdain for facts necessarily accompanies framing as manifested in the TEA movement, the import of this example is in how the movement rendered a very complicated bill (erroneously) simplistic for the mobilization of its constituency.

interesting encounter with a MEND representative in Warri, Delta state. Surprised at the operative's calm demeanor, youth and sophistication, Okonta asked: "Are you the MEND leader?" The young man responded:

> But exactly what do you understand by MEND? ... There is no such thing as MEND. What I know is that there are armed youth in the creeks who say they have had enough of the oil companies' double standards and are determined to put to an end the exploitation of their people by Shell, Chevron and the Federal Government. (Okonta 2006: 10)

Similarly, while conducting research for this book, I suspected that one of the political activists I interviewed was a member of MEND. He argued during the interview that "kidnapping for the sake of advancing the struggle is very proper" as a way of putting an end to the "bio-terrorism" of oil corporations. When I asked him about my suspicions, he stated with a chuckle that "I will neither confirm nor deny that". He added emphatically that "MEND chose to be anonymous, to be faceless. Anyone who says there is no MEND is as good as saying there is no air. Can you see the air?" The half-hearted denial of the existence of MEND encountered by Ike Okonta (2006) or refusal to confirm membership is part of the strategies that make MEND appear invincible.

Consequently, unlike the level of publicity and documentation Saro-Wiwa provided which served the triadic purpose of mobilizing MOSOP's constituents, legitimizing the SMO and the movement it represented in the eyes of international NGOs and greatly enhanced academic analysis (see Okonta 2008; Bob 2005, 2002), apart from the e-mails from MEND's spokesperson, Jomo Gbomo, no such pamphlets, articles, and publications are produced by MEND. This makes the task of understanding MEND more daunting. Therefore, the analysis draws on MEND's official e-mails, as well as interviews and focus group discussions with 42 ex-insurgents at the rehabilitation center established by the federal government of Nigeria in Obubra, Cross River state. As demonstrated below, more than any other sources, the official statements from MEND articulate the coalition's standpoint and serve as the clearest indication of how it wants allies, opponents and bystanders to understand its insurgent acts.

There are five major master frames in the MEND insurgency. These are the *imperative of violence master frame*, the injustice frame (Gamson et al. 1982; McAdam 1982), the human/minority rights frame (Bob 2005), environmental justice frame (Čapek 1993), and the return to democracy frame (Noonan 1995). These master frames are analyzed with a view to understanding how MEND uses them as discursive strategies to mobilize dissidents and appeal to bystanders. The following analysis builds upon over two decades of scholarly work on framing and master frames (Gamson et al. 1982; McAdam 1982; Snow, Rochford, Worden and Benford 1986; Snow and Benford 1992; Capek 1993; Swart 1995; Noonan 1995; Mooney and Hunt 1996; Benford 1997; Steinberg 1998; Benford and Snow 2000; Snow and Byrd 2007). While five master frames are identified in the MEND insurgency, the aim is not to establish artificial boundaries in MEND's framing cosmos. Rather, the various framing strategies operate concurrently and often glide into one another. The concordance of these framing accoutrements speaks to MEND's frame articulation and elaboration—the assemblage of seemingly disparate experiences and events into a coherent whole (Benford and Snow 2000).

The Imperative of Violence Frame

The metanarrative of the MEND insurgency is what may be termed the *imperative of violence master frame*. The imperative of violence frame is a fundamental characteristic of a *weltanschauung* of violence. Within this ambiance, violence is not merely a means to an end as the economies of war thesis presupposes, but becomes symbolic self-expression. As stated in Chapter 4, MEND insurgents adopt tactics that generate shock and awe in the opposition and bystanders. MEND insurgents set out to cut an image of frightening invincibility: The masks, intricate costume, labyrinthically worn amulets, war songs, dance, and performatively flaunted AK47 weapons are intended to instill fear and warn of looming danger and the possibility of violence.

Insurgents in the Niger Delta region are clear about consciously electing violent repertoires of protest. Even proponents of non-violent protest believe that "if you cannot kill people, if you cannot carry gun, the government will not listen to you".[2] Therefore, the episodes of kidnapping of oil workers, attacks on oil installations and disproportionate reprisal attacks by state forces constitute worrisome but unsurprising events in the unfolding real life drama set in the Niger Delta. The result is a pervasive state of disorder and insecurity conceptualized as "petro-violence" (Watts 2001; see also Zalik 2004).

Violence and violent resistance are commonplace in the Niger Delta and Nigeria as a whole due to historical factors related to British imperialist plunder (see Okaba 2009; Falola 1999) and numerous coups and the kaleidoscopic political process, as stated in Chapter 3. The result of such a violence-prone social milieu is that the loss of human life arguably becomes routine. Thus, MEND's operating environment guarantees that the outcome of the use of violent repertoires of protest is relatively unspectacular. The imperative of violence master frame is used to justify the use of violence.

MEND adopts the imperative of violence frame for several reasons. First, the failure of non-violent repertoires of protest—embodied in the hanging of the Ogoni Nine including Ken Saro-Wiwa and the decline of MOSOP (see Watts 2007; Bob 2005)—demonstrates that the language the Nigerian state understands is violence. Non-violent repertoires of protest are a charted territory, which has fallen to disuse. A strong belief exists that non-violent tactics and attempts to dialogue with the Nigerian state is a waste of time and have generated negligible

---

2   Interviewee 1.

results historically. As one insurgent puts it the "Nigerian state does not believe in dialogue. What they are interested in is violence".[3]

In addition, non-violent tactics arguably have little sense of urgency in the Nigerian political terrain as a responsive opposition is non-existent. MEND's attempt at peaceful resolution of the Niger Delta crisis in late 2009 to early 2010 was unsuccessful in spite of the group's initial optimism. The government contravened its amnesty program by raiding homes of militants, including a former MEND commander as noted earlier. MEND was disappointed that the government chose to negotiate "with a class of individuals it can very easily manage" rather than genuine agitators.[4] By January 2010, MEND resumed oil infrastructure sabotage and carried out two car bombings in March 2010. An inference from the point above is that the intransigence and imperviousness of the Nigerian state to peaceful entreaties arguably make violent repertoires of protest inevitable.

Second, the prevalence of corruption in the Nigerian state makes non-violent repertoires of protest highly susceptible to co-optation. The government's amnesty program provides a major example. The amnesty program was announced by President Umar Yar'Adua on 25 June 2009. It was aimed at encouraging insurgents to give up their arms and life in the creeks in exchange for state pardon, a monthly stipend (65,000 Naira or $430 [USD]) and employment training. MEND alleges that some insurgents were co-opted into the amnesty program in exchange for cash. MEND argued that the "government has been offering bribes to a number of militants who surrendered their birth rights under its amnesty program in the form of contracts. The government perceives this (sic) individuals to wield some kind of influence in the region".[5] There has been a series of demonstrations in the Niger Delta by former insurgents fighting to receive the money they were promised. Therefore, MEND contends that any attempt to relent will only provide avenue for being corrupted by agents of the Nigerian state without any benefits to the Delta people.

In one instance, in Yenagoa, Bayelsa state on 4 September 2009, former insurgents working with Ebikabowei Victor Ben (General Boyloaf) protested against the non-payment of the 10 million Naira (66, 357 [USD]) their boss allegedly promised each of them if they surrendered their weapons.[6] Therefore, some believe that "fraud, rent-a-crowd and monetary inducement" was part of

---

3   Interviewee 15.

4   Jomo Gbomo e-mail statement (number 6) "Amnesty Score Card". Wednesday 7 October 2009.

5   Jomo Gbomo statement (number 12).

6   Oyadongha, Samuel (2009, Sept. 5). "Amnesty: Militants Protest in Yenagoa". URL: http://www.vanguardngr.com/2009/09/amnesty-militants-protest-in-yenagoa/?utm_source=feedburner&utm_medium=feed&utm_campaign=Feed%3A+vanguardngr%2Fdleb+%28Vanguard+News+Feed%29 Accessed 17 November 2010.

the "amnesty charade".[7] Furthermore, allegations of contract inflation, bogus allowances for government representatives among others have bedeviled the amnesty program (Hubbard 2010).[8] Consequently, MEND treats insurgents who have accepted amnesty and denounced violence as people who have "capitulated" and bear "no significance to the continuation of the struggle".[9]

Third, MEND adopts the imperative of violence frame to explain to skeptical Niger Deltans and the general public why it believes that violent tactics are required to take what rightfully belongs to the Delta people. MEND insurgents speak of having no other option than to take up arms against the Nigerian state. This helps in mobilizing insurgents at the grassroots. During an interview conducted in Pidgin English, an insurgent[10] explains why he participated in pipeline vandalism and kidnapping episodes involving over 30 foreign oil workers:

Interviewer: Ahmm ... my question be say, ahmm ... the time wey una dey catch those oil worker, shay na oil workers wey be people fom this country, from our country, Nigerians na him una catch abi na oyibo (whites) wey him come work as oil worker here in Nigeria?

Respondent: Na oyibo

Interviewer: Na oyibo?

Respondent: Yeah

Interviewer: Like how many?

Respondent: Oyibo?

Interviewer: How many oyibo una catch?

Respondent: Ok, the oyibo, the oyinbo reach about 30 something because we catch for Bayelsa, Rivers, Delta.

Interviewer: Uhmm ... So when una catch dem like this, dem dey beg una? Those people wey una catch them, how dem dey react when una catch them?

---

7   Jomo Gbomo e-mail statement (number 2) "Cameroon Army Weapons at Bayelsa Disarmament Ceremony". Saturday 5 September 2009.

8   See Hubbard, Katherine. 2010. "Amnesty in Jeorpady in the Niger Delta", Centre for Strategic and International Studies, URL: http://csis.org/blog/areas-watch-amnesty-jeopardy-niger-delta Accessed 17 November 2010.

9   Jomo Gbomo statement (number 12).

10   Interviewee 27; militant 5. Ex-insurgent from Camp 5. Personal interview August 2010, Obubra Cross River state.

Respondent: Dey no do anything for we, because dem dey beg us, dem they
ask us wetin be our problem? We tell dem say our problem, dem dey tell say
Ok make we no worry ehn … make we take care of dem, make we no kill dem.
Na him we say yes *we no go kill una because after all we have to fight Federal
Government but we do, do like this so that Federal Government go fit reason
with us, that's why we dey catch una.* (emphasis added)

The insurgent justifies his participation in kidnapping as a way to make the Nigerian
government "reason" with his group. This standpoint is widespread among
insurgents. Henry Bindodogha (Egbema I), from another insurgent camp, NDFF,
stated that kidnapping was to "draw the attention of the government" to the pain,
neglect and bondage of the people. During a 2010 private tour of the creeks, where
four American oil workers kidnapped in 2007 were kept, Bindodogha claimed to
have explained to the victims that they had nothing against them and would be
released once the government agreed to build schools, roads and hospitals.[11] The
victims agreed (while in captivity) that "It's inhuman to treat Niger Deltans this
badly" (*Vanguard*, May 19 2009, p. 1).[12]

Many insurgents had a pariah status at the onset of their activities but were
later embraced by the people as heroes of the struggle. For instance, at the height
of the insurgency, Bindodogha suffered humiliation at the hands of members of
his community who regarded him as a criminal. Some threw stones, attempted
to attack him with machetes and called him all manner of names. Bindodogha
asserted that he avoided such people and refused to get provoked. Some community
members attempted to sabotage the group's boat engines by pouring salt in the
diesel they had kept at their camp.[13] The people received Bindodogha as a hero
when he and I visited Ofunama, Olodiama, Kosan, Tolofa communities in August
2010. Bindodogha believes that the people have come to appreciate why he took
up arms against the Nigerian state and the oil corporations.

Fourth, the imperative of violence frame has been enhanced by increased
militancy in the civil society. The experience of MOSOP provides rather persuasive
reasons why even non-violent activists became increasingly aggressive and
militant in their approach to protest since the 1990s. MOSOP issued the Ogoni Bill
of Rights in 1990 condemning the marginalization of the people and demanding
political autonomy and self-determination for the Ogonis from the military regime
of General Ibrahim Babangida. Although MOSOP was essentially a non-violent
group, which organized public protests, issued press statements, called for boycott
of the 12 June 1993 presidential elections, as tactics of protest, there is ample
evidence suggesting that the SMO was becoming increasingly impatient with

---

11   Interviewee 19.

12   This might have been a simple manifestation of Stockholm syndrome or mere
performance in a risky situation.

13   Interviewee 42. Militant 16. Protocol officer of NDFF. Personal Interview August
2010, Benin City.

the government and was becoming discursively militant in its approach. For instance, Garrick Leton, former president of MOSOP, argued that "(i)f the land is ours, irrespective of the law put in place by the major ethnic groups, anything that comes out of the land should be ours".[14] Saro-Wiwa told the Ogoni peoples that the Nigerian state "will have to shoot and kill every Ogoni man, woman and child to take more of their oil".[15] Dissident rhetoric influences repressive efforts by authorities (Davenport and Eads 2001).

Consequently, it was not a surprise to keen observers by the time the social movement in the Niger Delta took an overtly violent turn in the late 1990s after the Kaiama Declaration in 1998, the formation of the IYC and the NDPVF. In fact, the idea of "bloody revolution" to change the Nigerian system was no longer radical by the time MEND emerged in 2005. Academics and former political leaders continue to canvass the idea.[16] The imperative of violence frame resonates among a people who have already witnessed a series of violent incidents and believe bloodshed is fundamental to changing the system.

Finally, insurgents believe that the socio-political landscape of Nigeria could not have been sufficiently reconfigured to produce a president from the Niger Delta minorities without the use of violence. The presidential candidate of the ruling People's Democratic party (PDP), Umar Yar'Adua selected the governor of oil-rich Bayelsa state, Goodluck Jonathan, as running mate in the 2007 elections. In the previous year, 3, 674 incidents of pipeline vandalism were recorded, (up from 497 in 1999), at least 31 oil workers were kidnapped while 37 soldiers died in attacks on oil infrastructure by insurgents (Technical committee on the Niger Delta 2008). The selection of an Ijaw man as vice presidential candidate was generally seen as an attempt to assuage the insurgents and the peoples of the Niger Delta in order to reduce the level of violence. Violence, in this sense, was functional (see Ukiwo 2007). Insurgents view Jonathan's selection as VP candidate and subsequent elevation to the office of President of Nigeria as a culmination of their efforts and the fruit of their labor of violence:

> We believe that it was because of this struggle that took him (Jonathan) to a certain level ... it is because of the struggle that the former president (Obasanjo) ... picked our own to become a running mate to late Yar Adua because I feel if not for this struggle, they wouldn't have known that the people of Niger Delta were in existence. I believe this struggle was what gave us a voice ... So, in a nut shell, I will say his ascendency to that post was as a result of the struggle.[17]

---

14 See E. Efeni, "Agony of Ogoni Country", *The Guardian* 28 December 1992, pg. 7.

15 Cited in Osaghae (1995: 327)

16 Oyebode, Olayinka. 2010. "Danjuma, Nwabueze disagree on the Nigeria question", *The Nation*, URL: http://thenationonlineng.net/web3/news/4993.html Accessed 18 November 2010.

17 Interviewee 15.

Although insurgents acknowledge that Jonathan is "our man"[18] and a major beneficiary of their pains in the creeks, they believe the "issue of restoration of our sovereignty goes beyond Goodluck ... because there is a constitution that encumbers him".[19] This partly explains why the insurgency continues in spite of the Jonathan presidency.

More importantly, an erudite *war metaphor* prevails within the MEND universe. There is a strong belief that a *war situation* exists in the Niger Delta in particular and Nigeria in general. Anything goes under this circumstance. FNDIC's president, whose "non-violent" group kidnapped oil workers to provide human shield against military attacks on the people of Okerenkoko, gives the rationale behind kidnapping and pipeline vandalism:

> Nigeria has created a war situation and that is why you see people bursting the pipelines and holding hostages. In a crisis situation, it should not be seen as something special because there are more severe things ... like dropping bombs and people are dying. Hostage-taking and bombing, which one is more serious?[20]

Insurgents seem to be implicitly but unwittingly drawing on generations of scholarly work on the idea of the *social contract*. Social contract theorists, particularly Thomas Hobbes (1968 [1651]) in the *Leviathan* assert that people give up a part of their freedoms in exchange for the security and protection of their lives by the Sovereign. The authority of the Sovereign is "absolute" and "unlimited" (Hobbes, 1968: 257, 275). However, when and where the Sovereign fails to protect the people, Hobbes argues that citizens have the right to resist or disobey the state to save their lives. "(I)f the Sovereign command a man (sic) ... to kill, wound ... or abstain from the use of food, ayre medicine, or any other thing without which he cannot live; yet hath that man the Liberty to disobey" (1968: 268–9). Analyzing the idea of resistance in Hobbes, Steinberger (2002) argues that the purpose of the state goes beyond securing lives and extends to providing a minimal level of comfort for its citizens. Where a modicum of comfort cannot be provided by the state, he argues, citizens have no contractual obligation towards the state, since the contract had effectively become null and void. This is because a "life of unrelenting pain, of unbroken drudgery and oppression, of stupefying labor devoid of hope and meaning ... even if entirely safe and secure, would not be what individuals have in mind when they agree to the terms of the social contract" (858).

From this perspective, states are not naturally occurring phenomena. They are human creations intended to serve human ends. When the state fails to serve human needs, *the state does not exist* and resistance by rational thinking actors is not a crime, rather it is an act of war (Steinberger, 2002: 860). The absolute

---

18   Interviewee 26.
19   Interviewee 11.
20   Interviewee 38.

authority of the state thus exists *pari passu* with citizens' right to resist without any contradiction (Steinberger 2002).[21]

This suggests that under certain circumstances insurgent acts are not criminal activities but acts of war. By this logic, insurgents consider kidnapping a relatively minor irritation within an amphitheatre of war, where the Nigerian state drops bombs on its people. Many insurgents and activists articulate the idea that the Nigerian state has created a "war situation".[22] Asari Dokubo, for instance explicitly called for using violence against the Nigerian state in the late 1990s because he believed that was what the war situation required.[23] Dokubo believes that the insurgents are engaged in a "revolutionary struggle". Within this war logic, kidnapping is a contested empirical category:

> (F)rom the revolutionary viewpoint, there is nothing like kidnapping. We take into custody *enemy combatants* because the oil workers are actually enemy combatants. They give life to the Nigerian state to buy the weapons of mass destruction that is used against us (sic). So, for a revolutionary organization, to take into custody such people, it will be for furtherance of the revolution, for the good of the revolution, to serve as deterrents to these oil workers who are collaborators, who are formed as enemy combatant.[24]

Suffice to state that Delta insurgents believe a war is in progress in Nigeria. Hence, revolutionaries are simply rounding up soldiers of the other side— "enemy combatants"—as a quotidian "act of war". These "soldiers" happen to be oil workers, who supposedly support the Nigerian state by working for oil corporations. Not surprisingly, the JTF fundamentally disagrees with the idea of a war situation in the Niger Delta. General Bello describes the JTF operations— including aerial bombardment, infantry troops' battle with well-armed insurgents, naval reconnaissance and clandestine intelligence gathering—as a "simple law and justice operation".[25]

The Imperative of Violence master frame is a staple of many insurgent groups around the world. It is surprising that this framing strategy has yet to be clearly elucidated or generated deserved attention in the literature. Dissident groups adopting violent repertoires of protest generally give the impression that the violence they perpetrate is an act of war. Groups like Hezbollah, Hamas, FARC-EP and al-Qaeda frame terrorism in a way that suggests that violence is inevitable

---

21   This perhaps explains why Hume (1983) one of the critics of the idea of social contract paradoxically states that the doctrine of resistance be concealed from the masses. For a review of Hume's (1983) thought, see Merill (2005). Also, see Lefkowitz (2007) for a discussion of how morality may compel citizens to disobey.

22   Interviewees 11, 15, 19, 20, 27, 28–37 among others

23   Interviewee 11

24   Interviewee 11.

25   Interviewee 12. JTF Commander.

(see Snow and Byrd 2007) and part of a broader war. Al-Qaeda, for instance, targets the geo-political West, particularly the US supposedly as just dessert for the war in Iraq, among other factors (BBC 2005), while the Islamic Movement of Uzbekistan executes a vengeful jihad against the Uzbek government (Snow and Byrd 2007). The war metaphor allows insurgents to discursively minimize the damage caused by their actions: bad things happen in wars. For instance, Mohammad Sidique Khan, one of the al-Qaeda suicide bombers in the 7 July 2005 bombings in London provides rationale for targeting innocent civilians:

> Your democratically elected governments continuously perpetuate atrocities against my people all over the world. And your support of them makes you directly responsible, just as I am directly responsible for protecting and avenging my Muslim brothers and sisters. Until we feel security you will be our targets and until you stop the bombing, gassing, imprisonment and torture of my people we will not stop this fight. *We are at war and I am a soldier. Now you too will taste the reality of this situation.*[26] (emphasis added)

As one NDPVF insurgent puts it: "Until they give us what is rightly ours, we will never know sleep. The violence aspect, we have tried, the next strategy we are going to bring out, they will not know".[27]

The Injustice Frame

MEND uses the injustice frame in addition to the imperative of violence master frame. The injustice frame is a popular narrative among dissidents fighting for socio-political and economic transformation (see Benford and Snow 2000; Stewart 1995). The adoption of an *injustice frame* in the course of an encounter with authority demonstrates "a belief that *the unimpeded operation of the authority system ... would result in an injustice*" (Gamson et al. 1982: 14; italics in original). The said authority becomes defined as *unjust* when several participants adopt the injustice frame (Gamson et al. 1982: 14). The belief that the authority system is unjust may predate the specific encounter, when an injustice frame is adopted but the encounter increases the likelihood that participants will contemplate subversive collective action (Gamson et al. 1982). Many social movements in the world grew out of a high sense of injustice (Klandermans 1997). There may be moral indignation, which can lead to perceptions of injustice when grievances accumulate (see Klandermans 1997). The Civil Rights Movement is a well-

---

26   See http://www.youtube.com/watch?v=bPd1rbPz7_U Accessed 23 November 2010.

27   Interviewee 15, Chief of Staff to Asari Dokubo. Personal Interview, Port Harcourt, Rivers state, August 2010.

researched example of how injustice breeds life to social movements (Gamson et al. 1982; McAdam 1982).

MEND uses the injustice master frame in at least five major ways. First, it is used to assign blame for the Delta's many problems; second, it helps to accentuate and historicize the deplorable living conditions of the people of the Niger Delta. Third, MEND uses the injustice frame to provide rationale for its insurgency. Fourth, MEND harps on the theme of injustice to mobilize dissidents, supporters, and garner by-stander support. Finally, MEND uses the injustice frame to have its struggle nested in a universalist narrative of justice irrespective of social contours. A few examples from MEND's official statements may suffice:

> The Movement for the Emancipation of the Niger Delta is fighting against a *glaring injustice*. The land of the Niger Delta alone has been confiscated by the government from its owners and distributed to western oil companies and a few Nigerians from outside our region. *We have been declared landless* by the Nigerian government, yet without benefit. The government of Nigeria has been unable to cover-up this *crime against humanity* which has been exposed by every individual and organization that has visited the Niger Delta.[28] (emphasis added)

MEND views the conditions of the people of the Niger Delta as a "glaring injustice" comparable to "crime against humanity". The leader of a MEND affiliate explains that:

> Since there is no development, good schools, etc. in the Niger Delta maybe I could have been one of the graduates and topmost persons in the area. But when you cannot see those things, what about the children we born tomorrow (sic)? Or today, how do they look like. So when you think about that pain in yourself, you fight for your people and that is self-determination.[29]

The injustice frame allows MEND to embed itself in a discourse of fraternity of humanity. For instance, in its condemnation of the "attempted act of terrorism on Delta flight 253 into the United States by a misguided Islamic extremist from the Northern part of Nigeria",[30] MEND states that:

> Had the plan been successful, it would have left many families across the globe grieving on a day when Christians celebrate the birth of a peacemaker, Jesus Christ. *It should by now be evident that the threat to world peace will not emerge from the Niger Delta, a region agitating for justice* as is acknowledged

---

28   Jomo Gbomo e-mail statement (number 24). "MEND in Ghana Propaganda". Saturday 10 July 2010.

29   Interviewee 19.

30   The father of the young man made efforts to alert US authorities in Nigeria before the incident.

by every right thinking human being, but from the Islamic extremist northern part of Nigeria covertly supported by its elite who assume leadership of Nigeria to be the birthright of this region.[31]

For MEND, the "world should pay more attention to northern Nigeria with its threat to world peace than to agitation for justice in the Niger Delta which only threatens world oil prices". Therefore, from MEND's perspective, kidnapping of oil workers, car bombing select government buildings (which led to at least 19 casualties in 2010) and pipeline vandalism are not terrorist acts, as they do not purport to ruin Christmas or threaten "world peace".[32] MEND uses the failed airline bombing plot to demonstrate that it believes in world peace and underscore that it merely threatens "world oil prices"—a fact that must be considered a minor inconvenience by the international community—from MEND's standpoint.

In addition, MEND uses the injustice frame as a call for action, a mobilization tool for insurgents. For instance, a statement warning of further attacks in October 2009 states:

> MEND considers this next phase of our struggle as the most critical as we intend to end 50 years of slavery of the people of the Niger Delta by the Nigerian government, a few individuals and the western oil companies once and for all ... This government has gone ahead negotiating to sell off more lands of the people of the Delta without deeming its people fit to be consulted. We warn all those interested in buying off our land, they will not go unpunished. We will fight for our land with the last drop of our blood ... [33]

Conjuring images of slavery resonates lucidly in a region that played a pivotal role during the transatlantic slave trade and its concomitant social devastation (see Alagoa 1964). This frame is a major mobilization tool as it is widely shared by insurgents. One insurgent[34] who was married with seven children explained why he joined the notorious Camp 5, became a "gunman" and remained at the creeks despite losing some of his friends and comrades:

> *Interviewer*: So, in the course, that time when una dey do the struggle, how many people you don see wey don die go for your front or for your own side?
>
> *Respondent*: I don see more than 10 to 15 people

---

31   Jomo Gbomo e-mail statement (number 13). Sunday 27 December 2009.

32   This raises the issue of the global politics of categorizing entities as terrorist organizations. It is however beyond the purview of this book.

33   Jomo Gbomo e-mail statement (number 6) "Amnesty Score Card", Wednesday 7 October 2009.

34   Interviewee 29; militant 7. Gunman from Camp 5. Personal interview, August 2010.

Interviewer: Wey die?

Respondent: Wey die.

Interviewer: Ok. Why you join?

Respondent: Because suffer dey, oppression here and there. No money to chop, no money to feed family, no money to forward education those are the reasons why I join the game in 1995.

All other insurgents also considered the level of unemployment, schools, hospitals and hunger in the Delta an injustice that provides the rationale for their struggle against the Nigerian state and the oil corporations. One insurgent[35] who participated in a focus group discussion provides both an historical context for the insurgency and how he got actively involved:

Interviewer: Now, how about you? Why did you join?

Respondent 1: The whole Niger Delta is being marginalized not by only one particular area. We are not the ones that started it (the insurgency), Isaac Boro started it, he died on it; Ken Saro-Wiwa started it, he died on it and the same marginalization of these people has always arise from the Federal Government … we have not been answered. And every Nigerian man believes that the Niger Delta is contributing 80% of the national wealth, which is outrageous and due to that, we that are the young ones, we saw what our elders, our fathers passed through before we begin to fight now … *We're men, we have to gather ourselves and fight this injustice. That is why we start to carry gun.* The carrying gun is not deliberately to fight the Federal Government; it is to draw the attention of the Federal Government to this Niger Delta region that they marginalized. (emphasis added)

Interviewer: So what strategies did you use to get their attention? The specific … (cuts in)

Respondent: Yes, the specific attention that we can get from the Federal Government, we can go to any oil well and bomb blast it (bomb it), we can lay it right off, we can even hostage whites or …

Interviewer: You mean kidnap white oil workers?

Respondent: Yes, we hostage whites, it is through there the media came in then we express our feeling, the marginalization of the Niger Delta

---

35   Focus Group Discussion 5; respondent 1. Obubra, Cross River state, August 2010.

In summary, the injustice frame allows MEND to lay attribution, provide a relatively reverberating narrative of the conditions of the people of the Niger Delta, and the reason behind its insurgent activities. MEND also uses the injustice frame to situate its activities in a wider global discourse of fairness and justice as well as to mobilize insurgents.

The Human/Minority Rights Frame

MEND situates and contextualizes its struggle within a liberal universalist discourse of human rights, self-determination and respect for minority rights. While the Civil Rights Movement in the US appealed to the self-avowed creed of the American state (see Gamson et al. 1982; McAdam 1982)—such as the Declaration of Independence, asserting the gender-insensitive notion that "all men are created equal"—MEND looks beyond the Nigerian state in finding a rationale for using the human/minority rights frame. One fundamental reason why MEND talks past the Nigerian state in this regard is a widespread belief among insurgents that the Nigerian state is founded on injustice. Using any of Nigeria's stated creed—peace and unity, for instance —implies legitimizing the Nigerian state. Therefore, insurgents speak of the "stolen sovereignty of the people" of the Niger Delta. They argue that most of the kingdoms in the Niger Delta "were never conquered" but "Britain dubiously coerced them into signing treaties of protection after which Britain unilaterally abrogated these treaties".[36]

MEND's use of the human/minority rights frame has been enhanced by the military actions in Niger Delta communities. Several communities in the Niger Delta like Agge (2008), Okerenkoko in the Gbaramatu Kingdom, (2003, 2006, 2009) have seen their homes and other properties destroyed by JTF operatives in the quest to rid the communities of militants. Several people have also died from such military actions as stated earlier. The loss of lives and destruction of property give considerable credibility and resonance to MEND's human/minority rights frame within and outside the affected communities. MEND mobilizes dissidents, who seek to avenge the loss of their loved ones[37] by accentuating the consequences of such military actions.

MEND appears to be careful about its quest to be seen as a human rights champion and crusader. MEND always emphasizes that it does not strike a target unjustifiably, is not interested in wasting human lives during attacks and feels concerned about every life lost during its attacks. In one instance, MEND demonstrates its consciousness of the salience of human rights advocacy credentials. When rumors circulated in July 2010 that MEND was planning to attack the nascent oil industry in neighboring Ghana, MEND was quick to explain that:

---

36   Interviewee 11.
37   Interviewees 15 and 16.

Ghana is of no strategic importance in our fight against the Nigerian military. We respect the sovereignty of all nations bordering the Niger Delta and limit our operations to oil related facilities in Nigeria. The government and People of Ghana should therefore discountenance the un-intelligent and baseless claim of the Nigerian High commissioner, Musiliu Obanikoro intended to whip xenophobic sentiments against the Ijaws and other indigenous tribes of the Niger Delta legitimately visiting or residing in Ghana.[38]

Several inferences or claims are discernible from MEND's use of the human/ minority rights frame. The first is that the people of the Niger Delta did not choose to be part of Nigeria. Therefore, the opening statement of the 1999 constitution created by the military administration of General Abdulsalam Abubakar—"We the people of the Federal Republic of Nigeria (h)aving firmly and solemnly resolved, to live in unity and harmony as one indivisible and indissoluble sovereign nation under God"—is as someone puts it, "fraudulent".[39] With 252 ethnic groups, insurgents believe Nigerians are not one people and never agreed at any time to form a country. Consequently, MEND and many other insurgent groups propose a sovereign national conference of all ethnic nationalities to decide whether the various ethnic groups wish to remain in Nigeria. This pertains to the right to self-determination.

Second, MEND claims that the people of the Niger Delta are denied their human rights because they are an occupied people. MEND argues that the "people of the Niger Delta are peace loving people who simply cannot understand why a government which has confined us to slavery having stolen our lands, should expect peace". For MEND, the insurgency is to abolish an archaic institution— "slavery"— of the Delta people. This means that any actions by MEND are justified as they apparently aim at setting the Niger Delta people free from oppression.

Third, insurgents claim that the minority *qua* minority status of the people of the Niger Delta is a major reason behind the denial of their basic human rights. From this standpoint, the numerous military actions in Niger Delta communities, environmental degradation and marginalization in Nigeria's socio-political and economic life could not happen if they were one of the three majority ethnic groups. The argument is that if the more populous Igbos, Yorubas and Hausa-Fulanis had oil, they would not accept being unable to control their resources. In particular, insurgents decry being pawns in the hands of the "Hausa-Fulani ruling Oligarchy in the North".[40] This frame thus selectively highlights aspects of existing beliefs and values—perceived dominance by the Hausa-Fulani—and processes them into a rallying clarion call. This discursive strategy is imperative to movements whose success depends on their ability to mobilize constituents that have different identities from those likely to benefit from the movement

---

38   Jomo Gbomo (number 24).
39   Interviewee 11.
40   Interviewee 11.

activities (Benford and Snow 2000: 624). Once again, Southern Nigerians appear to be the intended conscience constituents. By so doing, MEND engages in frame amplification, which helps to idealize and elucidate the values or beliefs held by the target audience (Benford and Snow 2000: 624).

Fourth, for MEND, car bombings, kidnapping of oil workers, pipeline vandalism, illegal oil bunkering and so on are all a means to an end—liberation— of the Niger Delta peoples from the Nigerian state or at a minimum, ensuring a fair share from the national wealth. It is to MEND's credit that no kidnap victim has died in its custody as stated earlier (Okonta 2006). In particular, insurgents take extreme caution to ensure the safety of journalists and researchers in a way that suggests they see such professionals almost as partners. Michael Peel of the *Financial Times* of London was dumbfounded at the level of concern NDPVF insurgents demonstrated for his safety and well-being of his clothing during his visit to the creeks (Peel 2009). I was also flabbergasted to find that NDFF insurgents presupposed that I was their "guest" in the Niger Delta and went to great lengths to guarantee my safety during my field work. They prescribed what hotel to stay, provided (rather interestingly) government-sanctioned security during my visit to the creeks, a convoy, and made repeated phone calls to ensure I was safely back to Lagos.[41]

More significantly, this frame serves a major mobilization function for the insurgents. At Camp 5, an affiliate of MEND, one insurgent[42] who was a reggae artiste wrote a song "Suffering in Izon Ibe" based on many of the issues highlighted by MEND. *Izon* is the non-anglicized spelling of Ijaw, the most populous minority group in the Delta region, while *Ibe* means land. As others served as gunmen, cooks, and performed other relevant functions at the creeks, this insurgent helped to inspire his comrades to fight for the rights of the Ijaw people. His lyrics reveal the depth of his understanding of the conditions of the Delta minorities:

Verse 1:
We got no light in Izon Ibe
We got no water in Izon Ibe
We got no school in Izon Ibe
But there is gas flaring round the Izon Ibe
We got no road to Izon Ibe
We got no job in Izon Ibe
We got no medical care in Izon Ibe
But the highest oil-producing area is Izon Ibe
Without all this in Izon Ibe, how would mama, papa survive in Izon Ibe?

---

41   This welcome but unsolicited hospitality raises several ethical issues. These include researchers' responsibility to participants rather than vice versa.

42   Interviewee 34; militant 12. Raggae artiste from Camp 5. Personal interview, August 2010, Obubra, Cross River state.

Refrain:
Kala iye wa oh (It's not easy)
Kala iye wa oh, (It's not easy)
Kala iye wa oh, Tom Polo
The way we suffering in Izon Ibe

Verse 2:
There are this couple of wisemen in Izon Ibe
That say that they wanna bring freedom to Izon Ibe
But only one stands for Izon Ibe
And the rest turn dem back on the Izon Ibe
Because their papa did not tell them about the Izon Ibe
They don't know Oloibiri[43] is in Izon Ibe
They don't know Jones creek is in Izon Ibe
They don't know Batan is in Izon Ibe
They don't know Ogulagha is in Izon Ibe
They don't know Gelegelegbene is in Izon Ibe
They don't know Escravos is in Izon Ibe
That is why they are carelessly sleeping in Abuja Ibe

Refrain:
Kala iye wa oh (It's not easy)
Kala iye wa oh, (It's not easy)
Kala iye wa oh, Tom Polo
The way we suffering in Izon Ibe

Verse 3:
Egbesu owor dem that fight for dem freedom in Izon Ibe
You declare dem wanted in Izon Ibe
Five hundred shot dead in Izon Ibe
Our houses all burn down in Izon Ibe
Undermining CNN coverage in Izon Ibe or forgetting dem see how we suffering in Izon Ibe
But as soon as dem leave the Izon Ibe
Struggling, hustling, suffering continue in Izon Ibe

Refrain:
Kala iye wa oh (It's not easy)
Kala iye wa oh, (It's not easy)
Kala iye wa oh, Tom Polo
The way we suffering in Izon Ibe

---

43   Oloibiri was the first site in Nigeria where oil was discovered in 1956.

The lyrics present graphic details about the conditions of the people in Ijaw land. The lyrics also compare Ijaw land with Abuja, the federal capital, a fundamental distinction highlighted in Chapter 3. The overarching theme of the song is the suffering of the minorities of the Delta. Songs like this are intended to remind insurgents about the treatment meted out to peoples of the Niger Delta in spite of their contributions to Nigeria's economic survival and the essence of their cause.

The Environmental Justice Frame

The imperative of violence frame, injustice frame and human/minority rights frame are closely aligned with the environmental justice frame in MEND's narrative. The environmental justice frame has a long history in the Niger Delta struggle, particularly in the agitation for self-determination by the Ogoni people. Ken Saro-Wiwa led the Movement for the Survival of Ogoni People (MOSOP) to successfully adopt the environmental justice frame in 1993 (Bob 2005) after years of failure to garner international NGO support for addressing the concerns of the Ogoni people in the Niger Delta region. MOSOP turned what essentially began as a minority rights movement into an environmentalist one (Bob 2005, 2002). Organizations like Greenpeace, Friends of the Earth, among others that were not familiar with the Nigerian terrain and did not wish to be drawn into a political crisis became useful allies, when MOSOP adopted the environmental justice frame. Bob's (2005) analysis demonstrates that the social movement led by MOSOP, its organizational prowess, leadership acumen, resources, contacts and conscientious adoption of the environmental justice frame set the Ogoni cause on a distinctive pedestal from other minorities in the region facing similar problems and needs. Sadly, MOSOP appeared to have begun a trajectory of decline and fractionalization after the Ogoni Nine were hanged in 1995.[44]

The environmental justice frame comprises several claims related to environmental contamination or degradation (Čapek 1993). These claims include the right to "accurate information", "democratic participation", compensations for environmental degradation (see Čapek 1993: 8), ending "environmental racism" (Alston 1990, cited in Čapek 1993), among others. MEND adopts the environmental justice frame to emphasize the plight of the people of the Niger Delta people as derided "second class citizens" (Čapek 1993: 8) in the Nigerian state. MEND considers the presence of the JTF, northern Nigerians who possess oil blocs and transnational oil corporations in the Niger Delta without the consent of the people a symbol of environmental disrespect.

MEND emphasizes that the Nigerian government regards the Niger Delta as a constellation of oil blocs and assemblage of pipelines rather than a geographical area populated by people with basic human desires and aspirations. Furthermore, MEND believes that the people of the Niger Delta rarely receive any of the oil

---

44   Interviewee 4.

blocs on their land. MEND claims that: "The Niger Delta has been partitioned into oil blocks which have been distributed amongst mostly Northerners while indigenes of the Niger Delta can barely survive ... It is common knowledge that no southerner can lay claim to an inch of land in the North".[45] As indicated earlier, once again, MEND discursively divides Nigeria along ethnic lines to appeal to its intended audience, southern Nigerians, particularly the people of the Delta region.

The Nigerian constitution now confers land and resources on the Nigerian state through series of military decrees like the Land Use Act of 1978. This is a monumental change from the earlier system where federating units—the Northern, Western and Eastern regions—paid 50 percent of the revenue accruing from peanuts, cocoa and palm oil respectively to the federal government. Oil-producing states at present receive 17 percent of oil revenues from the federal government. MEND sees this as an environmental injustice: "The constitution before independence which offered resource control was mutilated by illegal military governments and this injustice is yet to be addressed".[46] In a particular instance, MEND describes as "preposterous" government suggestions of "concessions" aimed at "ceding 10% of its (federal government's) stake in the joint venture partnerships to oil producing communities and 9% to other interested Nigerians". MEND finds such proposals degrading and indicative of the low status of the Niger Delta people in the Nigerian body politic.

Similarly, MEND condemns the decision of the federal government of Nigeria to define "an oil producing community as one where oil installations are sited; where oil is drilled or where flow stations and other facilities" are located. MEND argues that all "communities in the Niger Delta without installations suffer the effects of gas flaring, spillages amongst others" in the same manner as those where oil is being drilled.[47]

MEND also challenges the "bleeding of the Niger Delta and exportation of its mineral resources" without the consent or payment of compensations to the people. This relates to the penultimate point. The Nigerian National petroleum Corporation (NNPC) signs joint venture agreements with oil corporations on behalf of the Nigerian state and by implication host communities in the Niger Delta. MEND regards the presence of oil corporations in the Niger Delta as a grave environmental injustice. It condemns the "occupation of our land and theft of our resources by the oil companies".[48] This frame is fundamental to mobilizing dissidents. One insurgent explains his participation in car bombings, pipeline vandalism and kidnapping oil workers during the insurgency:

---

45   Jomo Gbomo e-mail statement (number 20) "Bomb Alert in Warri". Monday 15 March 2010.

46   Jomo Gbomo e-mail statement (number 27) "Bomb Alert in Abuja". Friday 1 October 2010.

47   Jomo Gbomo e-mail statement—Ceasefire Called Off—(number 15). Friday 29 January 2010.

48   Jomo Gbomo (number 20).

where we even farm that place it is somehow the government land now. The army secure the land and people there; up till today they couldn't even go to their houses before they relocate them. The funny part of it is that when they survey the land, most of the land, the people's farm, they came into the reserve and there was no compensation even up till today.[49] (sic)

The environmental justice frame aligned with everyday experiences and inspired this insurgent who works for an affiliate of MEND. For him, the idea that the Nigerian state could confiscate farmlands, relocate whole communities without reasonable notice or adequate compensation and turn their land to a government reservation for oil extraction was a major motivating factor in joining the ranks of insurgents. Although this had been going on for years, the constant dissemination of this frame at the creeks made him to understand that the government could have adopted a more humane approach.

In addition, MEND insurgents believe that oil companies behave irresponsibly in the Niger Delta region. MEND argues that oil companies perpetrate acts that demonstrate little attention to environmental and health hazards. These include gas flaring, and oil spillage as well as water and land pollution. MEND accuses oil companies of conducting their business in a manner that is inconsistent with industry standards in their home countries in Europe and North America. This resonates strongly in the public. For example, the National Oil Spill Detection and Response Agency (NOSDRA) estimates that 3,203 oil spills occurred in the Niger Delta between 2006 and 2010. This implies that at least two oil spills occurred per day within the period. Of the total figure, 23 percent was due to equipment failure, operational or maintenance erosion and corrosion while 45 percent was as a result of sabotage or vandalism.[50] Only 859 of the oil spill sites had been "remediated and certified" by NOSDRA as of August 2010.

Estimates from the NNPC indicate that about 2,300 cubic metres of oil is spilled in 300 incidents every year, while the Department of Petroleum Resources states that 2,446,322 barrels of oil were spilled between 1976 and 1996 (*Daily Independent* 2010). An editorial in the *Daily Independent* demonstrates the credibility and resonance of the environmental justice frame. The editorial argues that "multinational oil companies in Nigeria violate the law with impunity and that the Niger Delta's "(m)angrove forest is particularly vulnerable to oil spills, because the soil soaks up the oil-like sponge and then releases it afresh every rainy season". The newspaper asks: "Where is the courage and political will, within the Nigerian government, to tame the *criminal excesses of the multinational oil companies* – which officially are joint venture partners with the Federal Government?"[51] (emphasis added).

---

49   Focus Group 5, respondent 2, Obubra, Cross River state, August 2010.

50   Minister of Environment John Odey in *The Guardian* (Nigeria) 24 August 2010, pp. 1–2.

51   See *Daily Independent* editorial "The Nation's 3,203 Oil Spills in Four Years", URL: http://allafrica.com/stories/201008130523.html Accessed 7 December 2010.

This charge also relates to *environmental racism*—discriminatory conduct of mining business in a manner that suggests that some operating environments are less socially valuable than others. Therefore, some extractive companies adjudged socially responsible corporate citizens in the developed world operate in developing countries in a way that makes host communities suffer disproportionately high levels of environmental damage because of equipment failure, outdated technologies, non-adherence to environmental safety protocols, and flagrant disregard for voiceless local communities. Such Western-based oil companies sometimes have an arguably inordinate influence over smaller nation-states and are occasionally implicated in human rights abuses in connivance with national or local governments in the developing world.[52]

In summary, the environmental justice frame enables MEND to make at least five fundamental claims. The first claim is that the people of the Niger Delta live in a peculiar and particularly difficult geographical terrain largely because of oil extraction. The second claim is an offshoot of the first: that because of its topography and revenue-generation machinery for the Nigerian state, the Niger Delta must be a priority in terms of developmental planning. These claims are not unique to MEND. The Willinks Commission report prior to Nigeria's independence in 1960 was unequivocal about the "special" problems of the minorities of the Niger Delta and called for the establishment of a government agency to plan and implement developmental projects concurrently with initiatives by the regional and federal governments as a panacea for the structural imbalance in the polity (Colonial Office 1958).

Third, the environmental justice frame enables MEND to make the claim that the people of the Niger Delta are not full citizens in the Nigerian nation-state. Embedded in this claim is the idea that the Niger Delta people have been "declared landless" by the Nigerian government and are victims of Nigeria's quest for oil and oil corporations' thirst for profits.[53] Fourth, MEND employs the environmental justice frame to allege that transnational oil corporations treat the Niger Delta region with disdain; are culpable in the human rights abuses in the region and ultimately guilty of environmental racism.[54]

---

52   Interviewee 14. Ken Saro-Wiwa (Jr.).

53   Jomo Gbomo. (number 24).

54   The same argument of discrimination has been used to explain the slow response of oil corporations to oil spills in the Delta. The argument that oil spills linger because of racism is understandable but tenuous although in terms of appointment, promotion and other emoluments, oil corporations are not above board. Oil corporations do not live up to their responsibility in Nigeria because the state is weak. Such corporations pay bribes to government officials and even community leaders to avert social responsibility or cleaning up oil spills. A relatively strong, stable and less-corrupt state would limit corporate irresponsibility. Oil corporations will attempt to operate with impunity wherever they can, as the 2010 oil spill in the Gulf of Mexico demonstrates. The onus is on the state to establish an effective regulatory framework for oil production.

Finally, MEND uses the environmental justice frame to draw attention to the consequences of the activities of transnational oil corporations. These include publicizing that Niger Deltans have lower life expectancy, live in chronic poverty even by Nigerian standards and suffer environmental hazards such as respiratory illnesses from gas flaring and destruction of the livelihood of the people—fishing and farming—as a consequence of environmental degradation from pipeline construction and routine oil spillage. The result is increased awareness of the Delta crisis, as MEND reiterates these issues after every insurgent action.

The Return to (True) Democracy Frame

Noonan (1995) outlines the *return to democracy* master frame in her research on the women's movement during the regime of Augusto Pinochet in Chile. Pinochet's introduction of "Catholic traditionalism", which mixes religion, patriotism, motherhood and *laisez faire* doctrine, enabled women in Chile to adopt a "maternal collective action frame" (Noonan 1995: 95). The irony in the use of patriarchal conservative ideology by women to fight the Chilean state is an interesting one (Noonan 1995). Chilean women used the same discourse as the regime rather than adopt potentially dangerous oppositional frames (common in much of the framing literature from advanced democracies). The women capitalized on the issue of traditional family values and integrity, which the regime promoted (Noonan 1995). The economic bust, and politicization of otherwise traditional (supposedly apolitical women), who were involved in protests ensured that a "return to democracy" master frame emerged circa 1978 (Noonan 1995: 98). Structural issues like employment, hunger and repressive tactics such as torture, murder, sexual harassment by state agents gave further gravitas to the frame.

A return to democracy frame is also part of the narrative of MEND. Although the clouds of the Nigerian insurgency have been accumulating for generations, would-be insurgents matured in the 1990s and reached an alarming level of operational finesse by the late 1990s and early 2000s. Nigeria returned to democratic rule on 29 May 1999 after decades of military dictatorship. As stated earlier, MEND as a name was formed late in 2005. This was during the civilian government of Olusegun Obasanjo. None the less, MEND claims that Nigeria's brand of democratic governance is foreign to the idea of democracy. Unlike the Chilean women under the Pinochet dictatorship, MEND does not call for a "return to democracy" but a return to *true* democracy. Several factors account for the use of a return to true democracy frame.

First, MEND posits that Nigeria's brand of democracy is an aberration because many foundational issues remain unresolved. These include devising a constitution that is fair to all, particularly the minorities. Instances of electoral malpractices and "executive recklessness" (Agozino 2003) also enable MEND to argue that politicians are "more concerned with looting their state treasuries and seeking a second term in office, even against the wishes of their people".[55] This standpoint is widely shared by civil society organizations and the public.

Second, the tenuous observance of the rule of law provides another basis for the use of the return to true democracy frame. The militarization of the Niger Delta and conduct of JTF operations provide incontrovertible evidence of state repression and human rights violation (Okaba 2009; Bot 2008; Omotola 2008; Thomas 2008; Akporaro 2008). In one instance, JTF operatives on August 20 2006 shot and killed 15 Ijaw youths who, unknown to the JTF, were returning from a mission to rescue a Shell oil worker at Letugbene Bayelsa state (Oboko 2010).

The final point is a corollary to the first two. The failure of the Nigerian state to behave like a democracy enables MEND to use the return to true democracy frame. In particular, MEND declared unilateral ceasefire on three occasions in the hope that the Nigerian government would "do the right thing"—engage the insurgents in meaningful dialogue to resolve the Niger Delta unrest and prevent "another cycle of violence".[56] MEND's Henry Okah met with President Umaru Yar'Adua on Monday, October 19, 2009. MEND was elated that the federal government had decided to engage the representatives of the insurgents in dialogue and declared an "indefinite ceasefire" on 20 October 2009 to facilitate the process. On Saturday, November 14, 2009 MEND's Aaron Team met with the president in Abuja. MEND expressed optimism that the "meeting heralds the beginning of serious, meaningful dialogue between MEND and the Nigerian government to deal with and resolve root issues that have long been swept under the carpet".[57] Three days later, MEND warned of a "threat to ceasefire" following a JTF operation in Kula community. This incident occurred at a time when the government had declared amnesty for the militants and had begun discussions with MEND. This was seen as another indication that the Nigerian state could not be trusted to honor agreements. One insurgent[58] explains that the lack of dialogue—a basic ingredient of democracy—in the Nigerian state made them resort to violence:

> Interviewer: It is on record, that your organization, Niger Delta People Volunteer Force was the first to explicitly call for the use of violence in the 1990s. Why did you resort to violence?
>
> Respondent: You see, *the Nigerian state does not believe in dialogue. What they are interested in is violence.* If you have a problem or you are quarreling with somebody, first and foremost, you have to apply dialogue. It is only when you

---

55 Jomo Gbomo statement (number 20).

56 Jomo Gbomo e-mail statement (number 3) "Indefinite Ceasefire". Tuesday 15 September 2009.

57 Jomo Gbomo e-mail statement (number 9) "FGN meets MEND Aaron Team". Saturday 14 November 2009.

58 Interviewee 15, Chief of Staff to Asari Dokubo. Personal interviewee, Port Harcourt, Rivers state, August 2010.

apply that dialogue, all the necessary avenues have been applied and they have refused to listen, then you give them the other language. May be, it will make them to give you a listening hear, because I can't just see you and begin to fight you. If I have a problem with you, there are elders, there are chiefs. You first of all present your matter or your issue with all those people and if the way they are handling issues or the way they are tackling the matter doesn't go down well with you, there are other avenues, but sometimes because when the verdict will be given, it is not in the favor or it is not in the favor of that person having the issue with you, you will not take it. At that point you have to try other ways and that is what we did. (emphasis added)

Some other factors in the political process in 2009/2010 enhanced MEND's use of the return to true democracy frame. The Nigerian president Umaru Yar'Adua became ill with pericarditis shortly after meeting with the insurgents' representatives in November 2009. This stalled the peace process. MEND was unimpressed that:

While the Nigerian government has conveniently tied the advancement of talks on the demands of this group to a sick president, it has not tied the repair of pipelines, exploitation of oil and gas as well as the deployment and re-tooling of troops in the region to the presidents ill health. While wishing the president a speedy recovery, a situation where the future of the Niger Delta is tied to the health and well-being of one man is unacceptable.

The illness of the president and attendant stalling of negotiations with insurgents points to the personalization of political power in Nigeria (see Bayart 2009; Richards 1986). This is intrinsically connected to the stranglehold leaders have on matters of policy and monopolization of decision-making as well as the failure to evolve enduring non-individuated institutions (see Bayart 2009; Mbembe 2001; Bayart, Ellis and Hibou 1999; Allen 1999).

Yar'Adua's ill-health launched an unprecedented succession battle. The Vice President Goodluck Jonathan was constitutionally required to take over as president. However, Yar'Adua neither officially handed over to Goodluck Jonathan nor wrote to the National Assembly to state that he would be away on leave as required by law. In addition, Jonathan was from the Ijaw ethnic group in the oil-rich Bayelsa state. Newspaper reports indicated that some political elites, particularly from the North, were opposed to a Christian Southerner serving out part of the presidency of a (Northern) Hausa-Fulani Muslim President. There was a palpable political vacuum for several weeks as Yar'Adua remained in a Saudi Arabia hospital from 23 November 2009. Rumors of an imminent military coup if Jonathan was not sworn in as president became widespread. Although MEND refused to join insurgent groups like the Joint Revolutionary Council (JRC) in calling for Jonathan's ascension to the presidency,[59] several militant groups were convinced that some Northern politicians refused to allow Jonathan to become president because he was a minority. The Network of Freedom Fighters in the Niger Delta, (NFF), a coalition of 50 insurgent groups, warned that if Section 145 of the 1999 Constitution, which makes provision for acting president was not implemented, there would be more violence in the Niger Delta.[60] This was an embarrassing development: A coalition of supposed "law-breakers" agitated for compliance with the rule of law. This case became another signifying moment: Nigeria was not a democracy after all.

The Supreme Court on 22 January 2010 ordered the Federal Executive Council to set up a team of doctors to determine the state of health of President Yar'Adua and ascertain if he was fit to govern. The Senate voted to allow Jonathan to become President in an acting capacity on 9 February 2010. Yar'Adua returned to Abuja on 24 February but Jonathan continued as acting president. Yar'Adua died on 5 May 2010 and Goodluck Jonathan took the oath of office as substantive President on 6 May 2010.

Concluding Thoughts: Nigeria's Political Process and MEND's Framing Strategies

This section analyzes how the political opportunity engendered by changes and fractures in the political structure of Nigeria have facilitated MEND's framing strategies. As stated in Chapter three, the *political opportunity* concept comprises three major claims (Koopmans 1999). These are the assertion that collective action is fundamentally shaped by variations in *opportunities*; second, as a result, variations in opportunity are a function of interactions of social movements with political and institutional actors (Koopmans 2009). Third, available opportunity is shaped by the structure of society, and not merely the strategic initiatives of social movement organizations (Koopmans 1999; Noonan 1995). The focus at this juncture is on how five major factors in Nigeria's political structure: the lack of counter-framing, failure of state interventionist programs, ethno-religious polarization, elite fragmentation and the "politics of the belly" (Bayart 2009) have unwittingly but fundamentally enhanced MEND's framing.

Constructing a collective action frame is an exercise in contestation (Benford and Snow 2000: 625). It is a complex, hydra-headed and multiplex endeavor involving constant negotiation by different actors. As this process is essentially about reality making and re-making, participants are engaged in what Benford and Snow

---

59   Jomo Gbomo e-mail statement (number 11) "JRC Disclaimer". Sunday 29 November 2009.

60   See Idonor Daniel and Samuel Oyadongha (4 February 2010). "MEND, 50 groups ready for fresh violence" URL: http://allafrica.com/stories/201002040029.html Accessed 17 November 2010.

(2000: 625), following Hall (1982), call the "politics of signification". Framing activities are delicate and mammoth processes whose mechanics are rarely monopolized by any set of actors. Framing activities involve considerable competition and negotiation. Activists face multiple challenges in the construction of collective action frames. These include counter-framing by movement opponents, (such as the state) bystanders and the media. There is also the possibility of disputes over appropriate and acceptable frames within a social movement organization. Saro-Wiwa learned this lesson during the Ogoni struggle as fellow activists in MOSOP, especially elites, openly disagreed with his strategies (see Bob 2002). Third, SMOs face possible tensions between their frames and collective action events (Benford and Snow 2000). Collective action frames are shaped by collective action events and vice versa. Collective action events can serve to attenuate or strengthen the kinds of frames adopted by a movement organization (Benford and Snow 2000). The interplay of these two antithetical phenomena shape framing processes because activists lack full control of both collective action frames and contentious events. MEND has been rather privileged in terms of the issues that may challenge a group's framing.

Besides spurts of unsystematic rebuttals, denials and name-calling from the JTF, MEND has largely enjoyed an unparalleled luxury of operating in an essentially non-competitive mono-framing field. The absence of a coherent and consistent response from the government to MEND's official statements and press releases is rather baffling. The JTF high command appears to have made the decision not to engage MEND in what they called "propaganda". The JTF commander, General Bello argues that "in conflicts of this nature, there is always propaganda. The first casualty is the truth…in the conflict in Niger Delta, the militants have had the upper hand in propaganda." He asserts that the crisis is an "internal conflict" and that the JTF does not "feel proud" to engage the insurgents, who are fellow Nigerians. Apart from this, General Bello notes that:

> in most conflicts in the world, the underdogs have better propaganda than the
> guys who are better. What I usually say to my soldiers is look; I would rather be
> more efficient in the operation than in propaganda than to be more efficient in
> propaganda and then I am losing men. So let us be more efficient in our operation,
> let us be more efficient as JTF in our operation, in the military operation, in the
> mandate, in the task we have been given; you know and then be less efficient in
> propaganda. Because I don't see what I stand to gain to demonize a portion of
> Nigeria in my quest to maybe have temporary victory.[61]

This intentional decision is perhaps one of the most significant opportunities handed to insurgents by the JTF. The JTF authorities' stance of "reactive press releases"[62] or responding on an ad hoc basis to specific incidents, confirming or

---

61   Interviewee 12. General Bello.
62   Interviewee 12.

denying figures and reports put out by MEND, arguably cedes the initiative and leaves MEND to win the battle of wits, hearts and minds in the Delta struggle.

This benefits MEND in several ways. First, many of MEND's claims are reported in the newspapers verbatim often with little contrary evidence. The public thus mainly hears MEND's side of the story. Second, MEND's routine official statements and occasional online interviews with journalists provide expansive material for the media to work with. This means that most of the "facts" reported are gleaned from MEND's sources rather than JTF's. Third, as a consequence of the above, MEND appears "open" and easily accessible—although none of these is completely accurate—while the JTF (and invariably the federal government) inadvertently earns a reputation of having something to hide because of its decision not to robustly engage MEND in "propaganda". These factors ensure that when opinions are formed by the public, bystanders and other interested persons, they predominantly evolve from what MEND put out.

In addition, the "supertribalization" (Osaghae 2003: 55) of young people in Nigeria is fundamental to understanding how Nigeria's political process nourishes MEND's framing strategies. It was noted in Chapter five that MEND focuses on Northern Nigeria in its diagnostic framing, as one of the loci of blame for the problems of the Niger Delta. This perspective resonates in other parts of Nigeria because Hausa-Fulani elites from the North are perceived as disproportionately benefitting from the system. This perception is widespread in Southern Nigeria and breeds contempt for Northerners occupying important offices in government. Such persons are often derided as beneficiaries of "federal character"—a cynical reference to the constitutionally sanctioned requirement that mandates distribution of public offices based on various ethnic, state and population dynamics.

The overwhelming number of military officers of Northern origins in the JTF and the supposed luxury in which they live[63] grant huge credibility to MEND's framing strategies among the people of the Delta and motivates them to fight against the Nigerian state. Most of the top brass of the JTF were from the North until the appointment of Major General Charles Osa Omoriege as Commander in September 2010. While this is a fairly benign point in theory, it enables MEND to accuse the JTF of occupying the Niger Delta with "Northern troops", who they claim trample on the rights of the people and perpetrate ethnic cleansing. This frames the presence of the JTF as a desecration of the Niger Delta by Northerners. A JTF staffed at the highest level by officers from the Niger Delta would arguably neutralize claims of ethnic cleansing and desecration.

Furthermore, two ethnically-charged incidents in 2008 and 2009 were probable blunders by a state accustomed to managing ethno-religious skirmishes. Management level appointments were announced at the NNPC in 2009. A huge public outcry followed the discovery that the Niger Delta was not well-represented in the government-owned company saddled with supervising crude oil extraction and revenue. Also, Professor Ibrahim Gambari, a Northerner and internationally

---

63　Interviewee 6. A soldier on assignment with the JTF. Personal interview. July 2009.

acclaimed diplomat, who worked closely with the General Sani Abacha regime that hanged the Ogoni Nine, was nominated in 2008 to serve as chair of the proposed Niger Delta Summit. The ensuing public condemnation led to the withdrawal of Gambari from the summit. The summit was eventually aborted altogether. These incidents lent the insurgency greater credibility among the people of the Delta and all over Nigeria, as insurgents pointed out the insensitivity of the Nigerian state to the Delta people.

The instability of political actors and availability of influential supporters (see Tilly and Tarrow 2007: 57) have had a significant impact on the framing strategies of MEND. The impressive array of elites in MEND's Aaron Team is one indication of the availability of influential supporters for MEND. A former Nigerian military Vice President, Vice Admiral Okhai Mike Akhigbe (rtd) and Nobel Laureate, Professor Wole Soyinka were two of the four eminent Nigerians who represented MEND at a meeting with President Yar'Adua on Saturday 14 November 2009, as stated in chapter three.

There is also a major schism among the political class besides the significant cultural and symbolic capital these elites bring to the cause of MEND. For example, the elites from the Niger Delta presumably have an extra-theoretical relationship with insurgents. There are instances where insurgents nominate members of government cabinets in the Delta,[64] as stated earlier. When the JTF visited Tom Polo's Camp 5, some payment vouchers of the Delta state government, among other documents, were reportedly discovered.[65] The vouchers indicated that the insurgents were receiving regular income from the government. Some political elites from the Delta seem to engage in double-speak with respect to the insurgency. While not openly supportive of the insurgents, they do not oppose them either. For some governors in the Delta, friendship with the militant commanders is an insurance against political violence in their states and possible guarantee of electoral victory. There is little doubt that MEND's framing strategies also receive considerable assistance from the sheer inanity of the Nigerian state. The chronic lack of capacity and failure to implement simple policies lend credence to the framing strategies of MEND. In particular, the Niger Delta Development Commission (NDDC), like other state interventionist programs in the Delta has been largely a failure (Adagbabiri 2006). The NDDC was established as a dedicated response to the lack of development in the oil-producing region. However, political brinkmanship and allegations of corruption are rife in the NDDC. This bureaucratic asininity at all levels of power in the Nigerian state draws widespread cynicism in the public. Therefore, insurgents who accuse the government of injustice and unfairness enjoy greater credibility than the Nigerian state. This point is further developed below.

MEND's framing strategies receive significant credibility and resonance in the public because of the entity represented by the Nigerian state *qua* state and its

---

64   Interviewees 1 and 20.

65   Interviewee 20. General Bello refused to make a comment on this point.

mechanism of operation. Jean-Francois Bayart (2009)[66] in *The State in Africa: The Politics of the Belly* develops a theoretical framework for understanding how states, particularly south of the Sahara, function. African states, he argues, function on *politique du ventre* or the *politics of the belly*. The belly is a metaphorical insignia and signification of the problematic socio-historical contours and dynamics of such states. The belly is also an organizing apparatus for the conduct of politics. Corruption and other means of self-aggrandizement are "simple" demonstrations of the politics of the belly (Bayart 2009: 235).[67]

The constellation of historical moments and flows: pre-colonial, colonial and neo-colonial, fundamentally shapes the operation of the postcolonial state. The relations of pre-colonial times, the brigandage, and brutality of the colonial era as well as the globalization of capital in the neo-colonial age provide the defining silhouette of the postcolonial state. The state "functions as a rhizome of personal networks, and assures the centralisation of power through the agencies of family, alliance and friendship, in the manner of ancient kingdoms, which possessed the principle attributes of a State within a lineage matrix, thereby reconciling two types of political organisation" (Bayart 2009: 261–2). Neither traditional nor bureaucratic in the Weberian sense, the postcolonial state is dictatorial and often personalized by the rulers (see Bayart 2009).

For the masses, the state re-presents the failure of independence (Bayart 2009: 249). Excessive use of force by the state and criminal misappropriation of government funds, however, "do not entirely prevent legitimacy or popular assent" (249) to the postcolonial state since everyone awaits their turn to "chop" or eat. The masses also develop a potent fatalism, which serves as a coping mechanism (250). Extra-state spaces are fabricated in the interstices of the political space. In Nigeria, Christianity and Islam are extra-state spaces and a huge part of the informal economy. It is not uncommon for corrupt contractors to pay tithes of unexecuted projects to the church with no questions asked.

More fundamental, the people merely pay "lip-service to their adhesion to the State" (Bayart 2009: 254). There is a lack of basic trust between the government and the governed. Consequently, in the unwritten hierarchy of credibility, a high level of cynicism surrounds any initiative by the state or any of its organs. The

---

66   First published in French in 1989. The first English version was published in 1993.

67   Institutionalization of social conflict by regimes as a matter of existential necessity is not uncommon (Bayart 2009: 250). For instance, the controversial 2007 elections in Kenya degenerated into violence that led to the ethnically-related death of at least 1200 persons. The International Court of Justice found that elites from both sides of the political divide—including Uhuru Kenyatta Deputy Prime Minister and finance minister, Francis Kirimi Muthaura, secretary to the cabinet and Mohammed Hussein Ali, former police chief, allies of President Mwai Kibaki as well as supporters of opposition leader Raila Odinga such as Henry Kosgey, minister for industrialization, William Ruto, suspended education minister and Joshua Arap Sang, a radio executive—were the "most responsible" for the crisis. See BBC News (15 Dec.). 2010. "Kenya election violence: ICC names suspects", URL: http://www.bbc.co.uk/news/world-africa-11996652 Accessed 15 December 2010.

public presupposition is that government officials are self-seeking corrupt people; hence their utterances are lies until proven otherwise. MEND's framing strategies thus often instantaneously receive an almost telepathic support from the public, civil society and even the media. A JTF spokesperson describes the situation succinctly:

> Because of working basically with any pro-government establishment, if you have an account of what has happened, their (the public and the media's) first impression is that I probably know something and or perhaps you have not told the truth. You have to go the extra mile to get to convince them that what you have said is the truth.

Nigerian citizens have a serious distrust of the state and its organs. Any public statement or policy initiative from the government is deemed to be another fraudulent scheme because of years of corruption and mismanagement. The NNPC, the parastatal that oversees matters of oil extraction, demonstrates this trend. A committee in the Senate in May 2009 publicly criticized the NNPC for running a "mystery budget".[68] In fact, the notion of "mystery budget" was a euphemism for the NNPC's failure to provide any budget for the Senate and the public to scrutinize. Interestingly, the Senate was infuriated in November 2010 when the Central Bank governor, Lamido Sanusi, declared that the two chambers of the National Assembly—the Senate and House of Representatives—received 25 percent of all the federal government's overhead in Nigeria.[69] Therefore, the Senate's criticism of the NNPC amounts to a profligate entity investigating another wasteful government agency. These allegations are in the public domain and erode confidence in the state and its organs. This inadvertently makes the framing strategies of insurgents more credible among the people.

In conclusion, this chapter analyzes the master frames—the imperative of violence frame, the injustice frame, the minority/human rights frame, environmental justice frame and the return to democracy frame—in the MEND insurgency. In MEND's discursive universe, pipeline vandalism, kidnapping of oil workers and car bombings are executed supposedly with hesitation and have to be understood within the *imperative of violence* master frame. This frame is an addition to the growing number of master frames in the scholarly literature. The imperative of violence master frame is the fundamental metanarrative of the MEND insurgency. Insurgents believe that the Nigerian state has created a war situation by bombing some oil-producing communities in the Delta, denying them inalienable human rights and failing to provide basic social services.

---

68   Ojeifo, Sufuyan. 2009. "Senate—NNPC Runs 'Mystery' Budget", *This Day*, May 27. URL: http://allafrica.com/stories/200905270205.html Accessed 6 December 2010.

69   Akogun, Kunle. 2010. "Standing Firm, Sanusi Meets Angry Senators", *This Day* (December 1). URL: http://allafrica.com/stories/201012020323.html Accessed 6 December 2010.

Therefore, insurgents discursively posit that the phenomenon of *kidnapping oil workers should be regarded by the public as a relatively minor irritation* within a war situation. Insurgents underscore the notion of a *war* situation. For MEND insurgents, kidnapped oil workers are *enemy* combatants working on behalf of the Nigerian state.

The analysis also shows that MEND uses the injustice frame to explicate the conditions of the people of the Delta. They attempt to create a link between the suffering of the people and the actions of the coalition. MEND also universalizes its struggle by appealing to humanity and the discourse of justice, human and minority rights. These narrative techniques present the people of the Delta as the oppressed victims of the Nigerian state and oil corporations that are exploiting its resources without adequate compensations and concern for the quality of life of the people. By so doing, MEND construes itself as the collective reaction of the Delta people and other Nigerians, who are committed to social justice, human rights, and self-determination.

This chapter also analyzes the environmental justice and the return to (true) democracy master frames in the MEND insurgency. It demonstrates that MEND uses the environmental justice frame to accentuate the Delta people's lack of participation in the drilling of oil and gas reserves and how the people are treated as second class citizens. This master frame also furnishes MEND with the tool to challenge the oil spill incidents and sundry environmental pollution in the Delta, which have had adverse effects on the health of the people. On the other hand, the return to (true) democracy frame enables MEND to put itself on a moral pedestal as a force for championing the cause of democratic reforms. MEND uses this frame to point out the contradictions in the polity, subversion of the rule of law and the privatization of the levers of power. All of these find resonance among people who have benefitted little from their country's enormous oil wealth. This chapter concludes by examining how the dynamics of the Nigerian political process helps MEND's framing strategies to resonate among the public. The failure of the Nigerian state and its organs, particularly the JTF, to engage in any consistent and rigorous counter-framing efforts is a windfall for MEND's framing aesthetics. The entire framing space is thus freely ceded to MEND. The availability of influential elite, who sympathize with the cause of the Delta struggle, has also granted considerable credibility to the frames. Among other factors, the government's poor reputation, the failure of many of its social programs, and corruption in the polity also contribute to making MEND's framing strategies align with the beliefs of everyday people. This alignment guarantees that the Nigerian state is always on the defensive relative to insurgents in the public domain.

Chapter 7
A Repertoire of Protest or Criminal Expropriation?

Introduction

This chapter focuses on a key issue: *Is kidnapping of oil workers a repertoire of protest or criminal expropriation?* This question is explored through, among several other sources, data garnered from field work in Agge community Bayelsa state (2009) and Okerenkoko in Gbaramatu Kingdom Delta state (2010). Kidnapping of oil workers in the Delta has gone through a process of evolution. For Okaba (2009), kidnapping began as a communal response to neglect and absence of basic social facilities. Okaba (2009) divides the episodes into three timelines. The first phase occurred between 1960 and 1990 (Okaba 2009). In this era, community members mobilized en masse to block access to oil infrastructure. Issues of provision of employment, and other social amenities as well as implementation of various memoranda of understanding between oil companies and communities were the major issues at stake (Okaba 2009). It was not unusual for local and foreign oil workers to be briefly held hostage by community representatives until an agreement was reached for providing needed services. Payment of ransom was non-existent at this period.[1] Kidnapping of oil workers was a form of communal agitation at this stage.

The second phase began in 1990 and ended in 2002 (Okaba 2009: 22). Foreign oil workers became targets of kidnapping by newly emerging groups during this period. The foreigners were considered "high value targets" because the attention of the international community could be easily secured, while local oil workers would not generate a serious reaction from the Nigerian state (Ikporukpo 2008, cited in Okaba 2009: 22). Okaba (2009) estimates the third phase of hostage-taking from 2003 to date. The targets, he argues are "individuals and institutions (local and foreign) within and outside the oil industry that have potentials for huge ransoms" (p. 22). Huge ransoms were demanded by kidnappers from 2003 onwards. Kidnappings also increased in intensity. There are contestations over the appropriateness of this tactic among the Nigerian public, elites, and even insurgent groups. The insurgent leader responsible for initializing the on-going phase of kidnapping, Asari Dokubo, argues that "Hostage-taking is a powerful tool in revolutionary struggle but what is happening is not what is done in other parts of the world. What is happening is that criminals have hijacked our struggle"

---

1   Interviewees 1 and 2.

(*The Punch*, 7 August 2007: 7). Dokubo particularly condemned the kidnapping of minors "who are still wearing napkins". This suggests that even among those directly involved, kidnapping is highly contested.

From a Hobsbawmian perspective, factors like unemployment, poverty, injustice, the presence of inaccessible creeks and waterways, societal transition from kinship structure to bureaucratic structure, weakness and division in the state and resistance against the destruction of a people's way of life are crucial to the rise of social banditry. All of these factors are present in Nigeria's Delta (see Oyefusi 2008, 2007; Omeje 2007; Ibeanu and Luckham 2007; Okereke 2006; Okonta 2005; Human Rights Watch 2005; Zalik 2004). What remains unaddressed is whether or not politically-motivated kidnapping in the Delta is an act of criminality or a repertoire of protest. In other words, is the kidnapping of oil workers a form of social banditry or a mere criminal act?

Hobsbawm's (1969: 13) theoretical specification offers a way to provide answers to this question. He argues that bandits are:

> outlaws whom the lord and state regard as criminals, but who remain within peasant society, and are considered by their people as heroes, as champions, avengers, fighters for justice, perhaps even leaders of liberation, and in any case as men to be admired, helped and supported. This relation between the ordinary peasant and the rebel, outlaw and robber is what makes social banditry interesting and significant.

For Hobsbawm, therefore, the key to ascertaining whether groups such as MEND are a gang of criminals or social bandits is to investigate the relationship between the said group and the opinions of members of their poor rural communities. This standpoint is theoretically and empirically useful for a number of reasons. First, MEND and its affiliates construct the people of the Niger Delta as voiceless victims whose interests they supposedly represent by engaging the current Nigerian system. Second, other actors in this struggle, such as political and economic elites, environmental and political activists, and the media, among others may have certain interests that are not necessarily the same as those of the everyday people of the oil-producing region. Political elites and the Nigerian state are essentially concerned with ensuring the ceaseless flow of oil, while the media are interested in covering stories they consider newsworthy, as demonstrated in Chapter two. Besides, many of these actors—political activists and those maintaining the status quo—do not necessarily have the same experiences as the people in rural areas in the Delta.

Consequently, the opinions of the rural population of the people of the oil-producing Delta region is treated as the most credible parameter for interrogating whether kidnapping of oil workers is sheer criminality or a repertoire of protest. This reflects a careful theoretical choice.

The Role of a *Benevolent Insurgent Commander:* The "Messiah" Called Tom Polo

The major finding is that any Delta community with at least one recognized *benevolent insurgent commander* specialized in kidnapping and other related activities like illegal oil bunkering will generally view kidnapping as a form of protest while a community without a benevolent insurgent commander will construe kidnapping as a criminal act. *Benevolent insurgent commander* means a founder, leader, or "General" in any of the many insurgent groups in the Delta who actively engages in executing humanitarian projects or provides basic social amenities like clean water and roads in his or her community. This category includes people like Henry Bindodogha who took me to the NDFF creeks. Bindodogha and I visited his parents' communities, Ofunama and Abere on Friday 27 August 2010. The reception we were accorded demonstrated that he was a beloved son. An entry in my journal shows that "a huge crowd quickly developed" to welcome us and that our visit "soon became a big ceremony and spectacle". Not surprisingly, there were community members who requested favors from Bindodogha at the welcome party in our honor.

However, not all insurgents enjoy the same level of public affection. The likes of "Ken", an insurgent commander from Kaiama and Priest Igodo were loathed by the people in their communities. Ken and Igodo represent *non-benevolent insurgent commanders*. The distinction between benevolent and non-benevolent insurgent commanders goes beyond semantics. One activist explains that:

> those militants who actually kidnapped expatriates and got money from there used the money for the youths and for the upliftment of their communities, but those who were sustained by the government like Ateke Tom, supported by Odili (former Governor of the oil-rich Rivers state) used the money against their own people ... Those that were sustained by the politicians used the money, that political resource that political patronage as element of oppression against their people.[2]

None the less, as explained below, an insurgent commander can engage in kidnapping as well as enjoy patronage from politicians, and yet use the revenue from both activities for the benefit of the people.

Agge and Okerenkoko, two oil-producing communities, provide fascinating evidence of the variability of how kidnapping in the Niger Delta is socially constructed, vacillating between criminality and protest. They also demonstrate how one insurgent commander can fundamentally shape the people's perceptions of the entire insurgency. Agge is in the Ekeremor local government area of Bayelsa state. The JTF carried out an operation in search of militants supposedly hiding in

---

2   Interviewee 2.

the community in August 2008.[3] The military action was a reprisal for the attack on soldiers along the Forcados River in Bomadi area of Bayelsa state. Two soldiers died and insurgents captured a JTF gunboat in that attack. Although newspaper reports indicated that some of the youths in the community engaged the JTF in a gun battle and were shot dead, the paramount chief of Agge confirms that the only casualty was his younger brother, who died the night after the military action "not from gun (shot) but fear" as "he was not so sound".[4] The people of the community stated that they ran for their lives as soldiers burned down all the houses except the town hall and churches. The JTF, however, claims that the houses caught fire because the people hoarded petroleum products in their homes.[5]

Okerenkoko has also had its share of military action. The JTF carried out aerial bombardment of three communities in the Gbaramatu Kingdom; Okerenkoko, Oporoza and Kunukuma communities in the Warri South West Local Government Area of Delta state on 15 May 2009. The military action was conducted after insurgents allegedly hijacked two NNPC vessels, kidnapped 15 oil workers, injured six soldiers and killed two soldiers in the same week. The palace of the king was bombed in the JTF reprisal. At least 37 persons died in the bombardment of Gbaramatu Kingdom by the JTF.[6]

Agge and Okerenkoko share many characteristics. First, both are oil-producing communities in the Niger Delta undergoing similar problems of socio-economic marginalization and environmental degradation. Second, as explained above, both communities have experienced brutal military repression: Agge in 2008 and Okerenkoko in 2003, 2006 and 2009. Third, the military attacks in both communities led to colossal destruction of property. Fourth, both communities were believed to be havens for militants. The rationale provided by the JTF for the attacks on both communities was that they harbored militants who kidnapped oil workers and/or attacked or killed soldiers.[7] Fifth, one can reasonably expect that these two communities would have grievances against the Nigerian state, which deployed the JTF troops as well as the militants who gifted the JTF reasons to attack them.

However, Agge and Okerenkoko differ in one fundamental respect: Agge does not have a recognized benevolent militant commander while Okerenkoko does. This does not mean that young people from Agge are not involved in the insurgency, rather there is no militant of *significant* rank from Agge community.

---

3   Interviewee 3, Colonel Rabe Abubakar, former Coordinator Joint Media Campaign Centre (JMCC) of the JTF. Personal interview, July 2009, Effurun, Warri Delta state.

4   Paramount Chief of Agge community. Personal interview, Agge community, July, 2009.

5   Interviewee 3.

6   See "37 feared killed as JTF invades Delta communities", URL: http://ndn. nigeriadailynews.com/templates/?a=17836&z=50 Accessed 7 December 2010.

7   Interviewees 3. Interviewee 10, Lt. Col. Timothy Antigha, Coordinator Joint Media Campaign Centre (JMCC) of the JTF. Personal interview, July 2010, Abuja. Antigha took over as media coordinator from Abubakar.

This means that Agge is unable to attract the patronage afforded by a "son of the soil" who is well-placed in the insurgency. Two focus group discussions were conducted in Agge in 2009. Participants were unequivocal in their condemnation of kidnapping. They claimed that groups like MEND, NDPVF, NDFF and others are not fighting for Agge, as they are a peace-loving people. The president of the youth association among others said that kidnapping gave the Niger Delta a bad name in Nigeria and overseas and was partly responsible for the brutal treatment they often received at the hands of soldiers. Participants argued that the kidnappers merely enriched themselves while hiding under the cloak of the struggle. The paramount chief expressed the readiness of the community to live in peace and attract significant infrastructural development.

On the other hand, "General" Government Ekpemupolo or "Tom Polo", an indigene of Okerenkoko, is one of several insurgent commanders who use some of the proceeds of the insurgency for the benefit of their communities. Tom Polo's generosity to the people of Okerenkoko and Gbaramatu Kingdom in general fundamentally shapes how kidnapping in particular and the entire insurgency are perceived in his community. Very few insurgent leaders have had as much impact on the insurgency as Tom Polo. Tom Polo's influence is arguably rivaled only by the repercussions generated by Asari Dokubo's NDPVF. Dokubo was the first to call for the explicit use of violence against the Nigerian state and his group pioneered the current trajectory of kidnapping in the Niger Delta.[8] Tom Polo was the mobilization officer of the Federated Niger Delta Ijaw Communities (FNDIC). Although Tom Polo has not been officially relieved of his duties at FNDIC, his relationship with the organization is no longer cordial. FNDIC president Oboko Bello said Tom Polo "used to be a very purposeful boy, cool headed and was relied upon truly as the mobilization officer".[9] Tom Polo is a pioneer member of MEND[10] and one of the primogenitors of the violent turn of the Niger Delta movement. Many insurgent commanders, including Henry Bindodogha of the NDFF learned the rudiments of the discipline from Tom Polo before establishing their own groups. Tom Polo has a messianic appeal among insurgents besides possessing enormous resources. Three young men who had served as reggae artistes at Camp 5 were interviewed at the Obubra camp, where ex-militants were being rehabilitated. All three had each recorded one album with songs dedicated to the prowess of Tom Polo although they had had little personal contact with Tom Polo. One of the artistes, "Young P" describes Tom Polo as "God-sent to deliver his people". Young P's lyrics portray Tom Polo as a transcendental figure:

Tom Polo is saying everybody unite
No betraying
Tom Polo says everybody come together

---

8   Interviewee 15.
9   Interviewee 38.
10   Interviewee 19

No backbiting
Tom Polo says everybody love your brother in this land ...[11]

Tom Polo is the brain behind the (in)famous Camp 5 in Gbaramatu Kingdom, where insurgents kept the 15 oil workers kidnapped in May 2009. This is only a fraction of Camp 5's prolific operations. One of the operatives from Camp 5 claimed to have personally participated in kidnapping at least 30 persons between 2007 and 2009.[12] Therefore, Tom Polo's activities were directly responsible for the military repression in Okerenkoko in 2009. There are also allegations of extrajudicial killings, and extortion against Tom Polo. He is believed to have gained his reputation largely because of the mysterious deaths of 29 young men from Gbaramatu Kingdom working at Camp 5 who dared to mutiny against him.[13] The Delta state government allegedly took credit for the killing of the Camp 5 men, who were presented to the public as "sea pirates".[14] This endeared Tom Polo to the Delta state government. Vouchers of the Delta state government were allegedly found at Camp 5 when the JTF raided it in May 2009.[15] However, Tom Polo remains phenomenally popular in Okerenkoko in spite of his alleged involvement in extrajudicial murder, extortion, and bribery.

Two focus group discussions were conducted in Okerenkoko in August 2010. The first comprised six adult males, while three adult females (18 and above) were the second group. Participants were eager to narrate how Tom Polo used the money he made from his activities to rebuild the bombed palace of their king and to ensure that the king was solvent. In addition, two of the six men in one of the focus group discussions claimed that Tom Polo's Camp 5 employed hundreds of young men from the community and ensured that they received regular income to take care of their families. The participants suggested that whatever Tom Polo did was to secure the survival of the people as many of them had benefitted from proceeds of the kidnapping of oil workers. The women narrated how Tom Polo distributed food items, provided clean water, electricity generators and scholarships for their children. It was particularly striking to hear from a woman who had lost a son in the aerial bombardment of Okerenkoko by the JTF in 2009. Amid tears, she blamed the JTF for her woes and praised Tom Polo for fighting for the rights of the people of the Niger Delta.

Tom Polo appears to be a charismatic leader in the insurgency. Other insurgent commanders look up to him for direction and occasional financial assistance.[16] Many insurgents in the Delta, including commanders with different camps refer

---

11   Interviewee 35.

12   Interviewee 27. Former Camp 5 insurgent. Personal interview at the Amnesty rehabilitation camp, Obubra, Cross River, August 2010.

13   Interviewee 20.

14   Interviewee 20.

15   Interviewee 20.

16   Interviewee 19.

to Tom Polo as their "master". As Max Weber argues, charismatic authority emanates from the recognition of the mission of an individual, who possesses strong determination and self-restraint. If the mission succeeds, such an individual becomes "their master—so long as he knows how to maintain recognition through 'proving' himself" (1968: 20).

The Delta is going through a period of crisis as is clear by now. A crisis is generally conducive to the emergence of charismatic leaders (see Weber 1968). There can also be little doubt that the weakness of the Nigerian state has facilitated (see Eatwell 2006) the emergence of charismatic insurgents like Tom Polo. Personality also matters in the rise of charismatic authority, as Eatwell (2006) observes (see also Lepsius 2006). In this case, Tom Polo's organizational prowess—while managing to remain outside the law—and ability to hire and coordinate better educated advisers are major strengths.

There are several other reasons why Tom Polo is the major figure in the insurgency. First, several of the boys working for Tom Polo at the Camp 5 have never actually met Tom Polo in person despite working for him for five years or more. Tom Polo surrounds himself with a plethora of lieutenants that ensures that his boys rarely, if ever, see him. Therefore, Tom Polo's itinerary is often talked about but he remains akin to a spirit whose presence can only be felt but never seen by the majority of his boys. This wraps the Tom Polo persona in mystique and ensures that he remains larger than life in the eyes of the boys who execute his commands. Second, Tom Polo rarely grants media interviews. His public appearances are also few. Tom Polo is difficult to reach and often delegates his lieutenants to speak or appear on his behalf while many insurgent commanders have become regular features in the media. This is interesting as Tom Polo is believed to have limited formal education, is far from articulate and employs ghost writers for his rare public statements.[17] Yet, his failure to grant interviews or appear in public has helped make him a towering insurgent figure, deflecting attention away from his supposed lack of oratorical gifts. His cultivated silence ensures that his followers, community members, other insurgent camps, the media and society at large remain enthralled, wondering what Tom Polo might do next.

Third, Tom Polo's generosity to his boys, members of rival groups and the people of Gbaramatu Kingdom is a major source of his authority. The magnitude of resources available to him and his willingness to distribute them help guarantee his adoration. In addition, his ability to circulate among conventional political elites has enhanced his legend among his boys, community members and rival insurgent commanders.

Tom Polo's situation in Okerenkoko in particular and Gbaramatu Kingdom in general aligns with Hobsbawm's (1969) notion of social banditry in several ways. First, while Tom Polo was a wanted criminal by the Nigerian state before the amnesty program,[18] the people continue to see him as a hero and champion

---

17   Interviewee 37.
18   Interviewee 12. JTF Commander, General Sarkin Yaki Bello.

of their cause. Second, he appears as a personal manifestation of Hobsbawm's (1969) prediction that banditry "may arise in sub-Saharan Africa on a more significant scale than we have had on record in the past" (1969: 19). The potent mixture of unemployment, poverty, injustice, favorable topography among others has contributed to making a social bandit out of Tom Polo even though his acts appear criminally outlandish. The failure and weakness of the Nigerian state also make everyday people in Okerenkoko look elsewhere for a hero. This is where the Tom Polo phenomenon reaps dividends as an extra-state benevolent militant commander. For example, an environmental justice advocate states that "I learnt he (Tom Polo) was doing reasonably well for his community people, that if you go to Gbaramatu that the place is really like a place you will cherish."[19] Tom Polo is a wealthy bandit and not a peasant contrary to Hobsbawm's schema. In fact, the enormous resources at his disposal are *sine qua non* to his status in an impoverished community.

Furthermore, today's bandits in Nigeria are experts at navigating rural and urban areas. In fact, they thrive in maneuvering the interstices of the rural and urban social space. Therefore, they are not necessarily rooted in rural areas as Hobsbawm (1969; 1959) suggests or urban-based as Mkandawire (2008) argues. Even urban-based groups can be explicitly concerned with issues affecting rural-based people, as Mkandire (2008) acknowledges in the case of the Ogoni movement led by MOSOP.

Tom Polo has used both government patronage and elements of genuine agitation to garner support from the people of Gbaramatu Kingdom. Although an active participant in the crass opportunism and exspoliation of the Niger Delta, Tom Polo is the metaphor for the bandit who robs the rich to give to the poor. Tom Polo is the figure of social protest and rebellion against the state (see Hobsbawm 1969) in the eyes of community members and the young men and women who participated in the struggle. He is the *de facto* government in a community where only oil wells remind the people of the Sovereign. The messianic phenomenon of Tom Polo is symbolic of the complexity of the Niger Delta movement and the interpellation (in an Althusserian sense) of everyone—rightly or wrongly—in the crisis. Tom Polo has managed to enrich himself, perpetrate spectacular acts of violence inimical to his community's well-being, entrench his personality in the political arena in Delta state as a power broker, while maintaining a level of popularity that most public figures can only wish they had.

At another theoretical level, Tom Polo and other benevolent insurgents partly owe their confounding popularity among the masses to the "criminalization of politics and the state" (Bayart, Ellis and Hibou 1999: 25). This phenomenon is fast rising on the continent of Africa. Arguably, nowhere is this phenomenon more accentuated than the Niger Delta region of Nigeria. A major characteristic of this phenomenon is that the legitimate organs of state are used for private purposes aimed at corrupt enrichment, and "organized gangs" are used for political

---

19   Interviewee 4

purposes as an essential part of the clandestine network surrounding political office holders (Bayart, Ellis and Hibou 1999: 25). In this environment, the state's "capacity to execute any form of policy has quite simply evaporated and its place has been taken, at least to some extent, by churches and religious solidarities, a burgeoning informal economy, and military organizations and militias or other armed movements" (Bayart, et al. 1999: 19). In essence, the state is increasingly reduced to a "legal fiction" (Bayart et al. 1999: 21) as established bureaucracies are circumvented by extra-state machineries.

The manner in which participants from Agge and Okerenkoko communities narrated their suffering, lack of access to basic social services and destruction of their livelihood demonstrates the failure of the Nigerian state. The people unwittingly evinced an overwhelming lack of confidence in the Nigerian state. The chief in Agge who was slightly more upbeat about the possibility of positive change in his community did not expect anything to happen soon. In addition, apart from the oil infrastructure, the people's experiential reality is an almost complete rupture from the Nigerian body politic. People in Agge and Okerenkoko communities seem to accept that theirs was a land under siege by a power they neither knew nor understood. In fact, a high level of communalism, strong religious beliefs, and a chronically fatalistic attitude to life are the three major coping mechanisms against violence and deprivation in both communities.

In summary, this chapter focuses on one key question: "Is kidnapping of oil workers in the Delta a repertoire of protest or criminal expropriation?" Agge community and Okerenkoko in Gbaramatu Kingdoms are used as case studies. The overall argument is that a community that has a *benevolent insurgent commander* who is able to distribute social goods like roads, schools, scholarships and food will perceive kidnapping and other acts of insurgency as a form of protest and self-help, while a community that has no benevolent insurgent commander will be strongly opposed to kidnapping and the insurgency in general. This chapter also focuses on Government Ekpemulo or Tom Polo, as a quintessential social bandit. Tom Polo remains hugely popular among the people because of his social welfare services and the mystification of his personality though he has become a major player and beneficiary of the insurgency as well as government patronage.

Chapter 8
Summary and Conclusions

Summary

This book investigates the phenomenon of kidnapping of oil workers in the Niger Delta region of Nigeria. The interstitial space invented through the processual deployment of kidnapping is interrogated on one hand as a form of protest and on the other hand, as sheer criminal expropriation. Episodes of kidnapping are explicated as the collective effervescence of Delta communities emanating from socio-economic flows, political trajectories, historical contours and moments. Kidnapping is the name of the social fact that interpellates everyone in Nigeria and (mis)appropriates all facets of the society.

In Chapter 1, the research problem is contextualized by situating the Niger Delta in the ethno-linguistic crossroads of Nigeria. The incessant ethno-religious conflicts, such as the Tiv-Jukun conflicts in Taraba state (Best, Idyorough and Shehu 2007), the Ife-Modakeke conflict in Osun state (Albert 2007a), and the Zangon-Kataf crisis in Kaduna state (Akinteye, Wuye and Ashafa 2007), *inter alia* are nothing new in Nigeria and pose a relatively negligible threat to its corporate existence. None of these crises fundamentally challenges the precarious socio-political infrastructure of the Federal Republic of Nigeria as the rise of the "mature insurgency" (Watts 2004) in the Niger Delta since the early 2000s. The peoples of the Delta have derived little benefit from the activities of transnational oil corporations and the billions of dollars flowing into the exchequer in spite of the stupefying network of oil facilities and the concomitant elevation of the Niger Delta to the status of the substantive income generating machinery of Nigeria. This has led to the deplorable living conditions of Niger Delta communities (Watts 2008a, 2008b; Courson 2007; Joab-Peterside 2007a; Omeje 2004) and guarantees the alienation of the people from the body politick (Joab-Peterside 2007b; Ikelegbe 2005b).

Social movement scholarship has yet to examine the political opportunities that catalyzed MEND and other insurgent groups as well as their framing strategies despite the impressive array of studies on the Delta. This academic oversight is traced to the fact that the adoption of violent tactics by social movement organizations often poses sheer consternation to social movement scholars because of the romanticization of peaceful repertoires of protests (see Seidman 2001).

The dynamics of kidnapping in the Niger Delta is investigated. A locational and ideational specificity to kidnappings in the Niger Delta is provided. Many of the kidnappings in Nigeria have little to do with the movement against transnational corporation exploitation and state marginalization. Three variants of *opportunistic kidnappings* in Nigeria are identified and delineated from kidnappings for the furtherance of the movement represented by MEND. This book embeds the on-going violent struggle in the Delta in the wider social movement literature as has been done with the rise and decline of MOSOP (see Okonta 2008; Bob 2005, 2002). Chapter 1 also provides insight into the data and methods of the study, its significance, scope and limitations.

The second chapter of this book, "Kidnapping as "public good": The actors, social benefits and harms of the Nigeria's oil insurgency" problematizes the roles of two sets of actors—first-order and second-order cast—in the kidnapping episodes in the Delta. These include the oil-producing communities, interventionists, insurgents, oil workers, and oil corporations, insurance companies, and security companies, among others. It draws on Goffman's (1973, 1967) microsociology to enunciate the theatricality of kidnappings and the ongoing mutually reinforcing impression management by the actors. Kidnapping in Nigeria is marked by performativity: Various actors have roles that are articulately scripted, organically orchestrated and meticulously delivered for impression management. The harms and benefits of the insurgency to the actors are highlighted.

The complexity of the phenomenon of kidnapping is highlighted in Chapter 3. Kidnapping is contextualized as one of the many effects of lingering structural issues like low income, lack of educational opportunities (Oyefusi 2008; Turner 1998) and excessive use of violence by the state in controlling dissent and other forms of expression of frustration by the socially marginal (Sanchez 2006). The concept of *social banditry* (Hobsbawm 1969) is used as a theoretical framework in analyzing kidnapping. The notion of "contentious politics"—a cardinal tenet of the political opportunity/process paradigm—as well as conditions undergirding adoption of repertoires of protest by dissidents are interrogated. This chapter also presents findings on the political opportunities for kidnapping oil workers in the Delta. Nigeria's political process is interrogated with a view to understanding the opportunities created for or invented by insurgents engaged in kidnapping oil workers. The relative openness of Nigeria's institutionalized political system, the instability of elite alignments inherent in the polity (see Goodwin and Jasper 1999), the Nigerian state's capacity and apparatus of repression (see McAdam 1996a; Goodwin and Jasper 1999), and the interactions of social movements with political and institutional actors (see Koopmans 1999) are underscored. In addition, how the structure of the Nigerian society influences opportunities for kidnapping is highlighted.

Kidnapping is not a mere expression of the strategic initiatives of MEND and associate groups like NDPVF but a product of Nigeria's political process (see Koopmans 1999; Noonan 1995). The overarching theme in this chapter is that the socio-political process, its economic contours, disjuncture and inequitable configurations have served to produce kidnappers. In addition, the Delta public perceives foreign oil workers as the colonialist Other that have historically reaped where they have not sown. Other fundamental emotional issues like the *Abuja-Oloibiri nexus* are examined. Oloibiri, it is submitted, is the metaphor for the tragedy of oil-producing communities and the signature of the Delta peoples' historical subjugation within the Nigerian rentier petro-state. Abuja, on the other hand embodies the front-stage and façade of a supposedly rich and flourishing petro-state; the architectural expression of the generational oppression of the Niger Delta people. This chapter concludes by making reference to the role of the Specters of the Past—Isaac Adaka Boro and Ken Saro-Wiwa and how the treatment meted out to them has re-defined the struggle in the Niger Delta.

In Chapter 4, Car Bombing "with due respect": The *Idea* called MEND, the rise of MEND is investigated. This chapter begins with an analysis of the historical and immediate factors that precipitated the meta-phenomenon of MEND. This uber-insurgent *thing*, its clinical precision in executing its intents, and its mode of operation are enunciated. MEND's loose structure and secrecy, fluid membership, public sympathy, the Niger Delta terrain, which favors asymmetrical warfare, enigmatic status, unique internal logic, and vast resources, technological savvy and media relations that are fundamental to the success of MEND are emphasized. Furthermore, the space represented by the creeks is theorized. The creeks are not epiphenomenal to kidnapping but of first-order significance. The "symbolic transformation" (Lofland 1973: 140) of the creeks from a public space—albeit a remote disattended one—into a conscientiously securitized space that serves an operational, socio-cultural, economic, religious and even psychological function for the insurgents is illuminated. It is contended that the space re-presented by the creeks is not a *glocal space*, where all belong and can participate; it is a fundamentally and unabashedly *essentialized space* (see Siccakan 2005) based on ethnic, religious and linguistic forms of belonging and identity. The discriminatory regime of differences (see Sennett 2002) or *spatial segregation of persons* (Lofland 1973: 78) based on skin colour, language and ethnicity effected in the creeks is noted. The non-lethal constellation of identity at the creeks is being black, Nigerian, Niger Deltan and Ijaw-speaking. Not all are welcome at the creeks because of the inverted form of multiculturalism and equal opportunity for "kidnappability".

This chapter argues that the creeks constitute, first, the Ìta Èèwò or abominable space to non-Deltans and second, the Ìta Òmìnira or freedom space for the insurgents. It concludes by providing a brief examination of the role of women in the insurgency. Women's roles in the insurgency as *ammunition merchants and gun-runners, mediators between insurgent groups, the Nigerian state and the oil corporations, nude protesters, combatants, emissaries,* and the *spiritual backbone of insurgents* are explicated.

In Chapter 5, "Framing the MEND insurgency", the factors intrinsic to MEND's framing strategies are analyzed. MEND uses strong religious overtones, which discursively dichotomize the situation into a struggle between the Christian South and Muslim North. It is demonstrated that MEND also humanizes its insurgency by presenting itself as a compassionate revolutionary coalition that takes human lives seriously. MEND's use of ridicule and irony and the symmetry between its demands and those of non-violent groups are noted. This chapter also underscores the role of MEND's spokesperson, Jomo Gbomo, in articulating the coalition's framing strategies. How MEND conducts its diagnostic, prognostic and motivational framing is explicated. MEND this chapter argues blames four major entities—the *British colonialist expansionism* and its offspring the *Nigerian state, Northern Nigeria, transnational oil corporations* and the *political elite in the Delta* for the problems of the people of the Niger Delta.

Chapter 6 "Master frames in the MEND insurgency" accentuates MEND's use of the *imperative of violence frame*, the injustice frame (Gamson et al. 1982; McAdam 1982), and the human/minority rights frame (Bob 2005). Overall, the meta-narrative of the MEND insurgency is *the imperative of violence frame*. This chapter draws attention to the erudite *war metaphor* inherent in MEND's framing strategies. The analysis indicates that MEND insurgents fundamentally believe that the Nigerian state has created a "war situation", and oil workers are "enemy combatants". Therefore, insurgents consider kidnapping as a *minor irritation* in an amphitheater of war, where the state drops bombs on its people.

In addition, the use of the environmental justice frame (Čapek 1993), and return to (true) democracy frame (Noonan 1995) by MEND is examined. MEND considers the presence of troops and exploitation of the Delta region's resources without adequate compensation as environmental disrespect. This frame also enables MEND to emphasize the environmental hazards generated through oil extraction by corporations. MEND is thus able to depict the conditions of the Delta people. This chapter also shows how MEND uses the return to (true) democracy frame. MEND articulates this frame by reiterating the failure of the Nigerian state to respect the rule of law and engage the insurgents in meaningful dialogue.

Chapter 6 concludes by explicating how several factors in Nigeria's political process contribute to the credibility and resonance of MEND's framing strategies among its intended audience. The absence of any systematic efforts at counter-framing by the JTF is a major opportunity for the insurgents, whose facts and figures are widely reported in the media, and thus, shape popular opinion. The level of ethno-religious polarization in Nigeria, the division among the elites and the failure of social programs designed to ameliorate the conditions of the Delta have contributed to aligning the framing strategies of MEND with the everyday realities of the Delta people and those sympathetic to MEND's struggle. Following Bayart (2009), this chapter also demonstrates how the "politics of the belly", a complex interplay of corruption, avarice, cronyism and pervasive personalization of political power, among others, erodes confidence in the Nigerian state, which gives insurgents a major narrative advantage in the public domain.

In Chapter 7, "A repertoire of protest or criminal expropriation?", it is submitted that any Delta community with at least one recognized *benevolent militant commander* specialized in kidnapping and other insurgent activities will generally view kidnapping as a form of protest while a community without a benevolent militant commander will construe kidnapping as sheer criminal expropriation. The messianic portrayal of Tom Polo by the people of Okerenkoko in Delta state is highlighted. This chapter argues that Tom Polo benefits from the crisis in Nigeria and the criminalization of the state and politics yet manages to remain popular at the grassroots because of the social services he provides among other personal characteristics.

Contributions to the Discipline

The opportunity to draw participants from the ranks of insurgents, who were involved in kidnapping; military authorities, journalists, NGO representatives, community members, environmental justice and human rights activists, access to MEND's official statements, unqualified admittance to the creeks and major sites and actors provide depth to this book. This multi-actor approach goes in tandem with the theoretical and methodological eclecticism adopted. Drawing on insights provided by social movement scholarship, the notion of social banditry by Eric Hobsbawm, among other theoretical concepts, furnished the analysis with the requisite tools to engage the research problem.

The findings signpost the need to eschew ahistorical analysis in criminology and other human sciences. A nuanced approach is employed by putting socio-political and historical conjunctions, ruptures, trajectories and flows into consideration. Kidnapping of predominantly foreign oil workers, in particular, cannot be extricated from the savagery of the transatlantic slave trade, the brigandage of colonialism and ongoing neo-colonial spread of global capital. The findings suggest that not all crimes are localized and spatially bounded. Therefore, criminologists should embed analysis of crime in its wider socio-political contexts as the role of international arms merchants and the international community in the Delta crisis demonstrates.

As explained in Chapter 1, this study adopts a critical criminological approach. This necessarily entails investigating the role of power, conflict and vested interests in criminality (Ratner 1989). However, there is the important question of why should criminologists/sociologists, policy makers and the global public care about the oil insurgency in Nigeria?

This book demonstrates that lack of social justice—perceived or real—can breed criminality. Crime may develop when people feel threatened or believe that their way of life is under siege. This is particularly salient when the state is perceived to favor one group over others in terms of resource distribution, social amenities, government patronage and other forms of socially desirable opportunities. Therefore, countries with minority populations or class disparities, in particular, have to act in a manner that ensures that all groups in society feel like they are part of the commonwealth. Tyler's (1990: 178) warning resonates more than ever before:

> (P)eople obey the law because they believe it is proper to do so, they react to their experiences by evaluating their justice or injustice, and in evaluating the justice of their experiences they consider factors unrelated to outcome, such as whether they had a chance to state their case and had been treated with dignity and respect.

The kidnapping phenomenon fundamentally challenges the Nigerian state. The appropriation of all the segments of society in the Delta crisis signals that the entire society is positioned in the commission of crime. As stated in Chapter 3, the nature of the Nigerian rentier petro-state is a major driving force behind kidnapping episodes in the Delta. Political elites, government officials, top military brass, government-owned NNPC corporate executives, and some of those responsible for miscellaneous assignments, such as maintenance of security, have largely created the social milieu or exacerbated pre-existing conditions generating kidnapping and kidnappers through their actions and/or inaction. The sale of Nigerian army weapons to insurgents, the involvement of state officials in illegal oil bunkering activities and patronage of some insurgents as political thugs constitute only a minuscule proportion of the involvement of the agents of the state in this *crime*. Therefore, "crime", at the risk of unnecessary repetitiveness, is in and of itself a highly contestable category and should be treated as such.

Similarly, the traditional criminological notion of *crime* subsists on a subset of society engaging in an act defined as criminal and (at least in theory) consensually designated as *criminal*. However, just as kidnapping in the Niger Delta is contestable, so are insurgent activities like illegal oil bunkering and operation of unlicensed refineries. These are not acts perpetrated by a few so-called war-lords; rather whole communities are involved as a means of "survival" against the backdrop of structural unemployment, poverty, social inequality, neglect and marginalization. This suggests that when the state fails to meet the basic needs of its citizens, it is inadvertently asking the people to engage in innovation in a Mertonian sense—for better or worse. This shows the need for criminologists to go beyond state-sanctioned definitions of crime and attempt to gain an understanding of the rationale from the actors' perspective without privileging any of the standpoints.

A corollary to the point above is that the nation-state and its agencies may rest on a very fragile foundation. The legitimacy of the state *qua* state is not a given; it is an endless becoming. It is open to constant negotiation. As a result, some sections of the society may not share the same morales, mores, or participate in what they may consider the "illusions" (see Bissoondath 2002, orig. 1994) being peddled by wielders of power. For instance, although the government rather naively and/ or performatively advertises and promotes the "unity" of Nigeria on state-owned television, for a lot of Niger Deltans, particularly those who participated in the historical moment invented by the insurgency, Nigeria has a long way to go to be accepted as a legitimate state.[1] The consent of the governed is necessary *a priori* and *a posteriori*, as social contract theorists understand. The kidnapping phenomenon in the Delta questions the legal-rational basis and basic legitimacy of the Nigerian state. As demonstrated, insurgents fundamentally challenge the right of the Nigerian state and by implication, oil corporations to drill oil in the Niger Delta. This indicates that state legitimacy should be put into cognizance in analyzing crime.

---

1   Interview 11.

The analysis in this book also demonstrates that the law and order approach can be counterproductive in some contexts. The Nigerian state inadvertently conducts the investiture of violence in the Delta through militarization. This approach often assumes a life of its own. It ends up exacerbating conflicts, goes too far in its reach and becomes a part of the problem it seeks to solve. Besides, this approach presupposes that every individual wishes to preserve their life. It obscures the fact that there are people who are socially situated in a manner that makes them ready and willing to die. As the Delta crisis demonstrates and other contemporary and historical events admonish us, for some people, life is meaningful only to the extent that they lose it to a cause they have defined as worth-while; however, non-rational the larger society may deem it. Many Delta youths enroll at various insurgent camps knowing that they may lose their lives and warmly embrace that mortal probability. In fact, assurances that aspiring insurgents may die in battle is one of the issues raised by commanders before youths are enlisted.[2] Several insurgents witness the death of their comrades in battle yet such incidents only reinforce their resolve to fight the Nigerian state and the oil industry.[3] To be sure, there may be moments when force is necessary but it should always be the last resort. For example, the amnesty program announced in the summer of 2009 has helped to calm the restive region at least temporarily. It is unclear if the crisis could have been significantly reduced had dialogue been the first option.

This book also signifies that outbreaks of violence may not necessarily be demonstrations of irrationality. Some insurgents use proceeds from kidnapping and other acts of violence in the Delta to provide water, electricity, scholarships, food and other services for the people in their communities. Therefore, in the context of the Niger Delta, where structural opportunities for communal advancement and individual desires for education and a decent lifestyle are non-existent or blocked, kidnapping and illegal oil bunkering embody rationality. They make sense in the context of the Delta though they may offend our moral propriety. Insurgents merely create an alternate opportunity structure to climb the conventional social ladder and attain socially valued goods, such as material wealth and esteem. As argued in Chapter 7, several ex-insurgents have endeared themselves to the people of their communities through the social services they render. Despite having little education, some insurgents like Henry Bindodogha now occupy important cabinet positions, thus effectively joining the political class. Some like Tom Polo have also become political juggernauts whose support is crucial to winning elections in their territory.

This book highlights the dynamics that extractive industries can create, especially in the developing world. This calls for focusing criminological binoculars on the activities of corporations and their impact on the environment, particularly those in industries like oil and gas in the developing world. The

---

2   Interviewee 19.
3   Interviewees 26-34.

actions of the state: its law-making, enforcement, interpretation, social policies and programs should also be a focus of criminological research.

The research provides an empirical example drawn from a country in the interstices of authoritarianism and democracy and how that liminality both enabled and disenabled various repertoires of protest. It accentuates the theoretical currency of the political process paradigm, particularly the notion of *contentious politics*. It reinforces the relevance of the framing perspective. This study is a testament to the relevance of master frames such as the injustice frame, environmental justice frame, return to democracy frame and human/minority rights frame. The *imperative of violence master frame* is an addition to the framing scholarship and will be a useful resource to researchers studying insurgent groups that elect violent repertoires of protest. The setting of this study—a quasi-democratic state—is a useful addition to the framing literature that privileges liberal democratic settings. In conclusion, this book contributes to disciplines like peace studies, political economy, the "resource curse" literature, sociology, political science, social movements, among others.

Areas for Future Studies

There are several areas for further investigation. First, a longitudinal study of insurgents who participated in the rehabilitation exercise at the Obubra camp, Cross River state will help to assess the success of the Amnesty program and how former insurgents are integrated into the larger society. This is particularly relevant as a way of understanding future trajectories of protest in the Delta region.

Second, interrogating the engagement of ex-insurgents in the political process is warmly recommended. As some insurgents enjoyed the patronage of politicians in the past in order to win elections, such a study will document whether history repeats itself and also highlight the link between political elites and violence in the Niger Delta.

Third, although in Chapter 4, the role of women is analyzed, the topic calls for a more directed study on women's contributions to the insurgency. Fourth, an in-depth study of the lives and times of Isaac Adaka Boro, who led the first insurgency in the Niger Delta and Ken Saro-Wiwa, who internationalized the Ogoni struggle through MOSOP is long overdue. A comprehensive study on each of these individuals is recommended. Such studies would investigate the dynamics of their situations, the choices they made, mobilization of dissidents and what future leaders may learn from them.

Finally, a cross-national comparison between MEND and groups like FARC-EP will provide a fascinating academic material. In addition, a comparison between the MEND insurgency and the on-going spates of piracy in Somalia may help to further understand the link between perceived absence of social justice and criminality as well as the link between legitimate protest and criminal expropriation.

Concluding Comments

The phenomenon of kidnapping of oil workers championed by MEND in the Niger Delta has, at its core, the appropriation of every facet of the Nigerian society. Kidnapping of oil workers *is a relatively minor irritation* for several reasons. This does not purport to support such a dangerous endeavor. First, the people of the Niger Delta, particularly the Ijaws, have always been socially marginal and have developed a strong quintessential *oppositional identity*. Consequently, Ijaws have historically deployed violent repertoires of protest against any entities they perceive as oppressors. In the Akassa war led by the people of Nembe-Brass, for instance, King Koko and his men not only killed 24 persons at the Royal Niger Company premises, the king personally participated in offering many of the 70 prisoners of war as sacrificial lambs to the god, Ogidiga, whom they believed guaranteed their victory against an oppressive monopoly (Alagoa 1964). The type of repertoire of protest adopted is a reflection of socio-historical forces, political opportunities and the collective identity of dissidents.

Second, the conditions of living that King Koko and the Nembe-Brass people fought against have shown little sign of improvement. The oppression symbolized by the Royal Niger Company is believed to be reposed in Shell and other transnational oil corporations with the active support of the Nigerian state. Consequently, the Niger Delta people, particularly the Ijaws continue to have long-standing unaddressed legitimate grievances about the destruction of their environment, erosion of the values of their communities by oil workers, endemic poverty, and poor social infrastructure such as schools, hospitals and road network.

Third, for Niger Deltans, the Federal Republic of Nigeria is a union they did not ask for. Therefore, the legitimacy of the Nigerian state is still being questioned and they believe that its agents like the JTF constitute an army of occupation that must be dealt with by any means. More than ever before, Niger Deltans realize that there is nothing inevitable or natural about their plight. The "cognitive liberation" (McAdam 1982: 48) or increased level of awareness has generated intense mobilization of Niger Deltans and a stronger degree of involvement in the struggle at all levels and across social demographics.

Fourth, MEND is the name of the meta-phenomenon that distils the historical grievances of the Delta people into a potent and lethal line of action. The MEND insurgency is a continuation of protest in the Niger Delta through an overtly violent methodology. Today's insurgents are not oblivious of history in spite of the low level of education among many of them.

In the final analysis, MEND has made its mark on the sands of time—rightly or wrongly. While legitimate questions can and should be raised about its mode of operation, its activities guarantee that certain steps are taken and fundamental tokens presented to the Delta people. MEND generated national and international attention to the plight of the Niger Delta people after the lull that accompanied Saro-Wiwa's death. Gloria Arroyo, president of the Philippines barred Filipino workers from travelling to Nigeria in January 2007 (*The Punch* 23 January 2007: 3).

The US government issued a similar warning in the same month (*Nigerian Tribune* 25 January 2007: 3).

MEND and other insurgent groups have engaged in a surgical reconfiguration of the Nigerian political landscape. Not even Saro-Wiwa could accomplish this feat although his hanging partly laid the groundwork for the insurgency as he predicted. MEND appears to have little to lose. Goodluck Jonathan's presidency is proof of the belief among insurgents that the only language the Nigerian state understands is violence. The challenge is not to make peaceful means of protest impossible or ineffective.

Finally, the "dénouement" predicted by Ken Saro-Wiwa is worthy of reiteration. MEND insurgents, as Ken Saro Wiwa (Jr.), points out, revolted against the Nigerian state using the tool with which they had been equipped—violence—in the same way that Ken Saro-Wiwa used his education and contacts to internationalize the Ogoni struggle.[4] Much has been written about "resource wars" and "resource curse". These concepts have taken on a life of their own with varying degrees of agency and rationality accorded the most oppressed actors in real life and death situations. The proposal is that academic and social policy attention shift to what may be conceptually designated as *resource frustration.* Resource frustration is a resource-rich community's collective feeling and outburst of disenchantment and alienation from the body politic because of its inability to benefit from its natural endowment. As this book demonstrates, resource frustration begins with non-violent protest and culminates in extremely violent architecture of protest. Rather tellingly, resource frustration ensures that all facets of society: men, women, youths and those too young to understand the goings-on are mobilized and (mis) appropriated. Whether there would be another catharsis akin to the episodes between 2003 and 2010 remains unclear but probable. I hope that the Nigerian state recognizes the legitimate grievances of the people of the Niger Delta and reaches an amicable resolution. Once again, the agenda is already being set.

---

4   Interviewee 14. Ken Saro-Wiwa (Jr.). Personal interview, Abuja, August 2010.

References

Abdullah, I. and Muana, P. 1998. The Revolutionary United Front of Sierra Leone: A revolt of the lumpenproletariat, in *African Guerrillas*, edited by C. Clapham. Oxford: James Curry, 172–93.

Achebe, C. 2010. Igbo women in the Nigerian-Biafran War 1967–1970: An interplay of control. *Journal of Black Studies*, 40 (5), 785–811.

Adagbabiri, M.M. 2006. An Assessment of the impact of the Niger Delta Development Commission (NDDC) on Rural Communities in the Niger Delta Region of Nigeria. Unpublished PhD Dissertation, Department of Public Administration Ambrose Alli University, Ekpoma Edo state, Nigeria.

Adamson, C. 1998. Tribute, turf, honor and the American street gang: patterns of continuity and change since 1820. *Theoretical Criminology*, 2(1), 57–84.

Afrique en ligne. 2010. Nigeria at 50: US$63m celebration amid hopes, uncertainties. [Online] Available at :http://www.afriquejet.com/news/africa-news/nigeria-at-50:-us%2463m-celebration-amid-hopes,-uncertainties-2010100157276.html [accessed 18 October 2010].

Agboola, F.A.O. and Amoo, E. 2008. Poverty situation among women in the Niger Delta: The way forward, Proceedings of the International Conference on the Nigerian state, oil industry and the Niger Delta, March 11–13, Yenagoa Bayelsa state. Port Harcourt: Harey Publications, 314–21.

Agozino, B. 2003. *Counter Colonial Criminology: A Critique of Imperialist Reasoning.* London: Pluto Press.

Ahmed, A.G. 2008. Multiple complexity and prospects for reconciliation and unity: The Sudan conundrum, in *The Roots of African Conflicts: The Causes and Costs*, edited by A. Nhema and P.T. Zeleza. Oxford: James Curry, 71–87.

Akinbuwa, A.A. 2008. Alternative dispute resolution: A key to peace building in the Niger Delta area: Proceedings of the International Conference on the Nigerian state, oil industry and the Niger Delta, March 11–13, Yenagoa Bayelsa state. Port Harcourt: Harey Publications, 300–313.

Akinteye, A., James M.W. and Ashafa, M.N. 2007. Zango-Kataf crisis: A case study, in *Community Conflicts in Nigeria: Management, Resolution and Transformation*, edited by O. Otite and I.O. Albert. Ibadan: Spectrum Books, 222–46.

Akinyele, R.T. 1996. States creation in Nigeria: The Willink Report in retrospect. *African Studies Review*, 39, (2), 71–94.

Akpabio, I.A. 2007. Women NGOs and rural women empowerment activities in the Niger Delta. *Environment, Development and Sustainability*, [Online]. Available at http://www.springerlink.com/content/4q03427930256787/ [accessed: December 11, 2008].

Akpan, N.S. 2010. Kidnapping in Nigeria's Niger Delta: An exploratory study. *Journal of Social Sciences*, 24, (1), 33–42.

Akpotor, A.S. 2002. Warri Crisis Survey Report—Urhobo Perspective, in *Conflict and Instability in the Niger Delta*, edited by T.A Imobighe, B. Celestine and J. Asuni. Ibadan: Spectrum, 156–85.

Alagoa, E.J. 1964. *The Small Brave City-State: A History of Nembe Brass in the Niger Delta*. Ibadan: University Press.

Albert, I.O. 2007a. Ife-Modakeke Crisis, in *Community Conflicts in Nigeria: Management, Resolution and Transformation*, edited by O. Otite and I.O. Albert. Ibadan: Spectrum Books, 142–75.

Albert, I.O. 2007b. Ethnic and religious conflicts in Kano', in *Community Conflicts in Nigeria: Management, Resolution and Transformation*, edited by O. Otite and I.O. Albert. Ibadan: Spectrum Books, 274–305.

Ali, A.G., Elbadawi, I. and El-Batahani, A. 2005. Sudan's civil war: Why has it prevailed for so long? in *Understanding Civil War: Evidence and Analysis*. Volume 1: Africa, edited by P. Collier and N. Sambanis. Washington: The World Bank, 193–219.

Alimi, E. 2009. Mobilizing under the gun: Theorizing political opportunity structure in a highly repressive setting. *Mobilization*, 14(2), 219–37.

Alison, M. 2009. 'That's equality for you, dear': Gender, small arms and the Northern Ireland crisis, in *Sexed Pistols: The Gendered Impacts of Small Arms and Light Weapons*, edited by V. Farr, et al. New York: United Nations University Press, 211–45.

Alison, M. 2004. Women as agents of political violence: gendering security. *Security Dialogue*, 35(4), 447–63.

Allina-Pisano, E. 2003. Resistance and the social history of Africa. *Journal of Social History*, 37(1), 187–98.

Aminzade, R. and McAdam, D. 2002. Emotions and contentious politics. *Mobilization*, 7(2), 107–9.

Amodu, L.O. 2008. MNCs and sustainable environmental development: An assessment of the Niger Delta and Texas: Proceedings of the International Conference on the Nigerian state, oil industry and the Niger Delta, March 11–13, Yenagoa Bayelsa state. Port Harcourt: Harey Publications, 322–33.

Anderson, E. 1999. *Code of the Street. Decency, Violence, and the Moral Life of the Inner City*. New York: W.W. Norton.

Arato A. and Cohen, J. 1984. The German Green Party: A movement between fundamentalism and modernism. *Dissent*, 31: 327–32.

Ardener, S. 1975. Sexual insult and female militancy, in *Perceiving Women, edited by* S. Ardener. London: Malaby Press, 29–53.

Aronowitz, S. 1992. *The Politics of Identity*. New York: Routledge.

Asakitikpi, Aretha. 2008. 'Representation of power: Reportage of the Niger Delta crisis in some Nigerian newspapers: Proceedings of the International Conference on the Nigerian state, oil industry and the Niger Delta, March 11–13, Yenagoa Bayelsa state. Port Harcourt: Harey Publications, 382–95.

Auvinen, J. 1997. Political conflict in less-developed countries, 1981–89. *Journal of Peace Research*, 34(2), 177–95.

Badom, B. 2008. Peace building and security strategies in the Niger Delta: Proceedings of the International Conference on the Nigerian state, oil industry and the Niger Delta, March 11–13, Yenagoa Bayelsa state. Port Harcourt: Harey Publications, 53–63.

Baines, Erin. 2003. Body politics and the Rwandan crisis. *Third World Quarterly*, 24(3), 479–93.

Bakuniak, G. and Nowak, K. 1987. The creation of a collective identity in a social movement: The case of "Solidarnosc" in Poland. *Theory & Culture*, 16(3), 401–29.

Ball, P. 2005. On the quantification of horror: Notes from the Field, in *Repression and Mobilization*, edited by C. Davenport, et al. Minneapolis: University of Minnesota Press, 189–210.

Bassey, N. (ed.). 2009a. *Knee Deep in Crude. Environmental Field Reports.* Volume 2. Friends of the Earth and Environmental Rights Action. Ibadan: Kraft Books.

Bassey, N. (ed.). 2009b. *Defending the Environment: The Role of Environmental Impact Assessment.* Friends of the Earth and Environmental Rights Action.

Bassey, N. (ed.). 2009c. *Knee Deep in Crude. Environmental Field Reports.* Volume 1. Friends of the Earth and Environmental Rights Action. Ibadan: Kraft Books.

Bassey, N. (ed.). 2008. *The Nigerian Environment and the Rule of Law.* Friends of the Earth and Environmental Rights Action. Ibadan: Kraft Books.

Bastian, M. 2005. The naked and the nude: Historically multiple meanings of *oto* (undress) in southeastern Nigeria, in *Dirt, Undress, and Difference: Critical Perspectives on the Body's Surface, edited by* A. Masquelier. Bloomington, IN: Indiana University Press, 34–60.

Bateson, G. 1972. [1954]. *Steps to an Ecology of the Mind.* New York: Ballantine.

Baumann, C.E. 1973. *The Diplomatic Kidnappings: A Revolutionary Tactic of Urban Terrorism.* The Hague: Martinus Nijhuff.

Baumann, C.E. 1985. Diplomatic kidnappings, in *Terrorism and Personal Protection*, edited by B. Jenkins. Boston: Butterworth Publishers, 23–45.

Bayart, J., Ellis, S. and Hibou, B. 1999. From kleptocracy to the felonious state? In *The Criminalization of the State in Africa*, by J. Bayart, et al. [Trans. By Stephen Ellis] Bloomington, Indiana: Indiana University Press, 1–31.

Baylor, Tim. 1996. Media framing of movement protest: The case of American India protest. *Social Science Journal*, 33(3), 241–55.

Benford, R. 1997. An insider's critique of the social movement framing perspective. *Sociological Inquiry*, 67(4), 409–30.

Benford, R. and Hunt, S. 1992. Dramaturgy and social movements: The social construction and communication of power. *Sociological Inquiry*, 62(1), 36–55.

Benford, R. and Snow, D. 2000. Framing processes and social movements: An overview and assessment. *Annual Review of Sociology*, 26: 611–39.

Berdal, M. 2003. How 'new' are 'new wars'? Global economic change and the study of civil war. *Global Governance*, 9: 477–502.

Bergen Risk Solutions. 2007. Security in the Niger Delta [Online]. Available at http://www.bergenrisksolutions.com/ [accessed April 10, 2008].

Bergen Risk Solutions. 2006. Niger Delta: Serious security incidents—2006 [Online]. Available at http://www.bergenrisksolutions.com/ [accessed April 10, 2008].

Bernstein, M. 1997. Celebration and suppression: The strategic uses of identity by the Lesbian and Gay Movement. *American Journal of Sociology*, 103: 531–65.

Best, S.G., Idyorough, A.E., and Shehu, Z.B. 2007. Communal conflicts and the possibilities of conflict resolution in Nigeria: A case study of the Tiv-Jukun conflicts in Wukari local government area, Taraba state, in *Community Conflicts in Nigeria: Management, Resolution and Transformation*, edited by O. Otite and I.O. Albert. Ibadan: Spectrum Books, 82–117.

Bettez-Gravel, P. 1985. Of bandits and pirates: An essay of the vicarious insurgency of peasants. *Journal of Political and Military Sociology*, 13(2), 209–17.

Biggs, M. 2006. Who joined the sit-ins and why: Southern Black students in the early 1960s. *Mobilization*, 11(3), 321–36.

Billion, P. 2007. 'Drilling in deep water: Oil, business and war in Angola, in *Oil Wars*, edited by M. Kaldor, et al. London: Pluto Press, 100–29.

Bissoondath, N. 2002. (Orig. 1994). *Selling Illusions: The Cult of Multiculturalism in Canada*. Toronto: Penguin Books.

Blee, K. and Taylor, V. 2002. Semi-structured interviewing in social movement research, in *Methods of Social Movement Research*, edited by B. Klandermans and S. Staggenborg. Minneapolis: University of Minnesota Press, 92–117.

Blinkhorn, M. 2000. Liability, responsibility and blame: British ransom victims in the Mediterranean periphery, 1860–1881. *Australian Journal of Politics and History*, 1(3), 336–56.

Blok, A. 1972. The peasant and the brigand: Social banditry reconsidered. *Comparative Studies in Society and History*, 14(2), 494–503.

Blommaert, J. 2005. *Discourse: A Critical Introduction.* Cambridge: Cambridge University Press.

Bob, C. 2005. *The Marketing of Rebelion: Insurgents, Media and International Activism.* Cambridge: University Press.

Bob, C. 2002. Political process theory and transnational movements: Dialectics of protest among Nigeria's Ogoni minority. *Social Problems*, 49(3), 395–415.

Bond, P. and Sharife, K. 2009. Apartheid reparations and the contestation of corporate power in Africa. *Review of African Political Economy*, 119:115–25.

Boro, I. 1982. *The Twelve-Day Revolution.* Tony Tebekaemi (Ed). Benin: Idodo Umeh Publishers.

Bot, D.E. 2008. Militarization of the Niger Delta: Implications for National Security: Proceedings of the International Conference on the Nigerian state, oil industry and the Niger Delta, March 11–13, Yenagoa Bayelsa state. Port Harcourt: Harey Publications, 466–74.

Braun, H. 2003. *Our Guerillas, Our Sidewalk: A Journey into the Violence of Colombia.* Lanham: Rowman & Littlefield.

Briggs, C. 2007. Anthropology, interviewing, and communicability in contemporary society. *Current Anthropology*, 48(1): 551–80.

BBC. 2010. Military coup ousts Niger president Mamadou Tandja. [Online: British Broadcasting Corporation] Available at http://news.bbc.co.uk/2/hi/8523196.stm [accessed March 15, 2010].

BBC. 2008 (28 May). Nigeria's "Baba-go-slow" one year on. [Online: British Broadcasting Corporation]. Available at http://news.bbc.co.uk/2/hi/7420327.stm [accessed 26 November 2010].

BBC. 2005. London bomber video aired on TV. [Online: British Broadcasting Corporation] Available at: http://news.bbc.co.uk/2/hi/uk_news/4206708.stm [accessed 18 November 2010].

Brockett, C. 1993. A protest-cycle resolution of the repression/popular-protest paradox. *Social Science History*, 17(3), 457–84.

Brookman, F., Bennett, T., Hochstetler, A. and Copes, H. 2011. The 'code of the street' and the generation of street violence in the UK. *European Journal of Criminology*, 8(1), 17–31.

Boudreau, V. 2005. Precarious regimes and matchup problems in the explanation of repressive problems, in *Repression and Mobilization*, edited by C. Davenport, et al. Minneapolis: University of Minnesota Press, 33–57.

Buckley, P.J. 2006. Multinational enterprises in less-developed countries: Cultural and economic interactions revisited, in *Multinational Corporations and Global Poverty Reduction*, edited by J.C. Subhash. Cheltenham: Edward Elgar, 31–58.

Buckley, P.J. and Casson, M. 1991. *The Future of the Multinational Enterprise.* London: MacMillan.

Buechler, S. 2004. The strange career of strain and breakdown theories of collective action, in *The Blackwell Companion to Social Movements*, edited by D. Snow, et al. Malden, MA: Blackwell, 47–66.

Cadena-Roa, J. 2002. Strategic framing, emotions, and *superbarrio*—Mexico city's masked crusader. *Mobilization*, 7(2): 201–16.

Campos, Alicia. 2008. 'Oil, sovereignty and self-determination: Equatorial Guinea and Western Sahara. *Review of African Political Economy*, 117: 435–47.

Čapek, S. 1993. The "environmental justice" frame: A conceptual discussion and an application. *Social Problems*, 40(1), 5–24.

Capotorto, G. 1985. How terrorists look at kidnapping, in *Terrorism and Personal Protection*, edited by B. Jenkins. Boston: Butterworth Publishers, 2–7.

Caramazza, I.F and Leone, U. 1984. *Phenomenology of Kidnappings in Sardina: Towards an International Perspective of a Local Crime Problem.* Rome, Italy: The United Nations Social Defence Research Institute.

Carey, S. 2006. The dynamic relationship between protest and repression. *Political Research Quarterly*, 59(1), 1–11.

Carroll, W. and Ratner, R. 1996a. Master frames and counter-hegemony: Political sensibilities in contemporary social movements. *Canadian Review of Sociology and Anthropology*, 33(4), 407–35.

Carroll, W. and Ratner, R. 1996b. 'Master framing and cross-movement networking in contemporary social movements. *Sociological Quarterly*, 37(4), 601–25.

Cesarz, E., Morrison, J.S. and Cooke, J. 2003. Alienation and militancy in Nigeria's Niger Delta, Africa Program, Center for Strategic and International Studies, Africa Notes, 16, 5 May, 2003; 1–4.

Chan, S. and Clark, C. 1995. Do MNCs matter for national development outcomes? Contrasting East Asia and Latin America, in *Foreign Direct Investment in a Changing Global Political Economy*, edited by S. Chan. London: St. Martin's, 166–87.

Chirayath, V. and De Zolt, E. 2004. Globalization, multinational corporations, and white collar crimes: Cases and consequences for transitional economies, in *The Changing face of Globalization*, edited by S. Dasgupta. London: Sage, 151–65.

Clemens, E. 1996. Organisational form as frame: Collective identity and political strategy in the American Labour Movement, 1880–1920', in *Comparative Perspectives on Social Movements: Political Opportunities, Mobilizing Structures and Cultural Framings*, edited by D. McAdam, et al. Cambridge: Cambridge University Press, 205–26.

Clutterbuck, R. 1978. *Kidnap and Ransom: The Response.* London: Faber and Faber.

Comaroff, J. and Comaroff, J. 2006. Law and disorder in the Postcolony: An introduction, in *Law and Disorder in the Postcolony*, edited by J. Comaroff and J. Comaroff. Chicago: University of Chicago Press, 1–56.

Concannon, D.M. 2008. *Kidnapping: An Investigator's Guide to Profiling.* London: Elsevier.

Collier, P. 2000. Rebellion as a quasi-criminal activity. *Journal of Conflict Resolution*, 44(6), 839–53.

Collier, P., Elliot, L., Hegre, H., Hoeffler, A., Reynal-Querol, M and Sambanis, N. 2003. *Breaking the Conflict Trap: Civil War and Development Policy*. Oxford: Oxford University Press.

Collier, P. and Hoeffler, A. 2005. Resource rents, governance, and conflict. *Journal of Conflict Resolution*, 49(4), 625–33.

Collier, P. and Hoeffler, A. 1998. On Economic Causes of Civil War. *Oxford Economic Papers*, 50(4), 563–73.

Conaghan, C. 2005. *Fujimori's Peru: Deception in the Public Sphere.* Pittsburgh: University of Pittsburgh Press.

Conway, D. and Heynen, N. 2006. Globalizations Dimensions, in *Globalization's Contradictions: Geographies of Discipline, Destruction and Transformation*, edited by D. Conway and N. Heynen. London and New York: Routledge, 3–34.

Costain, A.N. and McFarland, A.S. (Eds.) 1998. *Social Movements and American Political Institutions: People, Passions and Power.* Boulder: Rowman & Littlefield.

Costain, A.N. 1992. *Inviting Women's Rebellion: A Political Process Interpretation of the Women's Movement.* Baltimore, MD: Johns Hopkins University Press.

Courson, E. 2009. Movement for the Emancipation of the Niger Delta (MEND): Political marginalization, repression and petro-insurgency in the Niger Delta. Discussion Paper 47, Nordiska Afrikainstitutet, Uppsala.

Courson, E. 2007. The burden of oil: Social deprivation and political militancy in Gbaramatu Clan, Warri South West LGA Delta State, Nigeria. Niger Delta: Economies of Violence Working Papers, No. 15. Institute of International Studies, University of California, Berkeley, USA.

Crelinsten, R. and Szabo, D. 1979. *Hostage-Taking.* Massachusetts: Lexington Books.

Dalby, S. 1996. The environment as geopolitical threat. *Ecumene*, 3(4), 472–96.

Davenport, C. 2005. Introduction: Repression and mobilization: Insights from political science and sociology, in *Repression and Mobilization*, edited by C. Davenport, et al. Minneapolis: University of Minnesota Press, vii–xli.

Davenport, C. and Eads, M. 2001. Cued to coerce or coercing cues? An exploration of dissident rhetoric and its relationship to political repression. *Mobilization*, 6(2), 151–71.

David. S.R. 2008. *Catastrophic Consequences: Civil Wars and American Interests.* Baltimore: Johns Hopkins University Press.

Davis, S., Von Kemedi, D. and Drennan, M. 2006. Illegal oil bunkering in the Niger Delta, Niger Delta Peace and Security Working Papers (March).

Delamont, S. 2004. Ethnography and participant observation, in *Qualitative Research Practice*, edited by C. Seale, et al. London: SAGE, 217–29.

della Porta, D. and Diani, M. 1999. *Social Movements: An Introduction.* Malden, Massachusetts: Blackwell Publishers.

della Porta, D. 1996. Social movements and the state: Thoughts on the policing of protest, in *Comparative Perspectives on Social Movements: Political Opportunities, Mobilizing Structures and Cultural Framings*, edited by D. McAdam, et al. Cambridge: Cambridge University Press, 62–92.

della Porta, D. 1995. *Social Movements, Political Violence and the State: A Comparative Analysis of Italy and Germany.* Cambridge: Cambridge University Press.

de Soysa, I. 2002. Paradise is a bazaar? Greed, creed, and governance in civil war, 1989 –1999. *Journal of Peace Research*, 39(4), 395–416.

Diani, M. 2003. Introduction: Social movements, contentious actions, and social networks: From metaphor to substance?, in *Social Movements and Networks: Relational Approaches to Collective Action*, edited by M. Diani and D. McAdam Oxford: Oxford University Press, 1–18.

Diani, M. 1996. 'Linking mobilization frames and political opportunities: Insights from regional populism in Italy. *American Sociological Review*, 61: 1053–69.

Dicken, P. 2007. *Global Shift: Mapping the Changing Contours of the World Economy.* 5th Edition. New York: Guilford Press.

Douglas, O. 1999. Shell and the Niger Delta: Between rhetoric and practice: In *Economic, Social and Cultural Rights of the Ogoni. Proceedings of the*

Symposium on the Economic Social and Cutural Rights of the Sami, the Maasai and the Ogoni. Vol.III. The Ogoni. Edited by F. Horn. Rovaniemi: Lapland's University Press, 69–75.

Douglas, O., Okonta, I., Von Kemedi, D. and Watts, M. 2004. Oil and militancy in the Niger Delta: Terrorist threat or another Colombia?, Niger Delta Economies of Violence Working Papers, No. 4. Washington, D.C: The United States Institute of Peace.

Dunn, E.D. 1999. The civil war in Liberia, in *Civil Wars in Africa: Roots and Resolutions*, edited by T. Ali and R. Matthews. Montreal and Kingston: McGill-Queen's University Press, 89–121.

Earl, J. 2006. Introduction: Repression and the social control of protest. *Mobilization*, 11(2), 129–43.

Eatwell, R. 2006. The concept and theory of charismatic leadership. *Totalitarian Movements and Political Religions*, 7(2), 141–56.

Ebhuomhan, S. 2010. Amnesty programme in jeopardy, [Online: *Next Newspaper*]. Available at: http://234next.com/csp/cms/sites/Next/Home/5559239146/amnesty_programme_in_jeopardy___.csp [accessed 2 June 2010].

Edeogu, C. 2008. Peace building strategies for peace in the Niger Delta: A comprehensive four-phase peace model: Proceedings of the International Conference on the Nigerian state, oil industry and the Niger Delta, March 11–13, Yenagoa Bayelsa state. Port Harcourt: Harey Publications, 64–80.

Edmunds, H. 1999. *The Focus Group Research Handbook*. Illinois: NTC and Contemporary Publishing Group.

Edwards, B. and McCarthy, J. 2004. Resources and social movement mobilization, in *The Blackwell Companion to Social Movements*, edited by D. Snow, et al. Malden, MA: Blackwell, 116–52.

Efe, S.I and Mogborukor, J.O.A. 2008. Acid rain in Niger Delta region: Implication on water resources quality and crisis: Proceedings of the International Conference on the Nigerian state, oil industry and the Niger Delta, March 11–13, Yenagoa Bayelsa state. Port Harcourt: Harey Publications, 217–28.

Ehwarieme, W. 2008. 'Oloibirinization: Developmental future of a post-oil Niger Delta: Proceedings of the International Conference on the Nigerian state, oil industry and the Niger Delta, March 11–13, Yenagoa Bayelsa state. Port Harcourt: Harey Publications, 157–63.

Einhwohner, R. 2003. Opportunity, honour and action in the Warsaw ghetto uprising of 1943. *American Journal of Sociology*, 109(30), 650–75.

Eisinger, P. 1973. The conditions of protest behaviour in American cities. *American Political Science Review*, 81: 11–28.

Elechi, O.O. 2006. *Doing Justice without the State: The Afikpo (Ehugbo) Nigeria Model.* New York: Routledge.

Enweremadu, D. 2008. The vicious circle: Oil, corruption and armed conflicts in the Niger Delta: Proceedings of the International Conference on the Nigerian state, oil industry and the Niger Delta, March 11–13, Yenagoa Bayelsa state. Port Harcourt: Harey Publications, 445–57.

Erickson, S. 1997. The process of cognitive liberation: Cultural synapses, links and frame contradictions in the US-Central America peace movement. *Sociological Inquiry*, 67(4), 470–87.

Eseduwo, F.S. 2008. Petroleum prospecting, state violence and hostage-taking in Nigeria: A study of the Niger Delta region (1966–2007): Proceedings of the International Conference on the Nigerian state, oil industry and the Niger Delta, March 11–13, Yenagoa Bayelsa state. Port Harcourt: Harey Publications, 483–507.

Esteban, J. and Ray, D. 2008. Polarization, fractionalization and conflict. *Journal of Peace research*, 45(2), 163–82.

Etekpe, A. 2005. *Minority Politics in Nigeria: The Case of the South-South and Middle Belt Regions*. Port Harcourt: Kamuela Publications.

Evans, J. 1997. Multi-organisational fields and social movement organisation frame content: The religious pro-choice movement. *Sociological Inquiry*, 67(4), 451–69.

Falola, T. 1999. *The History of Nigeria*. Westport: Greenwood Press.

Fanon, F. 1968. *The Wretched of the Earth*. Trans. Constance Farrington. New York: Grove Press.

Fearon, J.D. 2005. Primary commodities exploits and civil war. *Journal of Conflict Resolution*, 49(4), 483–507.

Fearon, J.D. and Laitin, D.D. 2003. Ethnicity, insurgency, and civil war. *American Political Science Review*, 97(1), 75–90.

Fechter, A. 2005. The Other stares back: Experiencing whiteness in Jakarta, *Ethnography*, 6(1), 87–103.

Fern, F.E. 2001. *Advanced Focus Group Research*. Thousand Oaks: Sage.

Ferree, M. and Miller, F. 1985. Mobilization and meaning: Toward an integration of social psychological and resource perspectives on social movements, *Sociological Inquiry*, 55(1), 38–61.

Fine, G.A. 1995. Public narration and group culture: Discerning discourse in social movements, in *Social Movements and Culture*, edited by H. Johnston and B. Klandermans. Minneapolis: University of Minnesota Press, 127–43.

Firestone, T. 1993. Mafia memoirs: what they tell us about organized crime. *Journal of Contemporary Criminal Justice*, 9(3), 197–220.

Fiske, J. 1996. *Media matters: Race and gender in U.S. politics*. Minneapolis: University of Minnesota Press.

Flyghed, J. 2002. Normalising the exceptional: The case of political violence. *Policing & Society*, 13(1), 23–41.

Francisco, R. 2004. After the massacre: Mobilization in the wake of harsh repression. *Mobilization*, 9(2), 107–26.

Francisco, R. 2005. The dictator's dilemma, in *Repression and Mobilization*, edited by C. Davenport, et al. Minneapolis: University of Minnesota Press, 58–81.

Frazier, L.J. 2007. *Salt in the Sand: Memory, Violence and the Nation-State in Chile, 1890 to the Present*. Durham and London: Duke University Press.

Friedman, D. and McAdam, D. 1992. Collective identity and activism: Networks, choices and the life of a movement, in *Frontiers in Social Movement Theory*, edited by A. Morris and C.M. Mueller. New Haven and London: Yale University Press, 156–73.

Friedman, E. 2009. External pressure and local mobilization: Transnational activism and the emergence of the Chinese labour movement. *Mobilization*, 14(2), 199–218.

Frynas, J. 2000. *Oil in Nigeria: Conflict and Litigation between Oil Companies and Village Communities.* Hamburg: Lit Verlag.

Gallagher, R. 1985. Kidnapping in the United States and the development of the Federal Kidnapping Statute, in *Terrorism and Personal Protection*, edited by B. Jenkins Boston: Butterworth Publishers, 129–45.

Gamba, V. and Cornwell, R. 2000. Arms, elites and resources in the Angolan civil war, in *Greed and Grievance: Economic Agendas in Civil Wars*, edited by M. Berdal and D. Malone. Boulder: Lynne Rienner Publishers, 157–72.

Gamson, W. 2004. Bystanders, public opinion and the media, in *The Blackwell Companion to Social Movements*, edited by D. Snow, et al. Malden, MA: Blackwell, 242–61.

Gamson, W. 1995. Constructing social protest, in *Social Movements and Culture*, edited by H. Johnston and B. Klandermans. Minneapolis: University of Minnesota Press, 85–106.

Gamson, W. 1992a. *Talking Politics.* New York: Cambridge University Press.

Gamson, W. 1992b. The social psychology of collective action, in *Frontiers in Social Movement Theory*, edited by A. Morris and C.M. Mueller. New Haven and London: Yale University Press, 53–76.

Gamson, W. 1975. *The Strategy of Social Protest.* Belmont: Dorsey Press.

Gamson, W. and Meyer, D. 1996. Accessing public, media, electoral and governmental agendas' in *Comparative Perspectives on Social Movements. Political Opportunities, Mobilizing Structures and Cultural Framings*, edited by D. McAdam, et al. Cambridge and New York: Cambridge University Press.

Gamson, W. and Wolfsfeld, G. 1993. Movements and media as interacting systems. *Annals of the American Academy of Political and Social Science*, 528: 114–25.

Gamson, W., Croteau, D., Hoynes, W. and Sasson, T. 1992. Media images and the social construction of reality. *Annual Review of Sociology*, 18: 373–93.

Gamson, W.A., Fireman, B. and Rytina, S. 1982. *Encounters with Unjust Authority.* Homewood, IL: Dorsey.

Gans, H.J. 1972. The positive functions of poverty. *American Journal of Sociology*, 78(2), 275–89.

Gartner, S. and Regan, P. 1996. Threat and repression: The non-linear relationship between government and opposition violence. *Journal of Peace Research*, 33(3), 273–87.

George, T. 2008a. The silent ones: Women and development in the Niger Delta region: Proceedings of the International Conference on the Nigerian state, oil industry and the Niger Delta, March 11–13, Yenagoa Bayelsa state. Port Harcourt: Harey Publications, 1195–204.

George, T. 2008b. Women, environment and food production: The challenge of the Niger Delta: Proceedings of the International Conference on the Nigerian state, oil industry and the Niger Delta, March 11–13, Yenagoa Bayelsa state. Port Harcourt: Harey Publications, 475–82.

Gerhards, J. and Rucht, D. 1992. Mesomobilization: Organising in two protest campaigns in West Germany. *American Journal of Sociology*, 98(3), 555–95.

Ghazvinian, J. 2007. *Untapped: The Scramble for Africa's Oil*. Orlando: Harcourt Books.

Gibbs, D. 1997. International commercial rivalries and the Zai'rian copper nationalisation of 1967. *Review of African Political Economy*, 24(72), 171–84.

Girvan, N. 1976. *Corporate Imperialism: Conflict and Expropriation: Transnational Corporations and Economic Nationalism in the Third World*. White Plains, New York: M.E Sharpe.

Global Witness. 1998. *A Rough Trade: The Role of Diamond Companies and Governments in the Angolan Conflict*. London: Global Witness.

Goffman, E. 1973. *The Presentation of Self in Everyday Life*. Woodstock, New York: The Overlook Press.

Goffman, E. 1967. *Interaction Ritual: Essays on Face-to-Face Behaviour.* Garden City, New York: Doubleday & Company.

Goheen, M. 2000. Women's political movements in Cameroon, in *Curricular Crossings: Women's Studies and Area Studies, edited by* M.R. Hunt. South Hadley, MA: Five College Women's Studies Research Center.

Gokay, Bulent. 2006. A–Z Glossary, in *The Politics of Oil: A Survey*, edited by B. Gokay. London & New York: Routledge, 121–204.

Goldstein, J. 2001. *War and Gender.* Cambridge: University Press.

Gomez-Barris, M. 2009. *Where Memory Dwells: Culture and State Violence in Chile*. Berkeley: University of California Press.

Goodwin, J. and Jasper, J. 1999. Caught in a winding, snarling vine: The structural bias of political process theory. *Sociological Forum*, 14(1), 27–54.

Gottfredson, M. and Hirschi, T. 1990. *A General Theory of Crime*. Stanford: Stanford University Press.

Gould, D.B. 2002. Life during wartime: Emotions and the development of act up. *Mobilization*, 7(2), 177–200.

Greenbaum, L.T. 1988. *The Practical Handbook and Guide to Focus Group Research*. Lexington: Lexington Books.

Griffiths, S. II. 1978. *Mao Tse-Tung on Guerrilla Warfare*. New York: Anchor Press/DoubleDay.

Haggerty, K. and Erickson, R. 2000. The surveillant assemblage. *British Journal of Sociology*, 51(4), 605–774.

Hamilton, L. 1980. Political kidnapping as a deadly game. *Simulation & Game*, 11(4), 387–402.

Harnischfeger, J. 2003. The Bakassi Boys: Fighting crime in Nigeria. *Journal of Modern African Studies*, 41(1), 23–49.

Harrison, J. 2008. 'News', in *Pulling Newspapers Apart: Analysing Print Journalism*, edited by B. Franklin. London & New York: Routledge, 39–47.

Hart, D.M. 1987. *Banditry in Islam: Case studies from Morocco, Algeria and the Pakistan North West Frontier.* Cambridgeshire, UK: Middle East and North African Studies Press.

Hart, S. 1996. The cultural dimension of social movements: A theoretical reassessment and literature review. *Sociology of Religion*, 57(1), 87–100.

Hayes, J. T and Tatham, B.C. 1989. *Focus Group Interviews: A Reader*. Illinois: American Marketing Association.

Henderson, Errol. 2008. When states implode: Africa's civil wars 1950–92, in *The Roots of African Conflicts: The Causes and Costs*, edited by A. Nhema and P.T. Zeleza. Oxford: James Curry, 51–70.

Henderson, J. 1985. *When Colombia bled: A history of the violencia in Tolima.* Alabama: University of Alabama Press.

Hess, D. and Martin, B. 2006. Repression, backfire and the theory of transformative events. *Mobilization*, 11(2), 249–67.

Hobbes, T. 1651. *Leviathan or the Matter, Forme and Power of a Commonwealth, Ecclesiastical and Civil.* London: Andrew Crooke.

Hobsbawm, E.J. 1997. *On History.* London: Weidenfeld and Nicholson.

Hobsbawm, E.J. 1969. *Bandits.* Worcester & London: The Trinity Press.

Hobsbawm, E.J. 1959. *Primitive Rebels: Studies in Archaic Forms of Social Movement in the 19th and 20th Centuries.* New York: Norton & Company.

Holthouse, D. 2009. The year in hate: Number of hate groups tops 900 [Online] Available at http://www.splcenter.org/intel/intelreport/article.jsp?aid=1027 [accessed February 27, 2009].

Homer-Dixon, T.F. 1999. *Environment, Scarcity, and Violence.* Princeton: Princeton University Press.

Homer-Dixon, T.F. 1991. On the threshold: Environmental changes as causes of acute conflict. *International Security*, 16(2), 76–116.

Human Rights Watch. 2007. Chop fine: The human rights impact of local government corruption and mismanagement in Rivers State, Nigeria. Volume 19, No. 2(A). [Online] Available at: http://www.hrw.org/en/reports/2007/01/30/chop-fine [accessed 23 November 2010].

Human Rights Watch. 2005a. *Rivers and blood: Guns, oil and power in Nigeria's rivers state.* A human rights watch briefing paper [Online]. Available at http://hrw.org/backgrounder/africa/nigeria0205/nigeria0205.pdf [accessed July 20, 2008].

Human Rights Watch. 2005b. 'Rest in Pieces': Police torture and deaths in custody in Nigeria [Online]. Available at: http//:www.hrw.org/reports/2005/0705/ [accessed January 5, 2006].

Human Rights Watch. 2003. The Warri crisis: Fuelling violence. Human Rights Watch, 15, 18(A), 1–30.

Human Rights Watch 2002. The Niger Delta: No dividend of democracy, Human Rights Watch, 14, 7(A), 1–39.

Hunt, S. and Benford, R. 2004. Collective identity, solidarity and commitment, in *The Blackwell Companion to Social Movements*, edited by D. Snow, et al. Malden, MA: Blackwell Publishing, 433–57.

Hunt, S., Benford, R. and Snow, D. 1994. Identity fields: Framing processes and the social construction of movement identities, in *New Social Movements*, edited by E. Larana, et al. Philadelphia: Temple University Press, 185–208.

Ibaba, S.I. 2008. Promoting peace in the Niger Delta: Some critical issues: Proceeding of the International Conference on the Nigerian state, oil industry and the Niger Delta, March 11–13, Yenagoa Bayelsa state. Port Harcourt: Harey Publications, 193–206.

Ibanez, A.C. 2001. El Salvador: War and untold stories: Women guerrillas, in *Victims, Perpetrators or Actors? Gender, Armed Conflict and Political Violence*, edited by C. Moser and F. Clark. London & New York: Zed Books, 117–30.

Ibeanu, O. and Luckham, R. 2007. Nigeria: Political violence, governance and corporate responsibility in a petro-state, in *Oil Wars*, edited by M. Kaldor, et al. London: Pluto Press, 41–99.

Ibelema, M. 2000. Nigeria: The politics of marginalization. *Current History, May:* 211–14.

Ifeka-Moller, C. 1975. Female militancy and colonial revolt: The women's war of 1929, Eastern Nigeria, in *Perceiving women*, edited by S. Ardener. London: Malaby Press, 127–57.

Ikelegbe, A. 2008. Interrogating a crisis of corporate governance and the interface with conflict: The case of multinational oil companies and the conflicts in the Niger Delta: Proceedings of the International Conference on the Nigerian state, oil Industry and the Niger Delta, March 11–13, Yenagoa Bayelsa state. Port Harcourt: Harey Publications, 107–35.

Ikelegbe, A. 2005a. Engendering civil society: oil, women groups and resource conflicts in the Niger Delta region of Nigeria. *Journal of Modern African Studies*, 43(2), 241–70.

Ikelegbe, A. 2005b. The economy of conflict in the oil rich Niger Delta region of Nigeria. *Nordic Journal of African Studies*, 14(2), 208–34.

Ikelegbe, A. 2001. Civil society, oil and conflict in the Niger Delta region of Nigeria: ramifications of civil society for a regional resource struggle. *Journal of Modern African Studies*, 39(3), 437–69.

Imobighe, T.A. 2002. Warri crisis in historical and contemporary perspectives, in *Conflict and Instability in the Niger Delta*, edited by T.A Imobighe, et al. Ibadan: Spectrum, 36–52.

Iwuchukwu, M. 2003. Democracy in a multi-religious and cultural setting: The Nigerian context. *World Futures*, 59(5), 381–90.

Jackson, R. 1993. Sub-Saharan Africa, in *States in a Changing World: A Contemporary Analysis*, edited by R. Jackson and A. James. Oxford: Clarendon Press, 136–56.

Jasper, J.M. 1997. *The Art of Moral Protest.* Chicago, IL: Chicago Press.

Jenkins, B. 1985. Introduction, in *Terrorism and Personal Protection*, edited by B. Jenkins. Boston: Butterworth Publishers, xvii–xxv.

Jenson, J. 1996. What's in a name? Nationalist movements and public discourse, in *Social Movements and Culture*, edited by H. Johnston and B. Klandermans. Minneapolis: University of Minnesota Press, 107–26.

Joab-Peterside, S. 2007a. Oil transparency in the Niger Delta: improving public sector oil derived resource flows and utilization in Abia state, Nigeria, Niger Delta: Economies of Violence Working Papers, No. 20. Institute of International Studies, University of California, Berkeley, USA.

Joab-Peterside, S. 2007b. On the militarization of Nigeria's Niger Delta: The genesis of ethnic militia in Rivers state, Nigeria, Niger Delta: Economies of Violence Working Papers, No. 20. Institute of International Studies, University of California, Berkeley, USA.

Johnston, H. 2006. 'Let's get small: The dynamics of (small) contention in repressive states. *Mobilization*, 11(2), 195–212.

Johnston, H. 2005. Talking the walk: Speech acts and resistance in authoritarian regimes, in *Repression and Mobilization*, edited by C. Davenport, et al. Minneapolis: University of Minnesota Press, 108–37.

Johnston, H. 2002. Verification and proof in frame and discourse analysis, in *Methods of Social Movement Research*, edited by B. Klandermans and S. Staggenborg. Minneapolis: University of Minnesota Press, 62–91.

Johnston, H. 1995. A methodology for frame analysis: From discourse to cognitive schemata, in *Social Movements and Culture*, edited by H. Johnston and B. Klandermans. Minneapolis: University of Minnesota Press, 217–46.

Johnston, H. and Klandermans, B. 1995. The cultural analysis of social movements, in *Social Movements and Culture*, edited by H. Johnston and B. Klandermans. Minneapolis: University of Minnesota Press, 3–24.

Johnston, H. and Oliver, P. 2000. Breaking the frame. *Mobilization*, 5(1), 61–4.

Johnston, J. 2000. Pedagogical guerrillas, armed democrats and revolutionary counterpublics: Examining paradox in the Zapatista uprising in Chiapas Mexico', *Theory and Society*, 29(4): 463–505.

Johnston, J. and Laxer, G. 2003. Solidarity in the age of globalization: Lessons from the anti-MAI and Zapatista struggles. *Theory and Society*, 32(1), 39–91.

Joseph, R.A. 1987. *Democracy and Prebendal Politics in Nigeria: The Rise and Fall of the Second Republic.* Cambridge: Cambridge University Press.

Kabia, John. 2008. Greed or grievance: Diamonds, rent-seeking and the civil war in Sierra Leone (1991–2002), in *Extractive Economies and Conflicts in the Global South: Multi-Regional Perspectives on Rentier Politics*, edited by K. Omeje. Aldershot, Hampshire: Ashgate, 93–106.

Kaldor, M. 2007. Oil and conflict: The case of Nagorno Karabakh, in *Oil Wars*, edited by M. Kaldor, et al. London: Pluto Press, 157–82.

Kaldor, M. 1999. *New and Old Wars: Organised Violence in a Global Era.* Stanford: Stanford University Press.

Kaldor, M., Karl, T.L and Said, Y. 2007. Introduction, in *Oil Wars*, edited by M. Kaldor, et al. London: Pluto Press, 1–40.

Kalyvas, S.N. 2001. 'New' and 'old' civil wars. A valid distinction? *World Politics*, 54: 99–118.

Kaplan, R. 2000. *The Coming Anarchy: Shattering the Dreams of the Post Cold War.* New York: Vintage Books.

Karl, T. 1997. *The Paradox of Plenty.* Berkeley: University of California Press.

Keen, D. 1998. The economic functions of violence in civil wars. Introduction. *Adelphi Papers*, 38: 9–13.

Keenan, J. 2008. Resource exploitation, repression and resistance in the Sahara-Sahel: The rise of the rentier state in Algeria, Chad and Niger, in *Extractive Economies and Conflicts in the Global South: Multi-Regional Perspectives on Rentier Politics*, edited by K. Omeje. Aldershot, Hampshire: Ashgate, 161–80.

Kemedi, D. 2006. Fuelling the violence: Non-state armed actors (militia, cults and gangs) in the Niger Delta'. Niger Delta: Economies of Violence Working Papers, No. 10. Institute of International Studies, University of California, Berkeley, USA.

Kiikpoye, A. 2008. The failure of corporate social responsibility in the Niger Delta: Towards a reinterpretation: Proceedings of the International Conference on the Nigerian state, oil industry and the Niger Delta, March 11–13, Yenagoa Bayelsa state. Port Harcourt: Harey Publications, 267–74.

King, J. 1998. Repression, domestic threat and interactions in Argentina and Chile', *Journal of Political and Military Sociology*, 26(2), 191–211.

Klandermans, B. 1997. *The Social Psychology of Protest.* Oxford: Blackwell.

Klandermans, Bert. 1992. The social construction of protest and multiorganisational fields, in *Frontiers in Social Movement Theory*, edited by A. Morris and C.M. Mueller. New Haven and London: Yale University Press, 77–103.

Klandermans, B. and Goslinga, S. 1996. Media discourse, movement publicity and the generation of collective action frames: Theoretical and empirical exercises in meaning construction, in *Comparative Perspectives on Social Movements: Political Opportunities, Mobilizing Structures and Cultural Framings* edited by D. McAdam, et al. Cambridge: Cambridge University Press, 312–37.

Klandermans, B. and Staggenborg, S. 2002. Introduction, in *Methods of Social Movement Research*, edited by B. Klandermans and S. Staggenborg. Minneapolis: University of Minnesota Press, ix–xx.

Klandermans, B., Staggenborg, S. and Tarrow, S. 2002. Conclusion: Blending methods and building theory in social movement research, in *Methods of Social Movement Research*, edited by B. Klandermans, and S. Staggenbor. Minneapolis: University of Minnesota Press, 314–49.

Klare, M. 2001. *Resource Wars: The New Landscape of Global Conflict.* New York: Henry Holt and Company.

Klare, M. and Volman, D. 2004. Africa's oil and American national security. *Current History*, May: 226–31.

Klein, N. 2007. *The Shock Doctrine: The Rise of Disaster Capitalism.* New York: Metropolitan Books.

Knight, G. 2004. The mass media, in *New Society: Sociology for the 21st Century.* 4th edition, edited by R.J. Brym. Toronto: Thomson, 127–53.

Kohut, D., Vilella, O. and Julian, B. 2003. *Historical Dictionary of the "Dirty Wars".* Lanham: Scarecrow Press.

Koopmans, R. 1999. Political opportunity structure. Some splitting to balance the lumping. *Sociological Forum*, 14(1), 93–105.

Koopmans, R. 1997. Dynamics of repression and mobilization: The German extreme right in the 1990s. *Mobilization*, 2(2), 149–64.

Kriesi, H. 2004. Political context and opportunity, in *The Blackwell Companion to Social Movements*, edited by D. Snow, et al. Malden, MA: Blackwell, 67–90.

Krueger, R.A and Casey, M.A 2000. *Focus Groups: A Practical Guide for Applied Research.* Thousand Oaks: Sage Publications.

Kubal, T. 1998. The presentation of political self: Cultural resonance and the construction of collective action frames. *Sociological Quarterly*, 39(4), 539–54.

Lahai, J. 2010. Gendered battlefields: A contextual and comparative analysis of women's participation in armed conflicts in Africa. *Peace and Conflict Review*, 4(2), 1–16.

Lefkowitz, David. 2007. On a moral right to civil disobedience. *Ethics*, 117: 202–33.

Legal Oil. 2007. Shifting trends in oil theft in the Niger Delta [Online] Legaloil. com Information Paper No. 3 (January). Available at http://www.legaloil. com/Documents/Library/Legal%20Oil%20Information%20Paper%20No%20 3%20270207.pdf [accessed December 26, 2007].

Legal Oil, 2004. Fingerprinting oil [Online] Information Paper No. 2. Available at http://www.legaloil.com/Documents/Library/Legal%20Oil%20 Information%20Paper%20No.%202.pdf [accessed December 26, 2007].

Legal Oil, 2003. Oil theft in Nigeria — an overview [Online] Information Paper No. 1. Available at http://www.legaloil.com/Documents/Library/LegalOil-InformationPaperNo1.pdf [accessed December 26, 2007].

Lenning, E. and Brightman, S. 2009. Oil, rape and state crime in Nigeria. *Critical Criminology*, 17, 35–48.

Lepsius, R. 2006. The model of charismatic leadership and its applicability to the rule of Adolf Hitler. *Totalitarian Movements and Political Religions*, 7(2), 175–90.

Li, P. 2003. Social inclusion of visible minorities and newcomers: The articulation of "race" and "racial" difference in Canadian society: Paper presented at the Conference on Social Inclusion, Canadian Council on Social Development

March 27–28, Ottawa. [Online]. Available at: http://www.ccsd.ca/events/inclusion/papers/peter_li.pdf [accessed 2 December 2010].

Lichbach, M. 1995. *The Rebel's Dilemma.* Ann Arbour: University of Michigan Press.

Lichbach, M. 1987. Deterrence or escalation? The puzzle of aggregate studies of repression and dissent. *Journal of Conflict Resolution*, 31: 266–97.

Lichbach, M. 1984. An economic theory of the governability: choosing policy and optimizing performance. *Public Choice*, 44: 307–37.

Lloyd, P.C. 1963. The Itshekiri in the nineteenth century: an outline social history. *Journal of African History*, iv, 2: 207–31.

Lofland, L.H. 1973. *A World of Strangers: Order and Action in Urban Public Space.* New York: Basic Books.

Lowi, M. 2005. Algeria, 1992–2002: Anatomy of a civil war, in *Understanding Civil War: Evidence and Analysis.* Volume 1: Africa, edited by P. Collier and N. Sambanis. Washington: The World Bank, 221–246.

Lubeck, P., Watts, M and Lipschutz, R. 2007. Convergent interests: US energy security and the "securing" of Nigerian democracy,' International Policy Report, February, 1–23.

Maier, K. 2000. *This House has Fallen: Nigeria in Crisis.* London: Penguin.

Mamdani, M. 2000. *When Victims become Killers.* Princeton: Princeton University Press.

Marenin, O. and Reisig, M. 1995. "A general theory of crime" and patterns of crime in Nigeria: an exploration of methodological assumptions. *Journal of Criminal Justice*, 23(6), 501–18.

Maxted, J. 2006. Exploitation of energy resources in Africa and the consequences for minority rights. *Journal of Developing Societies*, 22(1), 29–37.

Maxwell, J.A. 2005. *Qualitative Research Design: An Interpretive Approach.* Thousand Oaks: Sage.

Mazrui, A. 2008. Conflict in Africa: An overview, in *The Roots of African Conflicts: The Causes and Costs*, edited by A. Nhema and P.T. Zeleza. Oxford: James Curry, 36–50.

Mazurana, D., McKay, S., Carlson, K. and Kasper, J. 2002. Girls in fighting forces and groups: their recruitment, participation, demobilization, and reintegration. *Peace and Conflict: Journal of Peace Psychology*, 8(2), 97–123.

Mba, N.E. 1982. *Nigerian Women Mobilized: Women's Political Activity in Southern Nigeria, 1900–1965.* Berkeley: University of California Press.

Mbembe, A. 2001. *On the Postcolony.* Berkeley and Los Angeles: University of California Press.

McAdam, D. 1982. *The Political Process and the Development of the Black Insurgency.* Chicago: University of Chicago Press.

McAdam, D., Sampsons, R., Weffer, S. and MacIndoe, H. 2005. There will be fighting in the streets: The distorting lens of social movement theory. *Mobilization*, 10(1), 1–18.

McAdam, D. and Sewell, W. 2001. It's about time: temporality in the study of social movements and revolutions, in *Silence and Voice in Contentious Politics*, edited by R. Aminzade, et al. Cambridge: Cambridge University Press, 89–125.

McAdam, D., Tarrow, S. and Tilly, C. 2001. *Dynamics of Contention.* New York: Cambridge University Press.

McCarthy, J. 1996. Constraints and opportunities in adopting, adapting and inventing, in *Comparative Perspectives on Social Movements: Political Opportunities, Mobilizing Structures and Cultural Framings*, edited by D. McAdam, et al. Cambridge: Cambridge University Press, 141–51.

McCarthy, J. and Wolfson, M. 1992. Consensus movements, conflict movements, and the cooptation of civic state infrastructures', in *Frontiers in Social Movement* Theory, edited by A. Morris and C.M. Mueller. New Haven: Yale University Press, 273–97.

McCarthy, J. and Zald, M. 1977. Resource mobilization and social movements: a partial theory. *American Journal of Sociology*, 82(6), 1212–41.

McCulloch, J. 2009. Counting the cost: gold mining and occupational disease in contemporary South Africa. *African Affairs*, 108(431): 221–40.

McCulloch, Jock. 2005. Beating the odds: the quest for justice by South African asbestos mining communities. *Review of African Political Economy*, 32(103), 63–77.

McKay, S. and Mazurana, D. 2004. *Where are the girls? Girls in Fighting Forces in Northern Uganda, Sierra Leone and Mozambique: Their Lives During and After War.* Montreal: Rights & Democracy.

McPhail, C. and McCarthy, J. 2005. Protest mobilization, protest repression and their interaction, in *Repression and Mobilization*, edited by C. Davenport, et al. Minneapolis: University of Minnesota Press, 3–32.

Meintjes, S. 2007. Political violence and gender: A neglected relation in South Africa's struggle for democracy. *Politikon*, 25(2), 95–109.

Mello, P.A. 2010. In search of new wars: The debate about a transformation of war. *European Journal of International Relations* 16(2), 297–309.

Melucci, A. 1995. The process of collective identity, in *Social Movements and Culture*, edited by H. Johnston and B. Klandermans. Minneapolis: University of Minnesota Press, 41–63.

Melucci, A. 1992. Frontier land: Collective action between actors and systems, in *Studying Collective Action*, edited by Mario Diani and Ron Eyerman. Newbury Park, California: Sage, 238–58.

Melucci, A. 1989. *Nomads of the Present: Social Movements and Individual Needs in Contemporary Society.* Philadelphia: Temple University Press.

Menhaus, K. and Prendergast, J. 1999. Conflict and the greater Horn of Africa. *Current History*, May: 213–17.

Mensah, J. 2005. On the ethno-cultural heterogeneity of blacks in our "ethnicities", in *Immigration and the Intersections of Diversity*, Spring, 72–7.

Merill, T. 2005. The rhetoric of rebellion in Hume's constitutional thought. *Review of Politics*, 67(2), 257–82.

Meyer, David. 2004. Protest and political opportunities. *Annual Review of Sociology*, 30: 125–45.

Meyer, D. and Whittier, N. 1994. Social movement spillover. *Social Problems*, 41: 277–98.

Miller, W. and Crabtree, B. 2004. Depth interviewing, in *Approaches to Qualitative Research: A Reader on Theory and Practice*, edited by H.S Nagy and P. Leavy. New York & Oxford: Oxford University Press, 185–202.

Mitee, B. 1999. The socio-cultural impact of oil exploitation on an indigenous people: The Ogoni case: *Economic, Social and Cultural Rights of the Ogoni. Proceedings of the Symposium on the Economic Social and Cutural Rights of the Sami, the Maasai and the Ogoni*. Vol.III. The Ogoni, edited by F. Horn. Rovaniemi, Lapland's University Press, 1–29.

Mkandawire, T. 2008. The terrible toll of postcolonial rebel movements: towards and explanation, in *The Roots of African Conflicts: The Causes and Costs*, edited by A. Nhema and P.T. Zeleza. Oxford: James Curry, 106–35.

Moodie, D. 2006. Ethnic violence on the South African gold mines, in *States of Violence*, edited by F. Coronil and J. Skurski. Ann Arbour: University of Michigan Press, 307–42.

Mooney, P. and Hunt, S. A repertoire of interpretations: Master frames and ideological continuity in US agrarian mobilization. *Sociological Quarterly*, 37(1), 177–97.

Morgan, D.L., Krueger, R.A. and King, J.A. 1998. *Focus Group Kit*. Thousand Oaks: Sage.

Morris, A. 1992. Political consciousness and collective action, in *Frontiers in Social Movement Theory*, edited by A. Morris and C.M. Mueller. New Haven and London: Yale University Press, 351–73.

Morris, A. and Staggenborg, S. 2004. Leadership in social movements, in *The Blackwell Companion to Social Movements*, edited by D. Snow, et al. Malden, MA: Blackwell, 171–96.

Morrison, W. 2006. *Criminology, Civilization and the New World Order*. London: Routledge.

Morvaridi, B. 2008. *Social Justice and Development*. Hampshire: Palgrave MacMillan.

Moser, C. and Clark, F. 2001. Introduction, in *Victims, Perpetrators or Actors? Gender, Armed Conflict and Political Violence*, edited by C. Moser and F. Clark. London and New York: Zed Books.

Münkler, H. 2005. *The New Wars*. Cambridge: Polity.

Myrdal, G. 1962. *An American Dilemma: The Negro problem and Modern Democracy*. Vol. 1. New York: Harper & Row.

Nafziger, W.E. 2008. Nigeria's economic development and Niger Delta grievance: Proceedings of the International Conference on The Nigerian state, oil industry and the Niger Delta, March 11–13, Yenagoa Bayelsa state. Port Harcourt: Harey Publications, 147–56.

Ndikumana, L. and Emizet, K. 2005. The economics of war: The case of the Democratic Republic of Congo, in *Understanding Civil War: Evidence and Analysis*, edited by P. Collier and N. Sambanis Volume 1: Africa. Washington: The World Bank, 63–84.

Ngoie, G.T. and Omeje, K. 2008. Rentier politics and low intensity conflicts in the DRC: The case of Kasai and Katanga Provinces, in *Extractive Economies and Conflicts in the Global South: Multi-Regional Perspectives on Rentier Politics*, edited by K. Omeje. Aldershot, Hampshire: Ashgate, 135–48.

Nigeria. 2008. *Report of the Technical Committee on the Niger Delta*. Port Harcourt: Prelyn Fortunes.

Nigerian Compass. 2010. (24 October). Nigeria mishandled Abuja bomb blast — US" [Online] Available at: http://www.compassnewspaper.com/NG/index.php?option=com_content&view=article&id=68892:nigeria-mishandled-abuja-bomb-blast-us&catid=43:news&Itemid=799 [accessed 26 October 2010].

Nnoli, O. 1978. *Ethnic Politics in Nigeria*. Enugu: Fourth Dimension Publishers.

Noonan, R. 1995. Women against the state: Political opportunities and collective action frames in Chile's transition to democracy. *Sociological Forum*, 10(1), 81–111.

Nwilo, P.C. and Badejo, O.T. 2008. Oil spill dispersion and trajectories on Nigerian open sea: Proceedings of the International Conference on the Nigerian State, oil industry and the Niger Delta, March 11–13, Yenagoa Bayelsa state. Port Harcourt: Harey Publications, 164–92.

Obi, C. 2008. Enter the dragon? Chinese oil companies and resistance in the Niger Delta. *Review of African Political Economy*, 35(3), 417–34.

Obi, C. 2007. *The Nigerian Private Sector under Adjustment and Crisis 1985–1993*. Malhouse Monographs on Africa. Lagos: Malthouse Press.

Obiaga, N. 2006. *Nigeria: The Instability of Military Governance 1983–1998*. Bloomington, Indiana: Author House.

Ogundiya, I.S. 2009. The cycle of legitimacy crisis in Nigeria: A theoretical exploration. *Journal of Social Science*, 20(2), 129–42.

Oha, O. 2005. Nation, nationalism, and the rhetoric of praying for Nigeria in distress. *Interventions*, 7(1), 21–42.

Okaba, B. 2009. *Political Economy of Militancy, Petroleum Pipeline Vandalisation and Hostage-Taking in the Niger Delta Region of Nigeria*. Lecture Delivered at the Niger Delta Students Association (NANDA) Meeting Port Harcourt, 27 June 2009.

Okaba, B. 2008. Petrodollar, the Nigerian state and the crises of development in the Niger Delta region: Trends, challenges and the way forward: Proceedings of the international conference on the Nigerian state, oil Industry and the Niger Delta, March 11–13, Yenagoa Bayelsa state. Port Harcourt: Harey Publications, 21–39.

Okafor, C. 2008. Empowering women: an alternative mechanism in resolving the Niger Delta crisis: Proceedings of the international conference on the Nigerian state, oil industry and the Niger Delta, March 11–13, Yenagoa Bayelsa state. Port Harcourt: Harey Publications, 396–405.

Okereke, C. 2006. Oil politics and environmental conflict: the case of Niger Delta, Nigeria in *The Politics of Oil: A Survey*, edited by B. Gokay. London & New York: Routledge, 110–18.

Okonta, I. 2006. Behind the mask: Explaining the emergence of the MEND militia in Nigeria's oil-bearing Niger Delta. Niger Delta: Economies of Violence Working Papers. Working Paper No. 11. Institute of International Studies, University of California, Berkeley, USA.

Okonta, I. 2005. Nigeria: Chronicle of a dying state. *Current History*, 203–8.

Okonta, I. and Douglas, O. 2001. *Where Vultures Feast: Shell, Human Rights and Oil in the Niger Delta*. San Francisco: Sierra Book Club.

Okorie, V. and Williams, S.B. 2009. Rural women's livelihood strategies: a case study of fishery communities in the Niger Delta, Nigeria. *Gender, Technology and Development* 13(2), 225–43.

Olayiwola, L.M and Adeleye, O.A. 2005. Rural infrastructural development in Nigeria between 1960 and 1990 – problems and challenges. *Journal of Social Science*, 11(2), 91–6.

Olzak, S., Beasley, M. and Oliver, J. 2003. The impact of state reforms on protest against apartheid in South Africa. *Mobilization*, 8(1), 27–50.

O'Malley, P. 1979. Social bandits, modern capitalism and the traditional peasantry: a critique of Hobsbawm. *Journal of Peasant Studies*, 6(4), 489–501.

Omeje, K. 2005. The Egbesu and Bakassi boys: African spiritism and the mystical re-traditionalisation of society, in *Civil militia: Africa's intractable security menace?* Edited by D.J. Francis. Aldershot: Ashgate, 71–88.

Omeje, K. 2004. The state, conflict and evolving politics in the Niger Delta, Nigeria. *Review of African Political Economy*, 31(101), 425–40.

Omotola, J.S. 2009. Dissent and state excesses in the Niger Delta, Nigeria. *Studies in Conflict & Terrorism*, 32(2), 129–45.

Omoweh, D. 2005. *Shell Petroleum Development Company, the State and Underdevelopment of Nigeria's Niger Delta: A Study in Environmental Degradation*. Trenton, New Jersey: Africa World Press.

Onimode, B. 1988. *A Political Economy of the African Crisis.* London: Zed Books.

Onimode, B. 1982. *Imperialism and Underdevelopment in Nigeria. The Dialectics of Mass Poverty.* London: Zed Press.

Opukri, C. and Etekpe, A. 2008. Conflict management and strategies for peace-building: Proceedings of international conference on the Nigerian state, oil industry and the Niger Delta, March 11–13, Yenagoa Bayelsa state. Port Harcourt: Harey Publications, 136–46.

Oriola, T. 2012. The Delta creeks, women's engagement, and Nigeria's oil insurgency. *British Journal of Criminology*, 52(3), 534–55.

Orluwene, O. 2008. 'Elite networks and conflicts in the Niger Delta region: Proceedings of the international conference on the nigerian state, oil industry and the Niger Delta, March 11–13, Yenagoa Bayelsa state. Port Harcourt: Harey Publications, 344–56.

Ortiz, D. 2007. Confronting repression with violence: inequality, military infrastructure and dissident repression. *Mobilization*, 12(3), 219–38.

Oruwari, Y. 2006. Youth in urban violence in Nigeria: a case study of urban gangs from Port Harcourt. Niger Delta: Economies of Violence Working Papers, No. 14. Institute of International Studies, University of California, Berkeley, USA.

Osaghae, E. 2003. Explaining the changing patterns of ethnic politics in Nigeria. *Nationalism and Ethnic Politics*, 9(3), 54–73.

Osaghae, E. 1995. The Ogoni uprising: oil politics, minority agitation and the future of the Nigerian state. *African Affairs*, 94(376), 325–44.

Osaghae, E. 1986. Federalism, local politics and ethnicity in Nigeria. *Commonwealth & Comparative Politics*, 24(2), 151–68.

Osha, S. 2006. Birth of the Ogoni protest movement. *Journal of Asian and African Studies*, 41(1/2), 13–38.

Oyefusi, A. 2008. Oil and the probability of rebel participation among youths in the Niger Delta of Nigeria. *Journal of Peace Research*, 45(4), 539–55.

Oyefusi, A. 2007. Oil and the propensity to armed struggle in the Niger Delta of Nigeria,' [Online: April 1]. World Bank Policy Research Working Paper No. 4194. Available at SSRN: http://ssrn.com/abstract=979666 [accessed on 2 January, 2008].

Palacios, M. 2006. *Between Legitimacy and Violence: A History of Colombia, 1875–2002*. Trans. Richard Stoller. Durham and London: Duke University Press.

Paoli, L. 2003. *Organized Crime, Italian Style*. New York: Oxford University Press.

Parasher, S. 2009. Feminist international relations and women militants: case studies from Sri Lanka and Kashmir. *Cambridge Review of International Affairs*, 22(2), 235–56.

Pearce, J. 2007. Oil and armed struggle in Casanare, Colombia: Complex contexts and contingent moments, in *Oil Wars*, edited by M. Kaldor, et al. London: Pluto Press, 225–73.

Peel, R. 2009. *A Swamp full of Dollars: Pipelines and Paramilitaries at Nigeria's oil frontier*. London: I.B. Tauris.

Peluso, N.L. and Watts, M. 2001. Violent environments in *Violent Environments*, edited by N.L. Peluso and M. Watts. Ithaca: Cornell University Press, 3–38.

Peretomode, V.F. 2002. Warri crisis survey report – Ijaw perspective, in *Conflict and Instability in the Niger Delta*, edited by T.A Imobighe, et al. Ibadan: Spectrum, 133–55.

Persaud, T. 1976. Conflicts between multinational corporations and less-developed countries: the case of bauxite mining in the Caribbean with special reference to Guyana. Doctoral Dissertation at the Texas Tech University.

Perry, E.J. 2002. Moving the masses: emotion work in the Chinese revolution. *Mobilization*, 7(2), 111–28.

Pfaff, S. 1996. Collective identity and informal groups in revolutionary mobilization: East Germany in 1989. *Social Forces*, 52: 817–68.

Pichardo, N. 1997. New social movements: A critical review. *Annual Review of Sociology*, 23: 411–30.

Pinheiro, P.S. 2007. Youth, violence and democracy. *Current History*, February: 64–9.

Pisano, V. 1985. The Italian experience, in *Terrorism and Personal Protection*. Edited by B. Jenkins. Boston: Butterworth Publishers, 64–87.

Polletta, F. 2006. Mobilization forum: Awkward movements. *Mobilization*, 11(4), 475–8.

Posado-Carbo, E. 2004. Columbia's resilient democracy. *Current History*, February: 68–73.

Purnell, S. 1985. Business and terrorism in Argentina, in *Terrorism and Personal Protection*, edited by B. Jenkins. Boston: Butterworth Publishers, 88–112.

Rajasingham-Senanayake, D. 2004. Between reality and representation: Women's agency in war and post-conflict Sri Lanka. *Cultural Dynamics*, 16(2/3), 140–68.

Rajasingham-Senanayake, D. 2001. Ambivalent empowerment: the tragedy of Tamil women in conflict, in *Women, war and peace in South Asia: Beyond Victimhood to Agency*, edited by R. Manchanda. New Delhi: Sage, 102–30.

Rapley, T. 2006. Interviews, in *Qualitative Research Practice*, edited by C. Seale, et al. London: SAGE, 15–33.

Rasler, K. 1996. Concessions, repression and political protest in the Iranian Revolution. *American Sociological Review*, 61(1), 132–52.

Ratner, R. 1989. Critical criminology: A splendid oxymoron. *Journal of Human Justice*, 1: 3–8.

Regan, P. and Henderson, E. 2002. Democracy, threats and political repression in developing countries: are democracies internally less violent? *Third World Quarterly*, 23(1), 119–36.

Reisigl, S.D and Wodak, R. 2001. *Discourse and Discrimination: Rhetorics of Racism and Anti-Semitism*. London: Routledge.

Reno, W. 2005. The politics of violent opposition in collapsing states. *Government and Opposition*, 40(2), 127–51.

Richardson, J. 2007. *Analysing Newspapers: An Approach from Critical Discourse Analysis*. New York: Palgrave MacMillan.

Ross, M. 2004. What do we know about natural resources and civil war? *Journal of Peace Research*, 41(3), 337–56.

Ross, M. 2003. Nigeria's oil sector and the poor: [Online] Paper prepared for the UK Department for International Development (DFID) 'Nigeria: Drivers of Change' Programme Available at: http://www.sscnet.ucla.edu/polisci/faculty/ross/NigeriaOil.pdf [accessed on 1 April 2010].

Rostow, W.W. 1960. *The Stages of Economic Growth.* Cambridge: University Press.

Rothgeb, J. 1995. Investment dependence and political conflict in developing countries: a comparative regional analysis, in *Foreign Direct Investment in a Changing Global Political Economy*, edited by S. Chan. New York: St. Martin's Press, 188–218.

Rucht, D. 1996. The impact of national contexts on social movement structures: a cross-movement and cross-national perspective, in *Comparative Perspectives on Social* Movements, edited by McAdam et al. Cambridge: Cambridge University Press, 185–204.

Ruggiero, V. 2006. *Understanding Political Violence: A Criminological Analysis.* London: Open University Press.

Ruggiero, V. 2005. Brigate Rosse: Political violence, criminology and social movement theory. *Crime, Law & Social Change*, 43: 289–307.

Russel, C. 1985. Kidnapping as a terrorist tactic, in *Terrorism and Personal Protection*, edited by B. Jenkins. Boston: Butterworth Publishers, 8–22.

Ryan, C. 1991. *Prime Time Activism.* Boston: South End Press.

Ryen, A. 2004. Ethical Issues, in *Qualitative research Practice*, edited by S. Cleave, et al. London: Sage, 230–47.

Sacks, H. 1972. Notes on police assessment of moral character, in *Studies in Social Interaction*, edited by D. Sudnow. New York: Free Press, 280–93.

Said, Y. 2007. Greed and grievance in Chechnya, in *Oil Wars*, edited by M. Kaldor, et al. London: Pluto Press, 130–56.

Sala-i-Martin, X. and Subramanian, A. 2003. Addressing the Natural Resource Curse: An Illustration from Nigeria. *IMF Working Paper* 03/139. Washington, DC: International Monetary Fund.

Sanchez, M. 2006. Insecurity and violence as a new power relation in Latin America. *Annals of the American Academy of Arts and Social Sciences*, 606: 178–95.

Saro-Wiwa, K. 1992. *Genocide in Nigeria: The Ogoni Tragedy.* Port Harcourt: Saros International.

Sater, W. 1985. Terrorist kidnappings in Colombia, in *Terrorism and Personal Protection*, edited by B. Jenkins. Boston: Butterworth Publishers, 113–28.

Saxton, G. 2004. Structure, politics and ethnonationalist contention in in post-franco spain: an integrated model. *Journal of Peace Research*, 41: 25–46.

Sayndee, T.D. 2008. Thugs' paradise, agencies' guinea pigs and the natural resource intrigue: The civil war in Liberia, in *Extractive Economies and Conflicts in the Global South: Multi-Regional Perspectives on Rentier Politics*, edited by K. Omeje. Aldershot, Hampshire: Ashgate, 149–60.

Scarritt, J. and McMillan, S. 1995. Protest and rebellion in Africa: Explaining conflicts between ethnic minorities and the state in the 1980s. *Comparative Political Studies*, 28(3), 323–49.

Schiller, D. 1985. The European experience, in *Terrorism and Personal Protection*, edited by B. Jenkins. Boston: Butterworth Publishers, 46–63.

Schulze, K. 2007. The conflict in Aceh: Struggle over oil?, in *Oil Wars*, edited by M. Kaldor, et al. London: Pluto Press, 183–224.

Seidman, G. 2001. Guerrillas in their midst: armed struggle in the South African anti-apartheid movement. *Mobilization*, 6(2), 111–27.

Sennett, R. 2002. Cosmopolitanism and the social experience of cities, in *Conceiving Cosmopolitanism: Theory, Context and Practice*, edited by S. Vertovec, and R. Cohen. Oxford: University Press, 42–7.

Shaw, C. and McKay, H. 1971. Male juvenile delinquency as group behaviour, in *The Social Fabric of the Metropolis: Contributions of the Chicago School of Urban Sociology*, edited by J.F. Short. Chicago: University of Chicago Press, 252–82.

Shaxson, N. 2008. *Poisoned Wells: The Dirty Politics of African Oil.* New York: Palgrave.

Shoham, E. 2010. 'Signs of Honor' among Russian inmates in Israel's prisons. *International Journal of Offender Therapy and Comparative Criminology*, 54(6), 984–1003.

Sicakkan, H. 2005. How is a diverse European society sossible? An exploration into new public spaces in six European countries. AMID Working Paper Series, 46.

Skillington, T. 1997. Politics and the Struggle to define: A discourse analysis of the framing strategies of competing Actors in "new" participatory forum. *British Journal of Sociology*, 48(3), 493–513.

Skurski, J. and Coronil, F. 2006. Introduction: States of violence and the violence of states, in *States of* Violence, edited by F. Coronil and J. Skurski. Ann Arbor: University of Michigan Press, 1–31.

Slatta, R. 2004. Eric J. Hobsbawms's social bandit: A critique and revision', *A Contracorriente* [Online]. Available at http://www.ncsu.edu/project/acontracorriente/spring_04/Slatta.pdf [accessed December 15, 2008].

Slatta, R.W. 1990. Banditry as political participation in Latin America, in *Criminal Justice History: An International Annual.* (Volume 11), edited by L.A. Knafla. Westport, CT: Meckler, 171–87.

Slatta, R.W. 1987. *Bandidos: The Varieties of Latin American Banditry.* New York, NY: Greenwood Press.

Smith, C. 1996. *Resisting Reagan: The US Central America Peace Movement.* Chicago: University of Chicago Press.

Smith, M.L.R. 2003. Guerrillas in the mist. Reassessing strategy and low intensity warfare. *Review of International Studies*, 29(1), 19–37.

Snow, D. 2004. Social movements as challenges to authority: resistance to an emerging conceptual hegemony. *Research in Social Movements, Conflict and Change*, 25: 3–25.

Snow, D. and Byrd, S. 2007. Ideology, framing processes, and Islamic terrorist movements. *Mobilization*, 12(2), 119–36.

Snow, D. and Benford, R. 1992. Master frames and cycles of protest, in *Frontiers in Social Movement Theory*, edited by A. Morris and C. Mueller. New Haven: Yale University Press, 133–55.

Snow, D. and Benford, R.D. 1988. Ideology, frame resonance, and participant mobilization. *International Social Movement Research* 1: 197–217.

Snow, D., Rochford, B., Worden, S. and Benford, R. 1986. Frame alignment processes, micromobilization and movement participation. *American Sociological Review*, 51: 464–81.

Steinberg, M. 1998. Tilting the frame: considerations on collective action framing from a discursive turn. *Theory and Society*, 27: 845–72.

Steinberger, P. 2002. Hobbesian resistance. *American Journal of Political Science*, 46(4), 856–65.

Stern, R. 2005. Unpacking adaptation: the female inheritance movement in Hong Kong', *Mobilization*, 10(3), 421–39.

Stevens, P. Jr. 2006. Women's aggressive use of genital power in Africa. *Transcultural Psychiatry*, 43(4), 592–99.

Stewart, D.W. and Shamdasani, P.N. 1990. *Focus Groups: Theory and Practice*. Newbury Park: Sage.

Stewart, W. 1995. The League of Nations and the Irish question: Master frames, cycles of protest, and "master alignment". *Sociological Quarterly*, 36(3), 465–81.

Suberu, R. 2001. Can Nigeria's new democracy survive?' *Current History*, May: 207–12.

Subhash, J. and Vachani, S. 2006. The role of MNCs in alleviating global poverty, in *Multinational Corporations and Global Poverty Reduction*, edited by J.C. Subhash. Cheltenham: Edward Elgar, 3–28.

Tabb, W. 2007. Resource wars, *Monthly Review*, January: 32–42.

Tarrow, S. 1993. Modular collective action and the rise of the social movement: why the French Revolution was not enough. *Politics & Society*, 21(1), 69–90.

Tarrow, S. 1992. Mentalities, political cultures and collective action frames: constructing meanings through action, in *Frontiers in Social Movement Theory*. A. Morris and C.M Mueller. New Haven and London: Yale University Press, 174–202.

Tarrow, S. 1989. *Democracy and Disorder: Protest and Politics in Italy, 1965–1975*. Oxford: Clarendon.

Taylor, V. and Rupp, L.J. 2002. Loving internationalism: the emotion culture of transnational women's organizations, 1888–1945. *Mobilization*, 7(2), 141–58.

Taylor, V. and Whittier, N. 1995. Analytical approaches to social movement culture: the culture of the women's movement, in *Social Movements and Culture*, edited by H. Johnston and B. Klandermans. Minneapolis: University of Minnesota Press, 163–87.

Taylor, V. and Whittier, N. 1992. Collective identity in social movement communities: lesbian feminist mobilization, in *Frontiers in Social Movement*

Theory. A. Morris and C.M. Mueller. New Haven and London: Yale University Press, 104–29.

Technical Committee on the Niger Delta. 2008. *Report of the Technical Committee on the Niger Delta*. Port Harcourt: Fortunes.

The Sun. 2009. Niger Delta war: Pa Juweigha, 102, oldest man in Gbaramatu bombed to death [Online: 25 May]. Available at: http://www.sunnewsonline. com/webpages/news/national/2009/may/25 [accessed 27 May 2009].

ThisDay. 2009. Kidnappers pocket N15bn. Illegal oil bunkering: US to train Nigerian Navy [Online 1 April]. Available at: URL:http://www.thisdayonline. com/nview.php?id [accessed 3 April 2009].

Thrasher, F. 1927. *The Gang*. Chicago: University of Chicago Press.

Tilly, C. and Tarrow, S. 2007. *Contentious Politics*. Boulder & London: Paradigm Publishers.

Tilly, C. 2004. *Social Movements, 1768–2004*. Colorado: Paradigm.

Tilly, C. 2003. *The Politics of Collective Violence*. Cambridge: Cambridge University Press.

Tilly, C. 1995. *Popular Contention in Great Britain, 1758–1834*. Cambridge: Harvard University Press.

Tilly, C. 1978. *From Mobilization to Revolution*. Reading, MA: Addison-Wesley.

Tilly, C., Tilly, L. and Tilly, R. 1975. *The Rebellious Century, 1830–1930*. Cambridge: Harvard University Press.

Tonwe, D.A. 2002. Warri crisis survey report – Itsekiri perspective, in *Conflict and Instability in the Niger Delta*, edited by T.A Imobighe, et al. Ibadan: Spectrum, 186–223.

Touraine, A. 1981. *The Voice and the Eye*. Cambridge: Cambridge University Press.

Transparency International. 2008. 'Corruption Perception Index 2008 [Online] Available at http://www.transparency.org/policy_research/surveys_indices/ cpi/2008 [accessed 27 September, 2008].

Turner, M. 1998. Kidnapping and politics. *International Journal of the Sociology of Law*, 26: 145–60.

Turner, R. 1996. The moral issue in collective behaviour and collective action. *Mobilization*, 1(1), 1–15.

Turner, T. 1980. Nigeria: Imperialism, oil technology and the comprador state, in *Oil and Class Struggle*, edited by P. Nore and T. Turner. London: Zed Press, 199–223.

Turner, T. and Brownhill, L. 2004. Why women are at war with chevron: Nigerian subsistence struggles against the international oil industry. *Journal of Asian and African Studies*, 39(1–2), 63–93.

Turner, T. and Oshare, M.O. 1994. Women uprising against the Nigerian oil industry in the 1980s, in *Arise Ye Mighty People: Gender, Class and Race in Popular Struggles*, edited by T. Turner and B. Ferguson. Trenton: Africa World Press.

Tyler, T. 1990. *Why People Obey the Law*. New Haven: Yale.

Tzanelli, R. 2006. Capitalizing on value: Towards a sociological understanding of kidnapping. *Sociology*, 40(5), 929–47.

Uesseler, R. 2008. *Servants of War: Private Military Corporations and the Profit of Conflict*. Jefferson Chase (Trans.). Brooklyn: Soft Skull Press.

Ukeje, C. 2004. From Aba to Ugborodo: Gender identity and alternative discourse of social protest among women in the oil delta of Nigeria. *Oxford Development Studies*, 32(4), 605–17.

Ukiwo, U. 2007. From "pirates" to "militants": A historical perspective on anti-state and anti-oil company mobilization among the Ijaw of Warri, Western Niger Delta. *African Affairs*, 106/425, 587–610.

Ukiwo, Ukoha. 1999. The political economy of endangerment: The Ogoni and the rentier state in Nigeria, in *Economic, Social and Cultural Rights of the Ogoni. Proceedings of the Symposium on the Economic Social and Cutural Rights of the Sami, the Maasai and the Ogoni*. Vol. III. The Ogoni, edited by F. Horn. Rovaniemi, Lapland's University Press, 33–66.

Van Allen, J. 1971. *"Aba Riots" or "Women's War"?: British Ideology and Eastern Nigerian Women's Political Activism*. Waltham, MA: African Studies Association.

van Stekelenburg, J. and Klandermans, B. 2007. 'It takes three to tango: How (P)POS and mobilizing structures influence motives and emotions of protesters: [Online]. Paper presented at the annual meeting of the American Sociological Association, TBA, New York, New York City. Available at: http://www.allacademic.com/meta/p185033_index.html [accessed 27 April, 2010].

Vidal, J. 2010. Nigeria's agony dwarfs the Gulf oil spill. The US and Europe ignore it [Online: *The Observer*]. Available at: http://www.guardian.co.uk/world/2010/may/30/oil-spills-nigeria-niger-delta-shell [accessed 2 June 2010].

Voss, K. 1996. The collapse of a social movement: The interplay of mobilizing structures, framing and political opportunities in the Knights of Labour, in *Comparative Perspectives on Social Movements: Political Opportunities, Mobilizing Structures and Cultural Framings*. D. McAdam, et al. Cambridge: Cambridge University Press, 227–58.

Walcott, S.M. 2006. Multi-local global corporations: New reach – same core locations, in *Globalization's Contradictions: Geographies of Discipline, Destruction and Transformation,* edited by D. Conway and N. Heynen. London and New York: Routledge, 49–64.

Watts, M. 2009a. Tipping point: slipping into darkness. Niger Delta: Economies of Violence Working Papers, No. 23. Institute of International Studies, University of California, Berkeley, USA.

Watts, M. 2009b. Crude politics: life and death on the Nigerian oil field. Niger Delta: Economies of Violence Working Papers, No. 25. Institute of International Studies, University of California, Berkeley, USA.

Watts, M. 2008a. Imperial oil: The anatomy of a Nigerian oil insurgency. Niger Delta: Economies of Violence Working Papers, No. 17. Institute of International Studies, University of California, Berkeley, USA.

Watts, M. 2008b. Sweet and sour. Niger Delta: Economies of Violence Working Papers, No. 18. Institute of International Studies, University of California, Berkeley, USA.

Watts, M. 2008c. Blood oil: An anatomy of a petro-insurgency in the Niger Delta'. Niger Delta: Economies of Violence Working Papers, No. 22. Institute of International Studies, University of California, Berkeley, USA.

Watts, M. 2007. Petro-insurgency or criminal syndicate? Conflict and violence in the Niger Delta. *Review of African Political Economy*, 34(114), 637–60.

Watts, M. 2004a. Human rights, violence and the oil complex. Niger Delta: Economies of Violence Working Papers, No. 2. Institute of International Studies, University of California, Berkeley, USA.

Watts, M. 2004b. The sinister political life of community: economies of violence and governable spaces in the Niger Delta, Nigeria. Niger Delta: Economies of Violence Working Papers, No. 3. Institute of International Studies, University of California, Berkeley, USA.

Watts, M., Okonta, I. and Von Kemedi, D. 2004. Economies of violence: petroleum, politics and community conflict in the Niger Delta, Nigeria. Niger Delta: Economies of Violence Working Papers, No. 1. Institute of International Studies, University of California, Berkeley, USA.

Weede, E. and Muller, E.N. 1998. Rebellion, Violence and revolution: a rational choice perspective. *Journal of Peace Research*, 35: 43–59.

Welch, C. 1995. The Ogoni and self-determination: increasing violence in Nigeria. *Journal of Modern African Studies*, 33(4), 635–50.

Whittier, N. 2004. The consequences of social movements for each other, in *The Blackwell Companion to Social Movements*, edited by D. Snow, et al. Malden, MA: Blackwell, 531–51.

Whyte, W.F. 1943. *Street Corner Society: The Social Structure of an Italian Slum.* Chicago: University of Chicago Press.

Williams, R. 1995. Constructing the public good: social movements and cultural resources. *Social Problems*, 42(1), 124–44.

Willink Commission, Colonial Office. 1958. *The Report of the Commission Appointed to Enquire into the Fears of Minorities and the means for allaying them.* London: Her Majesty's Stationery Office.

Wint, A.G. 2006. FDI and poverty alleviation in small developing countries, in *Multinational Corporations and Global Poverty Reduction*, edited by Jain C. Subhash. Cheltenham: Edward Elgar, 83–104.

Woodward, P. 2008. Politics and oil in Sudan in *Extractive Economies and Conflicts in the Global South: Multi-Regional Perspectives on Rentier Politics*, edited by K. Omeje. Aldershot, Hampshire: Ashgate, 107–18.

Zald, M. 1996. Culture, ideology and strategic framing, in *Comparative Perspectives on Social Movements: Political Opportunities, Mobilizing Structures and Cultural Framings*, edited by D. McAdam, et al. Cambridge: Cambridge University Press, 261–74.

Zalik, A. 2004. 'The Niger Delta: 'Petro violence' and partnership development. *Review of African Political Economy*, 31(101), 401–24.

Zdravomyslova, E. 1996. Opportunities and framing in the transition to democracy, in *Comparative Perspectives on Social Movements: Political Opportunities, Mobilizing Structures and Cultural Framings*. D. McAdam, et al. Cambridge: Cambridge University Press, 122–37.

Zeleza, P.T. 2008. The cause and costs of war in Africa: From liberation struggles to the "war on terror"', in *The Roots of African Conflicts: The Causes and Costs*, edited by A. Nhema and P.T. Zeleza. Oxford: James Curry, 1–35.

Zhao, D. 1998. Ecologies of social movements: student mobilization during the 1989 prodemocracy movement in Beijing. *American Journal of Sociology*, 103(6), 1493–529.

Zunes, S. 1999. The role of non-violent action in the downfall of apartheid. *Journal of Modern African Studies*, 37(1), 137–69.

Index

CPSIA information can be obtained
at www.ICGtesting.com
Printed in the USA
LVOW13*2048160317
527493LV00008B/87/P